CLEARING THE AIR

CLEARING THE AIR

THE AIR

The Real Story
of the War on Air Pollution

Indur Goklany

CATO
INSTITUTE
Washington, D.C.

Library of Congress Cataloging-in-Publication Data

Goklany, Indur M.
    Clearing the air :   the real story of the war on air pollution   /
Indur Goklany.
        p.   cm.
    Includes bibliographical references.
    ISBN 1-882577-82-5 — ISBN 1-882577-83-3
    1. Air—Pollution—United States—History.   I. Title.
TD883.2.G65   1999
363.739'2'0973—dc21   95-051980

Cato Institute
1000 Massachusetts Ave., N.W.
Washington, D.C. 20001

To Karen for her support and understanding, Maya for ceding the computer on demand (kind of), and Sam under whose watchful eyes this project was accomplished.

Contents

LIST OF FIGURES   viii

LIST OF TABLES   ix

LIST OF BOXES   ix

LIST OF ACRONYMS   x

INTRODUCTION   1

1. THE HISTORY OF AIR POLLUTION AND ITS CONTROL   9

2. TRENDS IN INDOOR AIR QUALITY, 1940 TO 1990   43

3. LONG-TERM TRENDS IN AMBIENT (OUTDOOR) AIR QUALITY IN THE UNITED STATES   49

4. EMISSIONS TRENDS AND TECHNOLOGICAL CHANGE   67

5. THE ENVIRONMENTAL TRANSITION   87

6. THE STATES AND AIR POLLUTION: A REASSESSMENT BASED UPON EMPIRICAL EVIDENCE   111

7. THE FEDERAL ROLE IN AIR POLLUTION CONTROL AND THE PATH TO REFORM   125

8. CONCLUSION   149

NOTES   157

INDEX   183

List of Figures

Figure 1-1   U.S. Energy Consumption, 1850–1995   12

Figure 1-2   Pittsburgh: Dustfall and Total Suspended
Particulate Concentrations, 1912–77   19

Figure 1-3   Growth of Municipal, County, and State Air
Pollution Programs, 1880–1980   22

Figure 1-4   Dust Collection Efficiencies, 1900–70   23

Figure 1-5   Los Angeles: Trends in Ozone, 1956–72   28

Figure 1-6   New York: Ambient SO_2 Concentrations, 1963–72   32

Figure 1-7   Trends in Dustfall in Various Urban Areas,
1920s–60s   32

Figure 2-1   Indoor Air Quality, 1940–90   45

Figure 3-1   TSP and PM-10 Mean Annual Average, 1957–97   53

Figure 3-2   Ambient SO_2 Concentrations Mean Annual
Average, 1962–97   57

Figure 3-3   Ambient CO Concentrations, 1963–97   59

Figure 3-4   Ambient Ozone, 1974–97, Average of Second High
Daily Maximum Value   61

Figure 3-5   Ambient NO_2, 1974–97, Annual Average
Concentrations (in ppm)   63

Figure 3-6   Ambient Lead Concentration, 1975–97   64

Figure 4-1 SO_2, VOC, and NO_x Emissions, with
Population (P), GNP per Capita (A), and
GNP (P×A), 1900–97   70

Figure 4-2   CO and PM-10 Emissions, with Population (P),
GNP per Capita (A), and GNP (P×A), 1940–97   71

Figure 4-3   Sulfur Dioxide, 1900–97: Emissions, Emissions per
GNP, and Emissions per Capita   75

Figure 4-4   Volatile Organic Compounds, 1900–97: Emissions,
Emissions per GNP, and Emissions per Capita   79

Figure 4-5   Nitrogen Oxides, 1900–97: Emissions, Emissions
per GNP, and Emissions per Capita   81

Figure 4-6   PM-10, 1940–97: Emissions, Emissions per GNP,
and Emissions per Capita   82

Figure 4-7   Carbon Monoxide, 1940–97: Emissions, Emissions
per GNP, and Emissions per Capita   84

Figure 4-8   Lead Emissions, 1940–97   85
Figure 5-1   The Environmental Transition   87
Figure 5-2   After the Transition   96
Figure 5-3   Examples of Single-Country Environmental
             Transitions   101
Figure 5-4   Ambient SO$_2$ Concentrations, Various OECD
             Countries, 1980–95   104
Figure 5-5   National SO$_2$ Concentrations for Various Rich
             Nations, 1993   105
Figure 7-1   Chronic Bronchitis: Prevalence, 1979–95   131

List of Tables

Table 1-1   Milestones for Various Substances in the
            Atmosphere   40
Table 4-1   Changes in Population (P), Affluence (A),
            Economic Activity (GNP = P × A), and Technology
            (T) for Criteria Pollutants, 1900–97   72
Table 4-2   Progression of T-Factors (or E/GNP) at Various
            Milestones, 1900–97   76
Table 5-1   Milestones and Transitions for Various Pollutants
            and Indicators   92
Table 7-1   Cost per Life-Year Saved Using Various
            Interventions   130

List of Boxes

Box 7-1   Asthma and Air Pollution   134
Box 7-2   Risk-Risk Analysis—Improvements in Ozone vs.
          Fine Particulate Matter   140
Box 7-3   How Successful Is the Acidic Deposition Control
          Program?   144

List of Acronyms

A	affluence measured in this book by GNP per capita
BACT	best available control technology
BEA	Bureau of Economic Analysis
BTU	British thermal unit, a measure of heat energy
CAMP	Continuous Air Monitoring Project
CB	cost-benefit
CEQ	Council on Environmental Quality
CO	carbon monoxide
CO_2	carbon dioxide
E	emissions
E/cap	emissions per capita
E/GNP	emissions per GNP
ED	environmental degradation
EKC	environmental Kuznets curve
EPA	Environmental Protection Agency
ESECA	Energy Supply and Environmental Coordination Act of 1974
ETH	environmental transition hypothesis
FEA	Federal Energy Administration
FPM	fine particulate matter
GDP	gross domestic product
GNP	gross national product
HC	hydrocarbons, used here synonymously with VOC, which technically only include non-methane hydrocarbons
HEW	Health, Education and Welfare, Department of
I	impact
IPCC	Intergovernmental Panel on Climate Change
LACAPCD	Los Angeles County Air Pollution Control District
m^3	cubic meter
mg	milligram
MST	million short tons
NAAQS	National Ambient Air Quality Standards
NAPCA	National Air Pollution Control Administration

NIMBY	not in my back yard
NO_2	nitrogen dioxide
NO_x	nitrogen oxides
NSPS	new source performance standards
O_3	ozone
OAQPS	Office of Air Quality Planning and Standards
P	population
p(P)	period of perception
PPP	purchasing power parity
p(T)	period of transition
PM	particulate matter
PM-10	particulate matter less than 10 micrometers in diameter
PSD	prevention of significant deterioration
QoL	quality of life
SO_2	sulfur dioxide
T or T-factor	technology, measured here as emissions per GNP
t(F)	time of federalization
tBTU	trillion BTU
TSP	total suspended particulates
$\mu g/m^3$	micrograms per cubic meter
VOC	volatile organic compounds, used here synonymously with HC

Introduction

The air in the United States is much cleaner today than it has been in several decades.[1] Gone are the soot and smoke characteristic of urban areas a century ago. Gone are the killer episodes of the 1940s, '50s, and '60s that struck Donora, New York, and Pittsburgh.[2] And photochemical smog, which first raised its ugly head in Los Angeles over half a century ago, while not yet gone, is in retreat everywhere.

How did this remarkable turnaround come about? What were the forces driving the improvements in air quality during the 20th century? When did these improvements start? Were technology and economic growth the problems, or the solutions, for air pollution? How much credit is due to federal regulation? Would these improvements have occurred in the absence of federal regulation?

This book attempts to answer those, and related, questions.

Most people credit the federalization of air pollution control accomplished by the Clean Air Amendments of 1970 for the air quality improvements of the past few decades.[3] Conventional wisdom is that prior to that federalization, state and local governments had been dragging their feet because they were engaged in an inevitable "race to the bottom" in which the environment was sacrificed in the relentless competition for jobs and economic growth, with a consequent lowering of net societal welfare and economic efficiency.[4] The same conventional wisdom was used to justify federalization in the first place.[5] Another argument for federalization is that air pollution knows no boundaries, state or otherwise.[6]

Despite the apparent success of the existing framework for controlling air pollution in the United States, some analysts have challenged the race-to-the-bottom rationale for federalization of environmental control.[7] That has provoked a swift counterattack from proponents of federalization.[8] Articles have appeared in law journals debating the virtues and failings of federalization and whether in its absence states would indeed race to the bottom, whether the current framework of air pollution regulation is justified by the fact that certain

1

air pollutants cross state boundaries, and whether devolution would roll back the hard-won environmental gains of the last generation.[9] Perhaps the most remarkable aspect of this debate is how long it has gone on, based largely upon idealized (i.e., theoretical) economic models of firms' decisions to locate new capacity under environmental standards of varying stringencies,[10] but with virtually no reference to empirical data on air quality or emissions estimates.[11]

This book attempts to redress that situation, and to "clear the air" by bringing such empirical data to this long-running debate. In it I examine long-term air quality and emissions data spanning the pre- and post-federalization eras for each of the original five traditional "criteria" (i.e., the major) air pollutants or their precursors—namely, sulfur dioxide (SO_2), particulate matter (PM), carbon monoxide (CO), nitrogen oxides (NO_x), and ozone (O_3) or one of its precursors, volatile organic compounds (VOCs), and—to a lesser extent—lead.

Specifically, I examine long-term trends for three separate sets of indicators for each of these air pollutants. The first set consists of national emissions estimates, which are available from 1900 onward for SO_2, NO_x, and VOC, from 1940 for PM and CO, and from 1970 for lead. Analysis of that data set is supplemented by an examination of trends in emissions per unit of economic activity as measured by gross national product (GNP) and emissions per capita. The emissions per GNP measurement is a surrogate for technological change.[12] In a society whose population and economy are expanding, emissions per GNP and emissions per capita serve as *leading environmental indicators*.

The second set of indicators examined is composed of outdoor air quality measurements—that is, ambient concentrations in the outdoor air—which are usually better indicators for the environmental, health, social, and economic impacts of air pollution than are total emissions.[13] In fact, trends in ambient air quality need not be similar to trends in emissions in either magnitude or direction; as we shall see, air quality may improve even as the emissions of certain pollutants increase. Based upon available data, I have developed *qualitative* trends in "national" air quality for the various pollutants: from 1957 onward for PM, from the 1960s for SO_2 and CO, and from the 1970s for O_3/VOC and NO_x.

The final set of indicators analyzed consists of estimates from 1940 to 1990 of residential combustion emissions per occupied household.

Those estimates serve as crude proxies for indoor air pollution, which ought to serve as a better indicator of the public health impact of various air pollutants than outdoor air quality.[14]

In order to gauge the effect of federalization on long-term trends in the various air pollution indicators, federalization must be viewed in the broader context of the social, economic, technological, and political factors that affect the generation and control of air pollution in the United States. Chapter 1, a brief review of the history of air pollution in the United States, provides that context. It also identifies two critical milestones for each of the traditional pollutants. The first is the "period of perception" or p(P)—that is, the period during which a substance in the air gains sufficient notoriety to be perceived as an air pollutant by the public and, perhaps more importantly, by policymakers. The second milestone is the "time of federalization," or t(F), which identifies when the federal government appropriated regulatory authority to itself for the pollutant in question. Trends in the various indicators after p(P) but before t(F) could help illuminate the importance of federalization in improving air quality, and whether state and local agencies had, in fact, been dragging their feet on controlling air pollution and participating in a race to the bottom.

To determine the period of perception, it is necessary to answer the following question: when was the substance recognized or, more importantly, perceived to be responsible for (or capable of having) significant adverse impacts, and therefore in need of control? Prior to such recognition, one cannot expect any societal action—whether at the local, state, or federal level—designed specifically to reduce the presence of the substance in the environment. Thus, trends (or lack thereof) before that time tell us little about a particular level of jurisdiction's sensitivity to, or ability to deal with, environmental pollution per se. Consider, for example, that the effects of air pollutants other than PM (or smoke) on public health and welfare were not generally known to, or acknowledged by, either the public or policymakers until mid-century, and that as recently as 1959 the *Encyclopædia Britannica* had no entry under air pollution but had two detailed pages on "Smoke and Smoke Prevention," an indication that, for the vast majority of the public, air pollution was synonomous with smoke.[15] That was the case despite scientific evidence suggesting that other substances, such as SO_2, might also be a problem. Hence, if substances other than PM were less noticeable in the

3

first half of this century, it would have to be due to purely economic factors, or happenstance, because sources of smoke (and of total suspended particulates, or TSP), which were being controlled, also emitted those other substances. Another example is sulfates, which were recognized as a pollutant well *after* the passage of the Clean Air Amendments of 1970—that is, after full-scale federalization of air pollution control as we now know it. Thus, it would be inappropriate to conclude anything about the race to the bottom based upon pre-1970 trends for sulfates (except to the extent that they were associated with substances generally recognized as pollutants before 1970).

Chapters 2, 3, and 4 develop and explain the "national" trends for indoor and outdoor air quality and national emissions, respectively. For the traditional pollutants the deterioration of air quality has, by and large, peaked and, nationwide, air quality today is generally the best it has been in decades. The trends in leading environmental indicators show that because of technology, emissions per GNP peaked in the 1920s for SO_2 and in the 1930s for VOC and NO_x, and have been declining since the 1940s, if not longer, for PM and CO (Chapter 4). By the time the Clean Air Amendments of 1970 had federalized air pollution control, smoke had been conquered in most urban areas, and air quality was improving substantially in the most polluted areas—particularly for the very pollutants perceived to be causing the worst problems.

Chapter 5 synthesizes the results from the previous chapters and provides a unified framework (or theory) for understanding why—and the order in which—the various peaks occurred for each pollutant and indicator. That framework helps to explain qualitatively why, in the historical record presented in the previous chapters, improvements in air quality for pollutants known (or perceived) to cause the greatest public health impact came before those for the "lesser" pollutants; in indoor air quality before outdoor air quality; in outdoor air quality before total emissions (for primary pollutants); and for primary pollutants before secondary pollutants.[16] The framework is based upon the notion that society is on a continual quest to improve its quality of life, which is determined by a host of social, economic, and environmental factors. The weights given to each of those factors vary constantly depending upon society's precise circumstances.

4

In the early stages of economic and technological development, which go hand in hand, a society improves its overall quality of life by placing greater emphasis on increasing affluence than on some other determinants, even if that means tolerating some environmental degradation. Greater affluence provides the means for obtaining basic needs and amenities (e.g., food, shelter, water, and electricity) and reducing the most significant risks to public health and safety (e.g., infectious and parasitic diseases and child and maternal mortality). As society gets wealthier, progress is made on those priorities but environmental degradation increases. So environmental problems automatically rise higher on society's priority list of unmet needs, and solving them becomes more urgent because those problems have worsened and become more evident. Thus, environmental quality becomes a more important determinant of the quality of life.

Generally, unless a priority is self-executing (or perhaps even then, for the sake of symbolism), a society will enshrine its priorities into laws and regulations. Moreover, the wealthier the society, the more it can afford to research, develop, and install the technologies necessary for a cleaner environment. As a result, society goes through an "environmental transition," and environmental degradation peaks. Then, further economic and technological development, instead of worsening environmental quality, actually improves it.

Because society has become progressively wealthier and technologically more advanced over the last century, such an environmental transition manifests itself as a peak in a temporal trend line for environmental degradation. In the United States, the transition was further aided by society's technology-assisted evolution from an agrarian to an industrial to a knowledge- and service-based economy. That evolution would, by itself, cause emissions per GNP and emissions per capita to first increase and then decrease. Those trends were also reinforced by the waxing and waning of the economic and demographic influence of the polluting sectors as their relative contributions to national employment and GNP rose and fell. Because ours is a democratic society, that process eventually cleared the way for the promulgation and enforcement of increasingly tougher environmental cleanup policies in the postindustrial era.

Chapter 5 also notes that prior to a society coming to an environmental transition for a specific pollutant—that is, during the early phases of economic and technological development—the "race to the top of the quality of life" may superficially resemble a "race to relax" or a race to the bottom of environmental standards. But once a society gets past the transition, the race to the top of the quality of life may look more like a race to the top of environmental quality, which could create a not-in-my-backyard (NIMBY) situation if the benefits of control for a particular segment of society are substantially less than its costs, or if the costs (but not the benefits) are shifted to the other segments. Thus, the *apparent* race to the bottom and the NIMBY effect are, in fact, two aspects of the same phenomenon—namely, the race to the top of the quality of life—but the former occurs before while the latter occurs after an affluence- and technology-driven environmental transition.

Chapter 5 also discusses the factors that affect the timing of an environmental transition, the level of environmental degradation at which it would occur, and the extent to which one country's experience with such a transition is applicable to other countries.

Chapter 6 examines whether the data provided in the previous chapters in fact support the contention that, prior to the federalization effected by the Clean Air Amendments of 1970, there had been little or no progress in improving air quality[17] and that states had been indulging in a race to the bottom.[18] It finds that the empirical data do not support these two arguments that were used to justify the 1970 federalization.

Chapter 7 identifies those features of federalization that seem to have contributed the most to improvements in air quality above and beyond what states and local agencies would, based upon the evidence, probably have brought about on their own. In this context, it examines the Environmental Protection Agency study on the costs and benefits of the 1970 and 1977 Amendments to the Clean Air Act. This chapter also briefly addresses the economic efficiency of the various measures undertaken pursuant to federalization.

Observing that the nation's remaining air pollution problems are more difficult to address than those that have already been solved, Chapter 7 also offers policy recommendations designed to make air pollution control more effective and efficient in the future without sacrificing the gains of the past. Noting that the likelihood of backsliding is relatively low because of how far the nation has traveled past its environmental transition and the possibility of a substantial political backlash, this chapter recommends a much more decentralized approach than exists today. It suggests that the federal government should continue responsibility for controlling motor vehicle emissions and establishing National Ambient Air Quality Standards (NAAQS), but that the latter should be viewed as idealized goals and the states should be free to choose their own schedules and measures for attaining and maintaining NAAQS with regard to intrastate pollution.

Chapter 7 recommends that control of interstate pollution be negotiated between affected states. It also recommends allowing emissions trades across new and old sources, and instituting "risk-risk" trades across pollutants and programs so that the public receives as much benefit as can be obtained from the moneys implicitly or explicitly allocated by society to improve public health and welfare.

Finally, Chapter 8 concludes the book with some observations regarding the future role of economic growth and technological change in bringing about environmental transitions for the remaining, less tractable pollution problems facing humanity.

1. The History of Air Pollution and Its Control

Introduction

Had the Ancients known about air pollution, Zeus would not have wreaked vengeance upon humanity for Prometheus's theft of fire by presenting Pandora, with her box, to Prometheus's brother, Epimetheus. Air pollution would have been vengeance enough.

Air pollution is at least as old as the first fire, but for millennia human beings simply endured it. Perceptions of air pollution began to change as wood, becoming scarcer and costlier with deforestation and urbanization, was replaced by coal.[1] Beginning in the 13th century, sea coal from Newcastle appeared in London, primarily in the smithies and lime burners.[2] Acceptance of coal as a household fuel came slower. Domestic consumption, originally concentrated in Scotland and northern England and apparently associated with the lower classes, spread to the south and London only after substantial price increases for fuelwood in the 16th century.

The first recorded complaint against air pollution in England came from Queen Eleanor when she visited Nottingham in 1257.[3] During King Edward I's reign, Parliament formed a body to rid London of smoke, the use of coal in furnaces was forbidden, and kilns were banned outright from functioning in the city of London when the Queen was in residence. Some modern writers on air pollution claim that a coal merchant was even tortured and hanged,[4] though at least one authority was unable to confirm this.[5] Reputedly, coal was taxed heavily by Richard III and Henry V. Nevertheless, despite taxes and fines, the shortage of fuelwood and the absence of economic alternatives led to a continual increase in the amount of sea coal imported into London.

In 1661, John Evelyn's *Fumifugium*, an "Invective against the *Smoake* of *London*"[6] and its smells, grime, and effects on health and visibility, offered "a few proposals for the meliorating of the *Aer* of

London: being extremely amazed that . . . [despite] . . . the affluence of all things which may render the People of this vast City, the most happy on Earth, the sordid and accursed Avarice of some particular Persons, should be suffered to prejudice the health and felicity of so many."[7] These included moving brewers, dyers, soap and salt boilers, and other trades using sea coal at least five or six miles outside the city and encircling the city with a greenbelt of hedges, "fragrant Shrubs, Trees and Flowers."[8] While he was about it Evelyn would also banish chandlers, butchers, and fishmongers for their "horrid stinks . . . and unwholesome smells."[9]

A few months later, John Graunt, a self-taught haberdasher, published perhaps the first-ever quantitative epidemiological study, *Natural and Political Observations . . . Upon the Bills of Mortality*.[10] In this remarkable book—also credited with having founded the science of demographics—Grant suggested, based upon 90 years of data on burials and christenings for a country parish and about 60 years for London, "whether a City, as it becomes more populous, doth not, for that very cause, become more *unhealthful*, I [am] inclined to believe, that *London* now is more *unhealthful*, than heretofore, partly for that it is more populous, but chiefly, because I have heard, that 60 years ago few *Sea-Coals* were burnt in *London*, which now are universally used. For I have heard, that *Newcastle* is more *unhealthful* than other places, and that many People cannot at all endure the smoake of *London*, not only for its unpleasantness, but for the suffocation which it causes."[11] In fact, between 1585–86 and 1667–68, coal imports into London had grown elevenfold.[12]

Graunt's epistle, which went through four printings and editions in the next three years and earned its author a fellowship in the Royal Society, surely qualified as a best seller for those times. Despite its substantial success, as Daniel Defoe of *Robinson Crusoe* fame wrote later, it was insufficient during the Great Plague of 1665 to stop the burning of "great quantities of coals . . . even all the summer long and when the weather was hottest, which was done by the advice of the physicians" because they believed that "the sulphurous and nitrous particles that are often found to be in the coal, with that bituminous substance which burns, are all assisting to clear and purge the air, and render it wholesome and safe to breathe in after the noxious particles, as above, are dispersed and burnt up."[13] Defoe noted that this was not universally accepted among physicians, but he believed the pro-burning school "prevailed with good reason; and the experience of the citizens confirmed it, many houses which had constant fires kept in the rooms having never been infected at all; and I must join my experience to it, for I found ... [that] ... keeping good fires kept our rooms sweet and wholesome, and I do verily believe made our whole family so."

Similar ideas persisted at least until the first part of the 20th century. In one of the first American surveys of the scientific literature on the relationship between atmospheric smoke and health, Cohoe (1914) noted that many people believed in the antiseptic power of smoke and coal dust; in fact, because of the popular notion that coal dust is beneficial for tuberculosis, it "has been for years a common custom for those affected with this disease to resort to coal mines, or to build fires and inhale the smoke."[14]

Such attitudes, the lack of real alternatives to coal, the existence of more visible and immediate causes of death and disease, which rendered life "nasty, brutish and short," and—once the industrial revolution got going—the association of smoke with industrialization and, therefore, jobs and prosperity ensured that there would be little progress in controlling smoke for the next two centuries.

Urbanization, Industrialization, and the Growing Smoke Problem

In the United States, as the frontier moved westward so did urbanization and industrialization. However, unlike the eastern seaboard, which was near the eastern Pennsylvania sources of "smokeless" (anthracite) coal, Pittsburgh and areas west of it were close to large supplies of "soft" or highly volatile bituminous coal, which was very smoky when burnt. As early as the late 18th century, Pittsburgh, with its unfavorable meteorology, poor geography, and ready access to soft coal, began to acquire a reputation that would make its name synonymous with smoke.[15] By 1860, U.S. fossil fuel combustion, which had been about 3 trillion British thermal units (tBTU) in 1800, had increased to over 520 tBTU, almost equally divided between anthracite and bituminous coal (Figure 1-1).[16] While this was still overshadowed in the aggregate by fuel wood combustion (at about 2,640 tBTU), cities in the Midwest were beginning to experience smoke problems.

Figure 1-1

U.S. ENERGY CONSUMPTION, 1850–1995

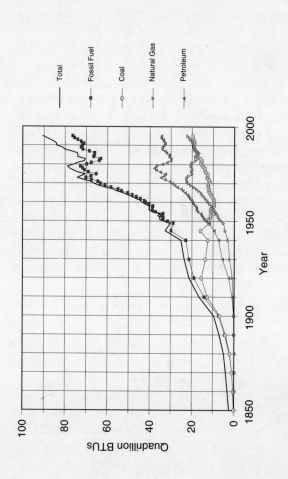

SOURCES: USBOC 1975; DOE 1966.

In 1864, a St. Louis man sued his neighbor, claiming smoke from the latter's shed rendered his house "almost untenantable."[17] In a judgment upheld by the Missouri Supreme Court, the plaintiff was awarded $50. Subsequently, St. Louis promulgated the first air pollution ordinance in the United States: a requirement that chimneys be 20 feet above the surrounding buildings. In 1868, Pittsburgh passed a smoke ordinance aimed at railroads, but this too apparently had little effect. In 1881, Chicago passed an ordinance declaring smoke from boats, locomotives, and chimneys to be a public nuisance subject to a fine of between $5 and $50.[18] In 1890, the state of Ohio granted municipalities the authority to regulate and "compel the consumption of smoke" due to coal burning and to prevent injury and annoyance resulting from the smoke.[19]

Meanwhile, U.S. fossil fuel consumption continued to grow. Wood combustion peaked in the 1870s and was overtaken by fossil fuel combustion in the 1880s. By 1890, bituminous coal—at 2,900 tBTU—had become the largest source of energy, supplying 41 percent of all needs (Figure 1-1).[20] By contrast, wood produced 2,520 tBTU; anthracite coal 1,160 tBTU; petroleum, which had been around since the 1850s, 156 tBTU; natural gas, a newer source, 257 tBTU; and hydropower for a brand new technology, electricity, provided 22 tBTU (fossil fuel equivalent). Smoke was becoming even more of a problem.

However, despite the numerous complaints, efforts by women's and other civic groups (composed generally of people from the upper middle class and the social elite), and local anti-smoke ordinances, there was little progress in the struggle against urban air pollution on either side of the Atlantic. Anti-smoke efforts continued to be stymied by the lack of viable alternatives to coal combustion where it existed, the notion that coal dust and smoke had antiseptic properties, and the general attitude that industrialization was for the common good and that "the smoky atmosphere . . . [was] . . . the index of prosperity of the town."[21]

As if these problems were not enough, in the 1890s some of the smoke control ordinances were overturned in court. St. Louis's was declared unconstitutional by the state Supreme Court on the grounds that it usurped the state's police powers.[22] Cleveland's was found wanting because its ordinance declared smoke to be a nuisance regardless of whether it contributed to injury and annoyance.

By that time, rapid urbanization and industrialization made smoke an issue even in the northeastern cities. Smoke would have been even more evident to the many immigrants who came from the relatively clean countryside to the polluted cities. A number of epidemiological studies done in the latter part of the 19th century in Britain and Germany suggested that smoke and coal burning might be affecting mortality.[23] In 1892, Pittsburgh's natural gas supply, which the city had used for about a decade, ran out.[24] Ordinances were passed to deal with the increased haze and foul air that year and in 1895, but to little avail.

In 1902, two passenger trains collided in New York's Park Avenue tunnel, killing at least 17 people.[25] The thick smoke and steam from the locomotives, which impeded the engineer's view of the lights in the tunnel, were blamed for the accident.[26] This led to several calls to electrify the railway.

The Progressive Era to the Second World War

The tide began to turn toward the end of the last century. The epidemiological studies mentioned above gave ammunition to civic organizations such as smoke abatement leagues, in Pittsburgh, Cincinnati, Boston, and elsewhere. In 1898, Maximilien Ringelmann, a French professor of agricultural engineering, proposed his smoke density chart, which allowed an observer to determine how dark was the smoke being emitted from a chimney.[27] The Ringelmann chart relied on objective measurements that were more or less reproducible from observer to observer, at least for black smoke. The U.S. Geological Survey began using the chart for its investigations of smokeless combustion in St. Louis in 1904, and made it available to the general public in 1908.[28] In 1910 it was written into Boston's smoke abatement ordinance.[29]

Modified versions of the Ringelmann chart served as the primary tool for monitoring and enforcing local smoke abatement regulations (which for practical purposes was synonymous with enforcing air pollution regulations, at least in the United States, until the 1960s and, in some cases, the 1970s[30]). These smoke abatement statutes were finally vindicated—but not until 1915—when the U.S. Supreme Court upheld their constitutionality in *Northwestern Laundry v. City of Des Moines*.[31] That same year it also upheld, in *Hadacheck v. Sebastian*, a Los Angeles ordinance banning manufacture or burning of bricks in a portion of the city because of the smoke associated with those processes.[32]

In the meantime, partly in response to the Park Avenue tunnel accident, New York State passed a law that, while providing other benefits to the New York Central Rail Road, banned steam locomotives from being used in or near New York City within five years[33] (although by the time the railway had been electrified, memories of the accident had apparently dimmed[34]). In 1907, Chicago took a step toward the control of industrial sources by requiring that new and reconstructed furnaces obtain preconstruction permits.[35]

By 1912, the federal Bureau of Mines reported that 23 of the 28 cities that had populations in excess of 200,000 were making some effort to control smoke.[36] Of the remaining five, Los Angeles and San Francisco relied on fuel oil rather than coal; Portland had no enforcement, but it too used fuel oil; Washington, D.C., was deemed relatively clean; and the outlier was New Orleans. The report provided sample smoke ordinances for small-, medium-, and large-sized cities as well as texts of the ordinances from Chicago, Pittsburgh, Des Moines, Milwaukee, and Boston.

But the real engines for progress on the urban smoke problem in the United States as well as in England were economics and technological change—forces that began in the late 19th century and have continued, for one reason or another, to the present day. New, cleaner energy sources such as natural gas, oil, and electricity became increasingly available as substitutes for coal and wood in homes, businesses, and industries. Urbanization, while responsible for many environmental woes, accelerated the process of substitution because higher population densities reduced access to wood and increased the cost-effectiveness and economics of distribution systems for natural gas and electricity. New technologies entered the marketplace that increased the efficiency of all types of combustion equipment, reducing the amount of soot produced and fuel burned for a given amount of usable energy. Those technologies included more efficient and cleaner furnaces and boilers for homes, businesses, industries, and power plants. In some places, underground and street railways powered by steam were electrified; in others, electrification replaced horse-powered street cars, reducing another, but no less real, form of pollution.[37] The automobile, which would later be viewed as an environmental villain, was still a relatively little-used luxury; in 1910 there were two automobile registrations for every 100 households.[38] In fact, the use of motor vehicles in urban areas served an environmental purpose by reducing the horse population and associated wastes, as did the electrification of street railways.

The realization that smoke signified unburnt fuel led industry, railroads, and even households to make efforts to reduce it. It was thought to be not only good economics but also good citizenship. That notion was clearly incorporated in the Ohio statute, which allowed municipal authorities to "compel the consumption of smoke." In time, even the Great War would be pressed into service against this foe; as the Pittsburgh Bureau of Smoke Regulation exhorted, "it must never be forgotten that loss of black smoke means loss of heat and that every unit of heat thrown away is so much aid given to the enemy."[39] On the other hand, the Bureau of Mines, part of the U.S. Department of the Interior, suspended its smoke abatement "campaign" during the war years.[40] At the other extreme, in Milwaukee, the war was used as justification to go, literally, full steam ahead; as a result, "smoky" days increased from 47 in 1916 to 212 in 1918.[41]

Thus, despite unsatisfactory and generally poorly enforced laws, progress was being made. Across the Atlantic, the "black fogs" of London had been largely eliminated by 1912.[42] The amount of sunshine in winter had almost doubled over the previous 30 years, due mainly to the electrification of underground railways; the use of more gas appliances for heating and cooking (which increased from about 50,000 in 1891 to 1.5 million in 1911); the efforts of the London Coal Smoke Abatement Society, which helped educate the public and improve operating practices to reduce smoke generation; industry's realization that smoke was due to inefficient combustion; and, possibly, a little bit of meteorological luck.[43] The Assistant Curator of the Kew Gardens even ascribed the improved health of a valuable "old Cedar of Lebanon" in the gardens to the improvement in the atmosphere.[44] It is useful to note that despite the increased use of gas, the worst problems "almost certainly were from domestic fires, for the darkest fogs have been on Sundays and Christmas Day," and between 7 a.m. and 9 a.m. and just before dinnertime.[45]

In the United States, a 1917 report from Pittsburgh's Bureau of Smoke Regulation noted that the days of dense smoke from January to June declined from 29 to 6 days between 1912 and 1917, and days of light smoke declined from 64 to 44 days even as consumption of coal increased threefold.[46] It attributed these improvements to increased combustion efficiency (largely achieved through modulation of fuel and air supply and the replacement of hand firing with mechanical stokers) and to switches to low-volatile coal. In one case, the amount of power produced almost doubled; the operators not only saved fuel, they also "released more than twenty (20) men from non-productive labor to productive labor." In another case, the annual fuel saving amounted to 50 percent of the cost of the mechanical stoker. Paradoxically, even though the air had become cleaner the laundry business prospered, because "people are wearing more light colored goods than ever before. It is only necessary to cite the increasing number of Palm Beach suits to be seen about town since their first appearance in the summer of 1915."[47]

Regulations do seem to have made a difference for Chicago. The 1907 preconstruction regulation gave the city's Department of Smoke Abatement the clout to successfully insist upon mechanical stokers for new and reconstructed furnaces. A 1912 report boasted that in one year the city had brought 1,040 suits and collected over $25,000 in fines and costs; 3,000 out of 14,000 stationary combustion sources had been reconstructed; under threat of suit, tugboats and marine vessels plying the Chicago River switched to "semi-smokeless" West Virginia coal; and both locomotives and stationary sources changed operating practices to reduce smoke generation. Those measures helped reduce smoke by 75 percent in the central city.[48] Just as important as the rules themselves and the apparent willingness to enforce them was the fact that the city employed experienced and knowledgeable engineers who reviewed designs and operating practices and worked cooperatively with coal-burning enterprises to help diminish the smoke from their operations, apparently threatening and instituting suits only as a last resort. No doubt it also helped that the regulations did not get ahead of what was economically doable.

The technological trends accelerated in subsequent decades. Increasing affluence made it possible for individual households and businesses to voluntarily purchase cleaner, new, more efficient technologies because they valued lower fuel bills and cleanliness and convenience for their homes and businesses. Moreover, once the new technologies were installed, gratification was immediate; people had no doubt that the premises were cleaner and their money had

17

been well spent. By 1932 the number of residential natural gas consumers had risen to 14.5 million—that is, to over 50 percent of nonfarm occupied housing units.[49] Because household and commercial emissions were released relatively close to the ground and in areas where a good part of the population spent much of their time, the health benefits of the resulting reductions in emissions would have been disproportionately large. (Recall that much of London's worst smoke problems, for instance, were due to domestic cooking and heating.)

Another major source of air pollution was the steam locomotive. Continuing efforts begun prior to the First World War, railroads improved the operations of their steam locomotives to reduce smoke generation, a number of urban rail systems were electrified, and the diesel electric locomotive began displacing coal-fired locomotives. The use of bituminous coal in Class I railroads peaked in 1920 at 135 million tons; during the Second World War it peaked again at 132 million tons. By 1950, it had declined to less than half that (61 million tons). In 1960 it stood at 2 million tons and by 1970 it was a footnote in statistical tables.[50]

The increased efficiency of coal use, and end users' preference for oil and gas, helped cause a reduction in the growth rate for coal consumption (Figure 1-1). Other factors also contributed. Despite efforts to make liquid fuel (coal oil) from coal, the product proved unsuitable for fueling the burgeoning demands of the internal combustion engine. Moreover, coal combustion for the production of electricity did not keep pace with the spectacular growth in the use of electricity: Technological change drove down the heat rate (i.e., the heat energy needed to produce one kilowatt-hour of energy, which had been 121,000 BTU in 1899 but declined to 58,900 BTU in 1913 and 23,400 BTU in 1929).[51] Since the mid-1960s the heat rate has more or less stabilized at today's level of 10,300 BTU. As a result, coal consumption peaked in the early 1920s, even as use of oil, gas, and electricity continued to climb (Figure 1-1). Any chance of a sustained comeback for coal was killed by the Great Depression. Consumption exceeded its earlier peak only after the next war effort had commenced.

Adoption of alternating current and improvements in the technology of transformers and transmission lines also made it possible to deliver electricity long distances without substantial energy losses,

Figure 1-2
PITTSBURGH: DUSTFALL AND TOTAL SUSPENDED PARTICULATE CONCENTRATIONS, 1912–77

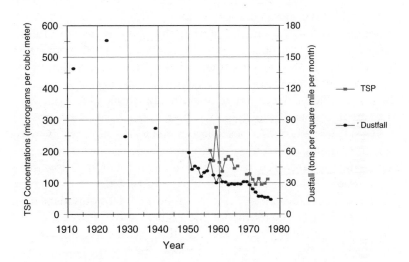

SOURCE: Davidson 1979.

allowing power plants to move initially to the outskirts of a city and, later, to the very mouth of the mine. Those locational changes improved urban air quality, even though they do not show up in national estimates of fossil fuel use or emissions.

Anecdotal information suggests that such market-driven choices and new technologies improved outdoor air quality in several urban areas. Smoke density in Chicago declined 50 percent between 1911 and 1933, although solid fuel consumption practically doubled.[52] Davidson's reconstruction of Pittsburgh's air quality indicates that between the two world wars, the number of hours of dense smoke decreased even though the total number of smoky (dense and moderate) days increased.[53] Those trends are not contradictory: perhaps Pittsburgh had more gray days, but the worst or really bad days were not that bad. This interpretation is consistent with measured declines in dustfall (see Figure 1-2).[54]

Some environmental historians have asserted that after the Great War, the nation turned to the business of prosperity; that as a result, public pressure for reducing smoke was much more muted in the 1920s; and that it more or less collapsed during the Depression, to the extent that Pittsburgh, for instance, dismantled much of its smoke abatement program.[55] While it is reasonable to think that the Depression would have dampened pressure to reduce smoke, there may be another explanation for the apparent apathy in the '20s: things were improving, particularly for the segments of the population most likely to protest against smoke. The trends noted above in the patterns of fuel use (Figure 1-1) and air quality support this rationale. The more affluent were not only switching to cleaner fuels, they were moving away from the city center to the cleaner suburbs—a movement initially made possible by streetcars and later, increasingly, by automobiles. Thus, homes and residential areas were getting cleaner, giving many women who spent most of their time there (see Chapter 2)—especially upper-middle-class women, among the prime movers of the earlier protests—less reason for dissatisfaction, at least as long as memories of the higher smoke levels had not faded. If they wanted even fresher air, they could drive out into the countryside in their automobiles; by 1930, there were 77 registered automobiles per every 100 households.[56]

With the onset of the Great Depression, the public's emphasis on controlling smoke waned. A survey by the Smoke Prevention Association in 1936, in the midst of the Depression, reveals active support among civic associations for smoke abatement in 7 of the 10 cities surveyed that had populations in excess of half a million, but virtually no involvement in those with lesser populations.[57] The three exceptions were Los Angeles, San Francisco, and Milwaukee, which were also among the exceptions noted in the 1912 Bureau of Mines survey.[58] In light of today's circumstances, it is ironic that one of the exceptions was Los Angeles. But it is hardly surprising, since Los Angeles depended on oil rather than coal; heating demand in its legendary climate was minimal; air conditioning was far less commonplace than it is today; what industry Los Angeles had also felt the effects of the Depression, which would have dampened enthusiasm for industrial controls; and, finally, the love affair with the automobile was still new enough that its benefits, but not yet its flaws, were evident.

Despite the decline in official interest in smoke reduction, indus-tries, businesses, and homeowners continued to switch to cleaner fuels and invest in cleaner-burning combustion equipment. As late as 1940, even though the economy and the war effort were picking up, many communities cited those factors as the reasons for improved air quality.[59] However, conditions in Pittsburgh and St. Louis, cities that were among the pioneers of air pollution control in the United States, seem to have deteriorated, which led to renewed smoke control efforts in those cities (Figure 1-2, for Pittsburgh). A new ordinance was passed in St. Louis in 1940 with substantial success.[60] Pittsburgh followed suit in July 1941, but compliance was postponed five years due to the war effort.[61]

The Post–World War II Period to the 1960s

After World War II there was rapid improvement in the smoke situation. The trends that had been arrested temporarily during the war years asserted themselves once again. In Cincinnati, between July 1, 1948, and June 30, 1949, airborne solids declined 17 percent, from 32,230 tons to 26,780 tons (some of the reduction may have been weather related).[62] Two-thirds of the improvement was due to reductions in fly ash and other incombustible portions of those sol-ids. A five-year study for Cincinnati confirms that suspended partic-ulates declined between 1946 and 1951.[63] In Pittsburgh, between 1946 and 1955, atmospheric visibility markedly improved.[64] The hours of heavy smoke dropped by 96.6 percent (from 298 to 10 hours) and hours of moderate and heavy smoke declined 88.8 percent (from 1,005 to 113 hours).[65] Railroads and river boats switched from coal to diesel. Industries and large commercial and apartment buildings purchased mechanical stokers and other smoke reduction devices. Private residences switched first to smokeless coals, then to natural gas. Tarr, the eminent environmental historian, has noted that between 1940 and 1950 the number of Pittsburgh households using coal declined from 80 to 31.6 percent while the number of those using natural gas increased from 17.4 to 65 percent, and that most of these changes occurred after 1945.[66] Dustfall records in Pittsburgh also show substantial improvements, declining from 56.3 tons per month per square mile in 1948 to 48.9 in 1955; in 1938 the figure had been 60.0.[67] Similar, though perhaps less spectacular, fuel switches by households occurred in other urban areas, including Chicago,

Figure 1-3
GROWTH OF MUNICIPAL, COUNTY, AND STATE AIR POLLUTION
PROGRAMS, 1880–1980

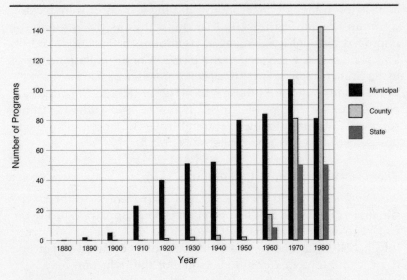

SOURCE: Stern 1982.

Cincinnati, Cleveland, Columbus, Louisville, Milwaukee, Pittsburgh, and St. Louis.[68] As a result of such developments, by the 1960s the smoke problem was virtually solved in most urban areas.

The progress in controlling the smoke problem can also be seen in Stern's tabulation of the number of agencies that were "implementing . . . their laws."[69] Despite greater public apathy, the number of "effective" municipalities increased from 23 in 1910 to 40 in 1920 to 51 in 1930, then leveled off before picking up substantially after the Second World War. See Figure 1-3, which also shows the shift of authority from the local to county and state levels in the 1960s, by which time the smoke problem was more or less solved.

Once it was accepted that the smoke problem was solvable, if not solved, smoke restrictions actually got tighter. In 1940, 81 percent of local ordinances allowed smoke denser than Ringelmann number 2 (or 40 percent opacity); that declined to 69 percent in 1950 and 41 percent in 1960. By 1975, only 3 percent would tolerate such levels.[70]

Figure 1-4
DUST COLLECTION EFFICIENCIES, 1900–70

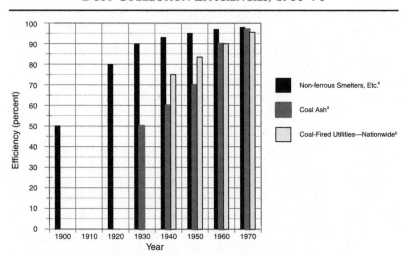

SOURCES: Tarr 1966; Moore 1966.

[a]For the Hudson-Raritan basin; see text and accompanying footnotes.

[b]The 1970 figure is actually for 1966; see text and accompanying footnotes.

These tougher requirements were matched by increased efficiencies of control of smoke and dust pollution, as indicated by Figure 1-4. For instance, Tarr and Robert U. Ayres estimate that control of coal ash averaged across all users (households, industries, and power plants) in the Hudson-Raritan region (which, in their study, included the New York Metropolitan Area, the lower Hudson River basin to Troy, New York, and a substantial portion of New Jersey) increased from 50 percent in 1930 to 60 percent in 1940, 70 percent in 1950, 90 percent in 1960, and 97 percent in 1970.[71] In the same region—once one of the nation's important centers of copper and lead smelting and refining—dust control of nonferrous smelters and related activities climbed from an estimated 50 percent in 1900 to 90 percent by 1930, 93 percent by 1940, 95 percent by 1950, and 98 percent by 1970.[72] Nationwide estimates of overall dust collection efficiency for power plants, which had been 40 percent pre-1940, had climbed to 75 percent by 1940, over 80 percent by 1950, 90 percent by 1960, and 95.5 percent by 1966.[73] Note that an increase

23

in efficiency from 90 to 95.5 percent sounds relatively trivial. In fact, it reduces emissions by 55 percent.

But just as the Hydra sprouted new heads as the old ones were cut off, new problems cropped up as old ones were solved.

First, elimination of smoke had increased fly ash from combustion, coal pulverization and better air mixing reduced smoke but caused more ash to be emitted, and the Ringelmann chart was not suitable for use with grey ash or brown smoke.

Second, in the early 1940s, Los Angeles began experiencing a new kind of smog quite unlike the traditional smoke problem experienced elsewhere in the industrialized world—a smog that irritated the eyes and reduced visibility. Los Angeles County, with the aid of the *Los Angeles Times*, enlisted the services of Professor Raymond Tucker of Washington University in St. Louis, who as smoke commissioner had been credited with solving St. Louis's smoke problems "against far greater odds than those faced in Los Angeles."[74] The County also hired a noted air pollution expert, Dr. Louis McCabe, formerly with the federal Bureau of Mines, as the first director of its Air Pollution Control District (APCD).[75] Despite a substantial, broad-based effort to control both sulfur dioxide (SO_2) and particulate matter (PM) from stationary sources[76]—which, for instance, helped reduce particulate emissions from known sources by over 50 percent between 1947 and 1949[77]—the citizens of Los Angeles perceived little, if any, progress in controlling smog. In 1950, A. J. Haagen-Smit, a professor of biochemistry at Caltech, proposed that motor vehicles might be implicated in the formation of Los Angeles smog. After several years of research—and in recognition of the fact that despite successful efforts to control PM and SO_2 sources the smog problem had still not been solved—by about 1957 most experts accepted that the smog was caused by the formation of "secondary" pollutants (such as ozone and other oxidants) formed by the reaction in sunlight of hydrocarbons (or volatile organic compounds) and nitrogen oxides emitted by motor vehicles and power plants and by other processes, and aggravated by Los Angeles' peculiar geography and weather conditions.[78]

Third, a series of air pollution episodes occurred in which excess deaths and sicknesses were noted and covered almost immediately in newspapers. The first one was the four-day inversion episode in Donora, Pennsylvania, in October 1948, resulting in 18 excess deaths in a population of 14,000. That is 15 percent of all the deaths we would expect today from all causes in a full year in a population of equivalent size. That translates into 37,000 additional deaths per week in a population the size of the present population of the United States. Retrospective measurements indicated that daily SO_2 and PM concentrations in Donora may have been at least 1,800 $\mu g/m^3$ and 5,320 $\mu g/m^3$, respectively.[79] By comparison, the 24-hour U.S. public health–related National Ambient Air Quality Standards (NAAQS) adopted in 1971 for SO_2 and PM were 365 $\mu g/m^3$ and 260 $\mu g/m^3$, respectively.[80] The second pollution episode was the infamous five-day London episode of December 1952. One-day mean SO_2 and smoke concentrations reached 3,830 $\mu g/m^3$ and 4,460 $\mu g/m^3$, respectively.[81] Visibility was down to between 1 and 5 meters.[82] Four thousand excess deaths were attributed to that episode out of a population of 8.5 million. For a population equal to that of the United States today, that would translate into about 100,000 excess deaths in less than a week![83]

These were not the first episodes in the industrialized world. At least one had occurred in the Meuse Valley in Belgium in 1930 but it had not left a permanent impression on the public, even though it was later estimated that mortality had increased to 9.5 times the background level.[84] Twenty-four-hour SO_2 and PM concentrations were later estimated at 25,000 $\mu g/m^3$ and 12,500 $\mu g/m^3$, respectively. But the post–World War II episodes were different. Donora was right here at home and London was almost home, not only because of a general anglophilia but also because the world had shrunk: millions had gone to or through England during or since the war, and familiarity with the land and its people made their tragedy that much more compelling. Moreover, the United States was no longer in a depression, nor was it fighting a war. Perhaps the decreases in mortality due to other causes also made these episodes more urgent. Certainly, decreases in death rates did make the job of detecting excess deaths easier and faster: In 1900 the national annual death rate was over 17.2 per 1,000; by 1948 it had declined to 9.9 per 1,000.[85] That may also explain why past episodes involving excess deaths had not been detected, though the air may well have been worse. Of equal importance, however—as Samuel B. Hays and others have noted—is the fact that increasing affluence made the general public more desirous of a better quality of life and less tolerant of pollution, a theme that will be examined in greater detail in Chapter 5.[86]

25

Other episodes occurred in the '50s and '60s in both London and New York.[87] About 170 deaths were ascribed to the last major one, which occurred in New York around Thanksgiving 1966.[88] Those episodes galvanized public support behind air pollution control and set the stage for sweeping regulations. The U.K. Clean Air Act was passed in 1956. In the United States, the initiative was taken by numerous local and state agencies (see Figure 1-3). By 1956, there were 82 local air pollution control programs.[89] The first state program began in Oregon in 1951, and by 1954 there were 14.[90] The federal government helped out by providing research, training, and technical assistance under the Air Pollution Control Act of 1955 and, under the Clean Air Act of 1963, grants for developing, establishing, or improving state and local programs.

The 1963 act also established a "conference" procedure to allow the federal Department of Health, Education and Welfare (HEW) to address interstate or, at the request of state and local agencies, intrastate pollution.[91] Under that procedure HEW could convene a conference involving representatives from the appropriate state and local agencies in order to analyze the sources, extent, and impacts of pollution in the affected area. Opportunity was provided for affected industry and other parties to be heard. If, at the end of the conference, HEW determined insufficient progress was being made to protect the general health and welfare, it could recommend specific actions and, if necessary, use federal court proceedings to enforce the recommendations. By 1968, the conference procedure was invoked in at least nine interstate areas that together involved over 10 percent of the nation's population. The general impression seems to be that the process did not lead to much pollution control because, the argument goes, only one case ever went to court.[92]

While other areas of the country focused on PM and SO_2 from stationary sources, Los Angeles (and California) were struggling against their own particular brand of automobile-generated photochemical smog. In 1959 California adopted ambient air quality standards for ethylene, nitrogen oxides (NO_x), photochemical oxidants, SO_2, and carbon monoxide (CO).[93] CO had long been known as the poisonous component of combustion gases that could kill indoors if not vented properly. Like volatile organic compounds (VOC), it had become a significant air pollutant with the increased use of motor vehicles. To help meet the ambient standards, California established motor vehicle emission standards. Beginning with the 1964 model year, no new vehicles could be sold in California unless they were equipped with a crankcase control device certified by the Motor Vehicle Pollution Control Board.[94] Already, beginning with the 1961 model year, motor vehicle manufacturers had started voluntarily equipping new vehicles sold in California with such devices.[95] (These crankcase controls were also voluntarily extended to the entire U.S. market in model year 1963.)[96] California's motor vehicle exhaust standards for new cars went into effect in 1966. Control requirements for used vehicles proved to be much more problematic and very unpopular with the public.[97] Eventually, because of a public outcry against these measures, the requirements were scaled back so that crankcase controls were only required for resales of cars from 1955 or later model years.[98]

The requirements came not a moment too soon: in the 1960s, 1-hour ozone concentrations often exceeded 1,000 $\mu g/m^3$ and, occasionally, 1,200 $\mu g/m^3$ in the Los Angeles air basin.[99] By the end of 1970, ambient monitoring data showed substantial progress (see Figure 1-5).[100] Between 1966 and 1970, the number of times the future (1971) oxidant NAAQS were exceeded annually in downtown Los Angeles dropped from 1,163 to 602.[101] CO air quality also improved. In 1965 CO concentrations in downtown Los Angeles exceeded the future 8-hour NAAQS 78 to 99 percent of the time; by 1970, that frequency had dropped to 40 percent.[102]

By the mid- to late '60s, the automobile was also becoming a problem in the urban areas of the Northeast. The New York and Pennsylvania legislatures even considered pollution control devices for new vehicles.[103] Based upon anecdotal evidence of damage to vegetation and rubber and a handful of ambient measurements in and around a few eastern and midwestern cities, Middleton and Haagen-Smit suggested that ozone and oxidants might be ubiquitous problems, and not just in the United States.[104]

Despite these warnings, the prevailing attitude among professionals seems to have been that "except for a few isolated instances which are somewhat doubtful, [cities outside California have not] been subjected to the . . . Los Angeles-type smog problem,"[105] and the initial focus on the automobile was due to CO rather than photochemical oxidants or their precursors, VOC and NO_x. As S. Smith Griswold, associate director of the National Center for Air Pollution Control, U.S. Public Health Service, noted, "Hydrocarbons appear

Figure 1-5
LOS ANGELES: TRENDS IN OZONE, 1956–72

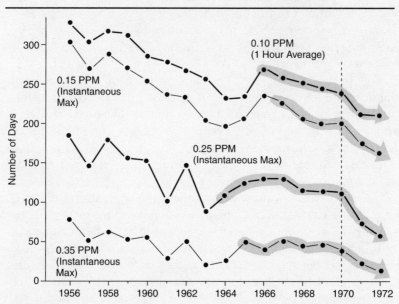

NOTE: Number of days that total oxidants reached one hour maxima of 0.10 ppm and instantaneous values of 0.15, 0.25, and 0.35 ppm in the L.A. Air Pollution Control District as compiled by California Air Resources Board (1974).

SOURCE: Ellsaesser (1995) based on data from L.A. Air Pollution Control District.

to be of most significance in Los Angeles. It may be found that carbon monoxide is of most concern in the canyons of Manhattan. . . . Worldwide, the vehicular pollutant of greatest concern to health officials is carbon monoxide."[106]

From today's perspective, it is remarkable that several *Reports for Consultation* issued from mid-1968 to late 1969 by the National Air Pollution Control Administration, the forerunner to today's Environmental Protection Agency (EPA), to support the designation of "air quality control regions" under the Air Quality Act of 1967 invariably deal with total suspended particulates (TSP), SO_2, and CO, but fail to mention *any* concern for oxidants or hydrocarbons except for regions in California.[107] As late as July 1970, New York City was assigning a much lower priority to oxidant pollution when, after a prolonged inversion, it was officially declared a problem.[108] Until that time, New York City too had been more concerned with the automobile as a source of CO.[109] At the time of the Clean Air Amendments of 1970, few areas knew they were not measuring up to the proposed total oxidant standard, and it was not until 1973, when an "unanticipated ... development [occurred] brought about by increased monitoring" that it began to be suspected that oxidants could be transported long ranges to nonurban areas.[110] The description by Laitos, an environmental analyst, of the events leading up to Wisconsin's first statewide ozone alert on July 19, 1973, captures well the astonishment of state air pollution officials at discovering high ozone levels in outlying areas of the state.[111] Similarly, the author remembers, when he was working in the Michigan Air Quality Division in the mid-1970s, the surprise with which state officials greeted monitoring results that indicated that nonmetropolitan areas of their state were exceeding the oxidant standard.

The idea that CO was a greater problem than ozone may have been reinforced by the tendency of participants in the policy debates to lump all pollutants together when describing the importance of motor vehicle emissions. For instance, during the debates in Congress leading up to the Clean Air Amendments of 1970, it was stated that, "by weight," CO was 47 percent of the nationwide emissions problem[112] and that transportation accounted for 42 percent of the national air pollution problem and 64 percent of the CO problem.[113]

California's foray into motor vehicle emissions control, and the broader concern about CO, energized Congress to pass the Motor Vehicle Air Pollution Control Act of 1965, which gave the federal government authority to regulate hydrocarbons (HC) and CO from motor vehicles. Under that law, California's vehicle emissions standards for the 1967 model year were extended nationally, starting with the 1968 model year. The rationale for this action was that a study (admittedly disputed) showed that any area with over 50,000 people would have "enough motor vehicles to create the potential for an air pollution problem."[114] As the argument went, control of vehicle emissions was necessary, but local controls over vehicles engaged in interstate commerce would be inadequate. Moreover, there would be tremendous confusion if each state had its own standards. The auto companies disputed the underlying premise but acquiesced in the outcome; they would rather be subject to 1 set of standards than 50.[115] As the Automobile Manufacturers Association stated later, "A minimum of variation in requirements is in the best interests of the public, the industry, and eventually the regulatory agencies themselves."[116]

But the 1965 Act was insufficient to deter other states from considering their own motor vehicle standards. For instance, in August 1966, Governor Nelson Rockefeller signed a law giving the New York Air Pollution Control Board the authority to establish motor vehicle emission controls "with due consideration being given to Federal laws and regulations."[117] In response, the Air Quality Act of 1967, signed by President Johnson on November 21, 1967, explicitly preempted state regulation of automobile emissions standards except for California.

The Air Quality Act of 1967 required the federal government to designate air quality control regions and publish air quality criteria and control technology documents. Based on these criteria and documents, states were to develop ambient air quality standards and formulate implementation plans for federal approval. By mid-1970, 21 states had established TSP and SO_2 ambient air quality standards and 20 air quality control regions had also proposed or promulgated such standards.[118] While several states received federal approval for their ambient standards, none of the 21 plans submitted received approval.[119] The process itself was deemed to be a failure.[120] The process may have failed, but, as we shall see later, available data suggest that air quality on the ground was improving for the pollutants most directly associated with mortality and morbidity—TSP and SO_2—especially in the worst areas.

State and local programs generally concentrated on controlling the density of smoke visible to the naked eye, open burning, incinerators in buildings and apartments, and rudimentary controls on industries. Some areas adopted sulfur-in-fuel regulations and established lower limits on stack heights to ensure that concentrations at or near ground level were not inordinately high.[121]

The increased use of oil and diesel also facilitated sulfur-in-fuel regulations. It is easier to desulfurize those fuels and to enforce the regulations since authorities need only focus on a few fuel distributors, and even fewer refiners, rather than on millions of consumers. Moreover, desulfurization of natural gas is self-enforcing because it is in the supplier's economic interest: any significant amount of sulfur in the gas creates an obnoxious odor and corrodes appliances as well as the distribution system.[122]

Power plants installed tall stacks, once "almost symbolic of good industrial air pollution practice" but now frowned upon officially in the United States, to reduce ground level concentrations in their immediate vicinity.[123] Finally, in response to regulations, control technology improved dramatically for all types of processes. For example, for control of TSP at power plants, cyclones (which were 60 to 75 percent efficient) were replaced, first by "high-efficiency" multicyclones (85 to 95 percent efficient), then electrostatic precipitators (initially, 90 to 97 percent) and, eventually, baghouses [99(+) percent].[124] As a result of such efforts (Figure 1-4), overall dust collection efficiencies increased substantially for fossil fuel combustion and other processes.

Between 1950 and 1970, SO_2, PM, and CO emissions from the residential sector declined 76, 73, and 66 percent, respectively.[125] The public health–related benefit of those reductions was very high because more of the reductions seem to have occurred in urban areas with higher population densities, low-level emissions magnify the ground-level impact of air pollution, and the reductions improved air quality in the area where most people spend the majority of their time, namely, in and around their homes (see Chapters 2 and 3).

These developments combined to result in remarkable progress, particularly for those pollutants that were responsible directly or indirectly for the crisis episodes. In New York City, SO_2 levels were reduced by more than half between 1964 and 1970 (see Figure 1-6),[126] while daily TSP levels, which had been as high as 1,000 $\mu g/m^3$ during the November 1953 episode, declined to 280 $\mu g/m^3$ by 1972.[127] TSP levels in Pittsburgh had also been cut by half between 1959 and 1970 (Figure 1-2).[128] Dustfall in Chicago had dropped from 395 tons per square mile in 1928 to 43 tons per square mile in 1963.[129] Measurements also declined in Cincinnati, Chicago, Detroit, and Philadelphia (Figure 1-7).[130] By and large, as we shall see in greater detail in Chapters 3 and 6, although TSP levels may have worsened in some rural areas, the era of major episodes with noticeably high mortality rates was over.

Full-Scale Federalization: The 1970 Clean Air Amendments and After

Some observers imply that the 1963 act was a failure because only one case ever went to court under the conference procedure;

Figure 1-6
NEW YORK: AMBIENT SO$_2$ CONCENTRATIONS, 1963–72

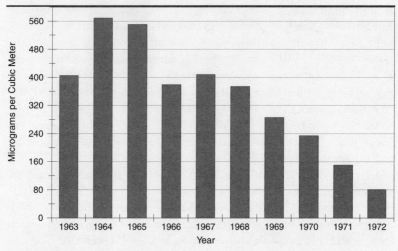

SOURCE: Schimmel and Murawski 1975.

Figure 1-7
TRENDS IN DUSTFALL IN VARIOUS URBAN AREAS, 1920s–'60s

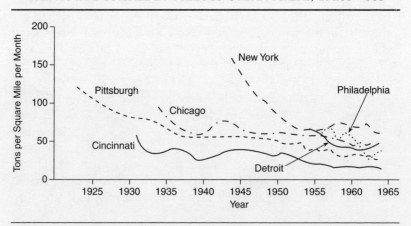

SOURCE: Ludwig et al. 1970.

similarly, the 1967 act has been labeled "fundamentally defective, because the enforcement provisions were weak."[131] This, of course, confuses form with substance, and "enforcement provisions" with progress in the air. In fact, as noted by the eminent environmental economists, Paul Portney of Resources for the Future[132] and Robert Crandall of the Brookings Institution,[133] there was impressive progress in improving air quality prior to 1970. This is consistent with the previously noted anecdotes concerning Pittsburgh (Figure 1-2), Los Angeles (Figure 1-5), and New York (Figure 1-6) and, as we shall see in greater detail in Chapter 3, with data nationwide.

Enforcement actions cannot, and should not, be the criteria for measuring success or failure. There are historical instances in which tough enforcement provisions and increases in enforcement action were due to massive failures in policy and did not necessarily result in any net improvement in public health or welfare. An extreme case is the situation following the establishment of prohibition. The only measures of success that count are the extent to which the risks to public health and welfare are reduced and at what social and economic cost.

Perhaps the failure of the *processes* envisaged by the 1963 and 1967 acts contributed to the perception that progress was too little and too late. Several arguments were offered for a larger federal role in air pollution control.[134] First, air pollution does not respect political boundaries, and state and local authorities would not make any effort to reduce pollution that originates in their own jurisdiction but affects adjacent jurisdictions. Second, in the absence of federal regulations, states and local jurisdictions competing for jobs and economic growth would inevitably sacrifice the environment. In other words, there would be a "race to relax" environmental standards, which would compromise net societal welfare—in other words, there would be a "race to the bottom."[135] The third argument claimed that the failure of the process outlined in the 1967 Air Quality Act proved that state and local authorities could not be trusted to improve air quality. Fourth, many industries saw federal regulation as a method of ensuring that they had a "level playing field," meaning that their out-of-state competitors did not have an advantage because of low cleanup requirements. Moreover, larger companies with plants in several states would rather deal with 1 powerful chief than 50 lesser chieftains. If nothing else, that would reduce their overhead costs, possibly giving them a competitive edge over smaller or new companies. Some companies may even have thought they could "capture" the federal regulators.[136] They would, in time, be in for a rude surprise.

Regardless of the merits of these arguments, larger factors were at work and, ultimately, politics prevailed. The political and social landscape was changing. The reports of numerous excess deaths associated with air pollution episodes in the 1960s had heightened concern. The air pollution problem cried out for a solution. And now that households were cleaner, industrial and downtown areas seemed, by contrast, that much dirtier and in greater need of control. People were living longer and healthier. And as old risks were conquered, the smaller, remaining risks seemed to be even more threatening. Had not the United States sent a man to the moon? If we could do that, certainly we could deal with more mundane problems on earth. All it took was ingenuity, money, and resolve.

Despite such optimism, opposition to the Vietnam War had stoked widespread suspicion about the military-industrial complex among certain segments of the population. Some establishment leaders may also have seen in the environment a way to channel youthful idealism away from anti-war protests and win back the support of the disenchanted for the institutions of government. As Senator Gaylord Nelson of Wisconsin would put it, "the failure of government or industry to move against air pollution strengthened the hand of those who argue that the Establishment could not solve the nation's problems."[137] Environmentalism was something that could—and, as events would prove, did—bring the establishment and anti-establishmentarians together.

Perhaps nothing better captures both the national spirit of optimism and the desire to coopt the energies of the young than Vice President Humphrey's call to arms in his address to the third quadrennial National Conference on Air Pollution more than two years *before* the landing on the moon:[138]

> Our Nation can do anything that it wills to do. We have proved it. We will build a supersonic transport . . . the engineers say we can. We are at a point where we can control genetics . . . transplant organs . . . [create life artificially].
>
> We are doing fantastic things when we will to do them. We are going to be able to put into orbit a manned orbiting laboratory. We will construct that laboratory in orbit. We will nail it together. We will have men going in and out of the laboratory just as we go in and out of an underground plant or factory . . . on earth. And it will all be in the next ten years. We know that.

We are able to do practically anything that we want to do, if we really want to do it and if we are willing to dedicate the necessary resources to it.

We will be communicating all over the world with communications satellites. We will have a University of the World in ten years. . . . We can do all this.

So don't tell me you don't know how to control some fumes coming out of a bus. Don't tell me that we are incapable of doing something about sulfur oxides. Don't tell me this— I don't believe it. I tell you we ought to make up our minds to do this. We *have* to do it. [Emphasis in original]

Or must we list the casualties every day, as we do in Viet Nam?

As a matter of fact, there are more people dying from emphysema than there are on the field of battle. [There is] "guerilla warfare" . . . loose in this country, a hidden enemy [amongst us] known as air pollution.

While the automobile was becoming a major problem, at least on the coasts, the millions of car drivers and owners were deemed relatively blameless. The blame was assigned—in the words of John Evelyn—to "the sordid and accursed Avarice of some particular Persons," namely, the automobile companies, who epitomized the military-industrial complex and who, it was widely rumored, had systematically conspired to keep cleaner cars and alternatives to the internal combustion engine off the market.

In 1969, in its waning days, the Johnson Administration's Justice Department sued the Automobile Manufacturers Association and the four major U.S. auto companies for antitrust violations and alleged a conspiracy to retard automobile pollution control.[139] The settlement of that suit by the Nixon Administration under a consent decree gave rise to several protests.[140] At least six cities and counties, including New York City and Los Angeles County, and 7 states filed suit against the association and four companies seeking restitution for damages to public buildings and higher welfare payments due to pollution-related diseases.[141] Subsequently, 15 other states filed a similar suit with the Supreme Court.[142] Ralph Nader started a campaign to "Make GM Responsible."[143] Eventually, proposals would be put forth in Congress to *ban* new auto sales in 1975 if 90 percent of the emissions were not removed.[144]

In the meantime, President Nixon labored to harness the forces of environmentalism, or at least to deny them to Senator Muskie— sometimes called "Mr. Clean"—the 1968 Democratic nominee for vice president and a potential presidential candidate in 1972.[145] Nixon established the Council on Environmental Quality on January 1, 1970.[146] The environment received special mention in his January State of the Union address. Nixon continued his offensive with a special message on the environment on February 10. That same day the administration bill on clean air was introduced in the House. It would have substantially expanded the federal role to include setting national ambient air quality standards and technologically feasible stationary source emissions standards for both new and old sources.[147] On March 4, Muskie introduced his own bill in the Senate. The success of the first Earth Day that year only escalated the stakes. On July 9, Nixon proposed establishing the EPA. By the time a bill emerged from the Senate subcommittee and committee, Muskie, in an effort to put his own mark on the legislation—and goaded by an earlier, widely publicized Ralph Nader report that questioned his environmental credentials[148]—had upped the ante considerably and not just with respect to motor vehicles. Claiming that "air pollution is more severe, more pervasive and growing faster than we had thought,"[149] Muskie said that "we have fallen behind in the fight for clean air, it is not enough to implement existing law. We must go further."[150] And he did, and Congress went with him. Ultimately, Nixon, despite any misgivings, ended that year as he had begun it—on an environmental high note. On December 31, he signed the new Clean Air Amendments of 1970 into law.

This law substantially expanded the federal government's role. It put in place the basic framework currently in place for air pollution control. Under it, the federal government has primacy; its relationship to state and local governments is that of a meddlesome and micromanaging superior to a group of recalcitrant and unreliable employees. Most important, the act

- Asserted federal responsibility for stationary sources whether or not they had an interstate impact;
- Established federally promulgated national ambient air quality standards;
- Set rigid deadlines to meet primary (health-related) NAAQS (originally 1975, but now replaced by a new set);

- Mandated a series of technology-forcing stationary source requirements—new source performance standards (NSPS) and national emissions standards for hazardous air pollutants—which are applied regardless of any need based upon ambient air quality and are therefore structurally divorced, to a large extent, from benefits;
- Established the concept of "prevention of significant deterioration" (PSD);
- Required that states obtain approval from the federal government for their programs and policies to ensure compliance with all the previous requirements;
- Mandated new motor vehicle emissions standards requiring 90 percent reductions (relative to pre-1968 vehicles) in HC and CO by 1975, and in NO_x by 1976, with a possibility of one-year extensions; and
- Established federal enforcement authority and provisions for citizen suits.

For practical purposes, except for the establishment of NAAQS, the effects of most of the 1970 act's provisions on air quality or emissions were not felt until 1973, or later.[151]

First, existing air quality was due to existing sources, but it was some time before the act's provisions related to those sources became enforceable regulations that then had to be acted upon by individual sources—partly because of the cumbersome centralized planning and approval process. In early 1971, EPA established NAAQS for SO_2, TSP, CO, oxidants, and NO_x. By mid-1972, EPA had only approved 14 state implementation plans designed to show how they would attain those standards; 41 more were approved in part; 19 plans were given two-year extensions to meet primary standards; and yet others were given extensions to submit plans for attaining the secondary standards.[152] On June 15, 1973, EPA disapproved 15 state implementation plans because their transportation control plans were inadequate (or missing), but approved 19 others in full or in part; another 9 had deficiencies that could be improved. In the interim, it had proposed a transportation control plan for California that would have curtailed auto use by 82 percent in Los Angeles from May to October.[153] Needless to say, it was never implemented.

Second, the technology-forcing NSPS made very little difference to air quality until the mid-1970s or even later. Utility (power plant) boilers were the first to be targeted. However, any unit that had already begun "construction"—defined as a unit that had received permit approval—was grandfathered. Thus, units actually subject to NSPS did not generally come on line until 1977 or later. That is, any unit coming on line prior to that was subject to state regulations in accordance with their state implementation plans.[154] Similarly, with respect to motor vehicles, except for relatively modest administrative tightenings (e.g., a less than 10 percent tightening of NO_x emissions standards for the 1972 model year[155]), the standards required under the 1970 amendments were postponed several times (in 1973, 1974, 1976, and 1977) before taking full effect.[156]

Third, by their very nature, standards for new sources, whether mobile or stationary, can only reduce emissions (or improve air quality) if there is turnover of existing stocks of vehicles and plants. But this is a gradual process. Moreover, to the extent that new standards add to the cost of new vehicles or equipment, it will dampen somewhat the desire for new equipment, slowing down the replacement rate.[157]

One of the beneficial byproducts of the motor vehicle emissions control program was that the auto companies resorted to catalysts to reduce unburnt VOCs and CO. Because catalysts could be "poisoned" by lead-based additives in gasoline, such gasoline was slowly phased out as newer, catalyst-equipped cars came onto the market. Just as reduction of lead in gasoline was incidental to reducing other motor vehicle emissions, lead emissions were reduced from stationary sources as a consequence of the cleanup of TSP sources. When a separate NAAQS for lead was issued in 1978, compliance was relatively painless for most areas of the country because of these associated control efforts.

The 1970s also saw the 1973 and 1979 oil shocks, which had a substantial effect on emissions and air quality. The oil shocks boosted fossil fuel energy prices across the board, which unleashed major energy conservation efforts in all economic sectors, including households. They arrested the growth of fossil fuel use, particularly the use of petroleum (Figure 1-1). Fossil fuel use, which had grown over 50 percent in the 10 years before 1973, grew only 6 percent in the following 20 years. Petroleum use in 1995 was still below 1973 levels (it peaked in 1979). Natural gas consumption in 1995 was also below 1973 levels.[158] On the other hand, the use of coal, which seemed to have more or less stabilized in the mid-'60s and early '70s, was 50 percent greater in 1995 than in 1973 and would have been even higher but for the increase in nuclear power. (Although the use of renewable energy sources has increased, its contribution to total energy consumption remains minimal.) In the absence of air pollution control requirements, these developments, by themselves, would have decreased VOC and CO emissions and increased SO_2 and TSP. However, control requirements accentuated reductions of the first two pollutants while reducing SO_2 and TSP.

Following the energy crisis of 1973, efforts to dilute the Clean Air Act in order to help move the country away from petroleum imports led to a compromise legislated into the Energy Supply and Environmental Coordination Act of 1974 (ESECA).[159] The ESECA required the Federal Energy Administration (FEA) to issue orders prohibiting power plants that were capable of burning coal from using oil or natural gas (in effect requiring them to burn coal). FEA was also given authority to issue similar prohibition orders to any major fuel-burning units. Compliance with air pollution limits required under federally enforceable state implementation plans could be waived until January 1, 1979. However, before any order could become effective, EPA had to determine that primary (public health-related) NAAQS would not be violated and that there be no risk to public health from pollutants for which NAAQS had not been promulgated. EPA also had to consult with the governors of affected states.

The ESECA generated a lot of activity, but ultimately only one utility converted to coal under that law.[160] That the compromise in that confrontation between energy use and the environment did not tilt further away from the environment—given the near-hysteria brought about by the energy crisis—is a testament to the country's desire for an improved environment.[161]

The 1977 amendments codified and tightened the PSD requirements, which, too, were not based on any balancing of costs and benefits. The 1977 amendments also replaced the old set of rigid deadlines with a new set because many areas had missed the previous ones, and established sanctions against states and areas that failed to meet those deadlines or did not have approved plans.[162]

The latest amendments to the Clean Air Act were written in 1990. With respect to the traditional pollutants, the amended act established a formal program to reduce SO_2 and NO_x because of their

Table 1-1
MILESTONES FOR VARIOUS SUBSTANCES IN THE ATMOSPHERE

Substance	Year or Period When Substance Was	
	Perceived or Recognized to Be a Pollutant [p(P)]	First Federally Regulated [t(F)]
PM	Before 1900	1971[b]
SO$_2$	1949 to early 1950s	1971[b]
CO	Approximately late 1950s or later[a]	1967[c]
VOC/O$_3$	California: mid- to late 1950s	1971[d]
	Rest of the nation: 1960s or later	1967[c]
NO$_x$	California: mid- to late 1950s	1971[d]
	Rest of the nation: 1960s or later	1971[b]

[a]CO was long known to be deadly indoors, but its status as an outdoor air pollutant was recognized much later.

[b]The Clean Air Amendments of 1970 was signed on the last day of 1970, but most regulation went into effect later.

[c]Model year 1968 for automobiles.

[d]Although federal motor vehicle emissions standards went into effect in 1967, they had no effect in California since it already had the same standards in place.

contribution to acid rain and decreased visibility, and, once again, changed the deadlines for nonattainment areas. However, recognizing finally that the magnitude of, and solutions to, the ozone problem varied from area to area, the amended act allowed deadlines for NAAQS attainment to be determined by the severity of the problem. The seeds of acid rain and visibility controls had previously been implicit in the requirements, which had

- Outlawed "tall" stacks and intermittent control systems;
- Mandated the requirement for "best available control technology" (BACT) in the PSD program;
- Established air quality increments as part of the PSD program, which meant that in many areas air quality would necessarily have to be substantially better than NAAQS; and
- Authorized imposition of "best available retrofit technology" to improve visibility in various parks.

The 1990 act made these stipulations more explicit and established quantitative emissions reduction targets for SO$_2$. It also took a small

The History of Air Pollution and Its Control

step away from its command-and-control mindset by allowing emissions trading for acid rain control.

"Periods of Perception" and "Times of Federalization"

Based upon the above discussion, we can identify the period during which the general public and policymakers began to recognize or, more importantly, to perceive that various substances in the air were, in fact, air pollutants that needed to be controlled. I denote this period the "period of perception," or p(P). Table 1-1 shows the substances and the time period when the federal government assumed responsibility for the control of each pollutant, designated as the "time of federalization," or t(F). This table will help us decipher the reasons for the empirically derived long-term trends in U.S. air quality and emissions that will be discussed in the following three chapters.

2. Trends in Indoor Air Quality, 1940 to 1990

Governments and international bodies such as the World Health Organization define healthy air in terms of the air quality at a fixed point outdoors. Air quality standards are specified for each pollutant in terms of its concentration in outdoor air (e.g., in parts per million, or ppm) or its mass in a fixed volume of outdoor air (e.g., in micrograms per cubic meter, or $\mu g/m^3$). However, indoor air quality, particularly in the home, is a far better indicator of the impact of air pollution on public health.

First, virtually no one spends an entire day, let alone an entire year, rooted at the same spot outdoors. In fact, most people spend the majority of their time indoors, generally at home. Studies of human activity patterns in the United States indicate that the average person spends about 93 percent of his or her time indoors, 5 percent in transit, and the remainder (2 percent) outdoors.[1] About 70 percent of the average person's time is spent indoors *at home*. The average homemaker spends an even greater amount of time indoors at home (88.7 percent).

Second, the quality of air is often worse indoors than outdoors. Traditional air pollutants have both sources and sinks indoors. Sources include heating and cooking equipment that use fossil fuels and biofuels (e.g., wood and, in developing countries, dung), smoking, solvents, and various cleaning solutions used or stored in the home. Thus, the relationship between indoor and outdoor concentrations is often weak. For instance, levels of CO, NO_x, and TSP are generally higher in homes that use natural gas than outdoors, while levels of SO_2 and O_3 are higher outdoors, by almost a factor of two to five.[2] Another factor contributing to this weak relationship is that the rate at which outdoor air comes into a building (i.e., the air exchange rate) is relatively low, particularly in winter and, where air conditioning is prevalent, in summer. This precludes equilibrium between outdoor and indoor concentrations.

Not surprisingly, empirical studies of human exposure show that the concentration of a pollutant in outdoor air contributes only a small amount to the total dose of that pollutant received by human beings. For example, a U.S. study showed virtually no correlation between CO levels in the blood, the physiological route by which CO affects people, and outdoor monitored levels; the latter explained less than 3 percent of variation in blood CO levels.[3] Similarly, outdoor concentrations of nitrogen dioxide (NO_2) are relatively poor predictors of total population exposure while average indoor concentration explains 50 to 60 percent of total exposure.[4] In an EPA study, major stationary and mobile sources accounted for only 2 to 25 percent of personal exposure to VOC and pesticides. Smoking, dry-cleaned clothes, and chloroform from heated water in the home were found to be 2 to 5 times larger sources of exposure than outdoor emissions sources.[5] Finally, calculations for the United States indicate that 1 gram of indoor PM emissions can have a greater effect on total exposure of the population than 1 kilogram (1000 grams) released by a power plant from a relatively high stack.[6]

Despite the fact that indoor air quality in the average home is the single most important indicator of air quality with respect to public health, no measurements of long-term indoor air quality are available for the home or elsewhere. A crude proxy for long-term trends for in-home concentrations, particularly applicable to nonsmoking households, can be constructed for some pollutants by dividing EPA estimates of residential fuel combustion emissions by the corresponding number of occupied housing units.[7] (Fuel combustion is the major source of residential emissions for the traditional pollutants.) Moreover, residential emissions contribute a relatively high fraction of total outdoor human exposure because such emissions are exhausted at low heights where people live and spend most of their time.

Using this approach, one estimates that the average "nonsmoking" household's in-home concentrations between 1940 and 1990 declined 91 percent for PM-10 (a standard that includes only PM less than 10 micrometers [microns] in diameter), 90 percent for CO, 97 percent for SO_2, and 51 percent for NO_x (Figure 2-1). For PM-10, over 99 percent of these improvements occurred prior to 1970, i.e., before the imposition of any federal regulation on stationary sources. The corresponding figures for CO, SO_2 and NO_x are 97, 92, and 27

Figure 2-1
INDOOR AIR QUALITY, 1940–90

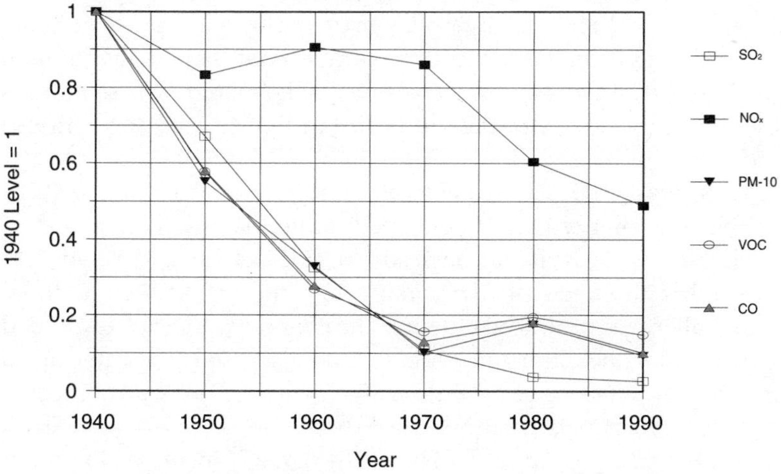

SOURCES: USBOC 1975; EPA 1995.

percent, respectively. The relatively smaller effect on NO_x was due to the fact that switching from wood and coal to oil and gas decreases NO_x less than it does SO_2 or PM-10, and many methods to burn fuel efficiently result in higher temperatures during combustion, which increases NO_x formation.

There are, however, a number of complicating factors with respect to these estimates. On one hand, the improvements in indoor air quality could be underestimates because they ignore several factors that may have further reduced indoor concentrations over the past 50 years, such as increases in the average house size, improvements in capturing, exhausting, and filtering combustion gases, and increased vacuuming of dust (as opposed to sweeping). Much of the improvement in indoor air quality would be masked in smokers' homes because tobacco smoke contributes substantially to indoor levels of CO, NO_x, and TSP[8] (although the average home should have become cleaner with respect to tobacco smoke because the annual number of cigarettes sold per capita dropped from 4,000 to 2,800 between 1970 and 1990[9]). On the other hand, through the years, the air exchange rate between the indoors and outdoors has been

45

reduced for the average home because of greater reliance on air conditioning (in summer) and the increased emphasis on energy conservation, particularly since the oil shocks of 1973 and 1978–79. While lowered air exchange rates may result in a cleaner in-home environment if the pollutant concentration outdoors is higher than that indoors, it would, ceteris paribus, make matters worse indoors by allowing concentrations of pollutants produced (or emitted) indoors to build up.

Thus, while the massive federal effort initiated during the 1970s to conserve energy may have helped reduce energy use somewhat, at least temporarily, it may have added, at least a little, to the adverse public health effects of fuel combustion indoors, as well as those due to allergens produced indoors. The long-term effect of any added risk to public health is uncertain but, as discussed in greater detail in Chapter 7 (see Box 7-1), the cases of and deaths attributed to asthma, which had declined dramatically in the 1960s and early 1970s, began to go up in the late 1970s. Even if increases in indoor concentrations of combustion emissions and allergens contributed to the increases in asthma, it would be difficult to allocate to the federal government its share of responsibility, since the population was probably responding more to the economics of energy use than to government's exhortations to conserve. At best, government-supported energy conservation campaigns would have helped accelerate the population's "education" regarding available conservation options. To the extent that people locked themselves into some measures before energy prices went down again, there may have been some net negative effect from the federal energy conservation campaign on public health.

Using the above methodology, one estimates VOC concentrations in a "nonsmoking" house due to fuel combustion also declined 85 percent. This improvement, however, may have been offset by increases in indoor emissions of solvents and other volatile substances stored or used in the house.

The improvements in the proxies for indoor air quality are due to the same factors that improved outdoor air quality in urban areas: technological change and affluence, which allowed households to switch to cleaner fuels. These improvements, which probably constitute the greatest reduction in the general population's exposure to traditional air pollutants, began decades before the promulgation of federal legislation—proving that where the need is obvious and the cause and effect are determinable with confidence, people will voluntarily take measures to improve their personal environment, with or without the government's intervention and at some expense to themselves. Remarkably, the costs of such improvements are not included in any accounting of air pollution control costs, even though, as noted above, they are probably the most effective measures for reducing total human exposure.

3. Long-Term Trends in Ambient (Outdoor) Air Quality in the United States

After indoor air concentrations (or appropriate proxies), the next best indicators for the public health impacts of air pollution are outdoor (or ambient) air concentrations at approximately ground level.

Systematic national efforts to monitor the air began in 1953, when the U.S. Public Health Service's Division of Sanitary Engineering began sampling suspended particulate matter using "high-volume samplers" in 17 cities in cooperation with local (and a few state) agencies. By 1956, particulate sampling had expanded to 66 communities nationwide. In 1957, the National Air Sampling Network, which planned to operate about 100 sampling stations each year in urban and nonurban areas, was established, followed in 1959–60 by the Gas Sampling Network, which was to collect 24-hour samples of SO_2 and nitrogen dioxide. Then in 1962, the six-city Continuous Air Monitoring Project (CAMP) was begun to continuously measure CO, NO_x, SO_2, total hydrocarbons, and total oxidants.[1] The order in which these monitoring programs came into being also reflects the order in which the various pollutants intruded into the consciousness of national policymakers and the public as having significant real or potential effects on public health (see Table 1-1).

Data from these sampling networks—which, at any one time, used more or less consistent protocols and procedures for gathering, handling, analyzing, and reporting data for each pollutant—allow us to construct national trends for the various pollutants. Using these data and data from successor networks managed by—or reported by states and local agencies to—EPA, it is possible to construct "national" trends provided measurements are appropriately adjusted to account for any changes in protocols, procedures, instruments, and instrument placement that may have occurred from time to time, and provided there are sufficient valid measurements during the year (see below). Thus, "national" trends can be developed for PM air quality going back to the mid- to late 1950s, and for SO_2 from the early 1960s onwards. For CO, some data are available from the early to mid-1960s. Data for the other pollutants, however, are insufficient (in quantity and quality) to derive robust national trends until the early 1970s.

Every year national ambient air data are published in EPA's annual report on air quality trends[2] and in the *Statistical Abstract of the United States*. The Council on Environmental Quality (CEQ) also used to publish an annual report (*Environmental Quality*) supplemented by other reports on environmental statistics. All these reports are based on EPA data. Until recently these publications provided data for a few (8 to 12) years at a time, but now the EPA's documents on air quality trends report trends over the previous 20 years. The data are presented as nationwide averages for each criteria pollutant for each time period for which a national ambient air quality standard is specified.

There are some problems associated with combining these time series to construct longer-term trends: Most monitoring networks are not developed with the notion of collecting a representative sample either geographically or, as we saw in the discussion on indoor air quality, with respect to population exposure. Monitoring systems are often funded, if not operated, by regulatory agencies. Other systems are also operated at their behest—for example, as a condition for permitting construction of new plants or to satisfy other legal requirements. But regulatory agencies generally seem to be driven by the desire to determine (or, possibly, in some instances, not determine) compliance with the NAAQS. This affects the placement of individual monitors in communities. As a consequence, it is not possible to establish average pollutant concentrations in the air inhaled by the average person or in the average volume of air in the United States. The averages determined and reported from existing monitoring systems are often merely the averages for an ensemble of unrepresentative monitors.

Moreover, measurements made today may not be comparable with those made even a decade or so ago. Monitoring methods are constantly refined, if not altered, as better and more accurate instruments are developed. For example, measurements taken of

NO$_x$ in the 60s used the Jacob-Hochheiser method, which was shown to overestimate NO$_x$ concentrations at low levels. This invalidated much of the NO$_x$ data collected prior to 1972, when a modified measurement method was deployed as part of the National Air Surveillance Network.[3] Older methods may be replaced without undertaking detailed side-by-side comparisons with newer ones to allow trends to be developed in the future. The number and precise locations of the monitoring stations that form the basis of the reported national trends keep changing continually; about 10 percent of National Air Monitoring System stations are phased out or replaced each year.[4] Microenvironments (the environment in the immediate vicinity) may have changed for monitoring stations. The area adjacent to the stations may have been paved over, its land use may have been altered, or an industry may have moved near it or away from it. Sometimes, even if the monitor is located at the same address, the height at which the air is drawn into it may have changed—but the concentration of a pollutant in the atmosphere may vary with height. Over time, individuals and laboratories gathering and analyzing the data are replaced, and the result is inconsistent handling and, potentially, the trading of one set of systematic biases for another.

Changes and fluctuations in climatic conditions can also mask changes due to emissions. Year-to-year and longer-term variability in meteorological (i.e., natural) factors at all geographical scales affect air pollutant concentrations. Variability in those factors—which include temperature, precipitation, cloud cover, and wind speeds—can cast doubt on long-term trends, particularly for "extreme" short-term concentrations (e.g., the highest, second highest, or highest 1 percent of the concentrations for 3, 8, or 24 hours) because these extreme levels are just as likely to be determined by meteorological extremes as by emissions, if not more likely. But, in fact, many ambient environmental quality standards are specified in terms of extreme concentrations for very short time periods. This makes it difficult to confirm attainment or nonattainment of the ambient standard until several years of monitoring data have been collected so that the effects of weather-related factors can be averaged or filtered out mathematically. However, since emissions (or pollutant loadings) can also fluctuate (though often not as dramatically as natural variability), averaging out several years of data may be insufficient to eliminate the effects of emissions, while mathematically filtering their effect can be tricky. Nevertheless, for ozone, in particular, EPA and some researchers have used mathematical models to adjust monitor data to reflect typical, rather than actual, meteorology.[5]

 Despite these difficulties, many of the time series provided in the publications mentioned above overlap, and averages based upon different, but large, ensembles of monitors indicate that while the mean values may differ between ensembles, the series are more or less parallel.[6] Thus, it is possible to combine several of these series to construct a much longer series. This has been done, and the results are presented in Figures 3-1 through 3-6 for the criteria pollutants: TSP (or PM-10), SO_2, CO, O_3, NO_x, and lead, respectively. The series go back as far as is possible with the available data. (For TSP they go back to 1957, and for SO_2 to 1962; for the other pollutants the data are more recent.) No effort was made to reconcile ensemble averages for each series based upon changes in factors such as instrumentation and location because, ultimately, one would have to resort to the heroic—and, as we have seen, probably incorrect—assumption that outdoor monitoring data are good indicators of the impacts of pollutants on public health. Thus, despite the fact that numbers, sometimes into four significant figures, are attached to the ensemble averages, the trends suggested by Figures 3-1 through 3-6 are, in reality, qualitative. Accordingly, in the discussion that follows, estimated changes in ambient air quality over the long term are rounded off to the nearest 5 percent. To avoid "data clutter," not all available series are shown in the figures.

Figures 3-1 through 3-6 indicate that nationwide air quality has improved for all of the traditional pollutants. The largest improvements have been for lead, followed by SO_2, TSP, and CO, and the smallest for NO_2. For reasons discussed earlier, TSP and SO_2 improvements came first; in fact, significant improvement occurred before most of the new requirements mandated by the 1970 Clean Air Act became effective—that is, about 1972 or earlier.[7] Because much of the reduction in emissions occurred at low-level sources while increases occurred at sources with taller stacks, improvements in ambient TSP, SO_2, and CO air quality levels are, as we shall see, greater than would be indicated by trends in total emissions. In fact, for some periods, air quality may well have improved even though aggregate emissions increased.

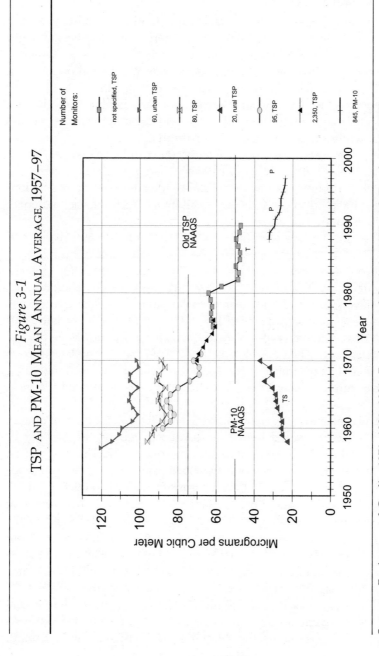

Figure 3-1

TSP AND PM-10 MEAN ANNUAL AVERAGE, 1957–97

SOURCES: *Environmental Quality* 1971, 1981, 1991; *Environmental Statistics* 1978; *AQ Trends* 1996, 1997.

Particulate Matter

We have seen (Figure 1-2) that dustfall in Pittsburgh has probably been declining since the early 1920s. There may have been a slight upturn in the late '30s and during World War II, after which it continued to drop more or less continuously.[8] Dustfall data shown in Figure 1-7 for Chicago and Cincinnati from the '30s, for New York from the '40s, and for Detroit and Philadelphia from the '50s are consistent with the general pattern indicated in Figure 1-2.[9] These data, while suggestive of a broad pattern and consistent with emissions estimates (to be discussed later), must still be considered anecdotal. It was not until the mid-1950s, when the federal government initiated a program to monitor total suspended particulates nationwide, that there began to be sufficient data to formulate a "national" composite for TSP air quality.

The oldest series of data starts in 1957 for about 60 urban—and in 1958 for 20 rural—areas. Figure 3-1 combines these time series with others to give an overview of "national" trends for ambient air quality for PM from 1957 to 1997.[10] It shows that the "nationwide" TSP levels, based on the mean of the annual average concentrations for several monitors, declined 40 to 50 percent between the late 1950s and 1990. The national "average," which used to be above the old primary (public health–related) NAAQS of 75 $\mu g/m^3$, had declined to 35 percent below that by 1990. As the previous discussions regarding Pittsburgh and New York indicated, urban areas showed the most improvement.

Ambient air quality data (Figure 3-1) indicate that urban air quality for PM, as measured by TSP, has been improving at least for as long as the data have been available—since 1957. The mean of an ensemble of 60 urban monitors shows that these annual average levels declined from 121 to 102 $\mu g/m^3$ from 1957 to 1970.[11] On the other hand, the data plotted in Figure 3-1 show that the average of 20 rural monitors rose from 23 to 37 $\mu g/m^3$ between 1958 and 1970.[12] However, it is worth noting that those "rural" data, obtained from the CEQ's 1971 annual report,[13] seem to be inconsistent with subsequent trend analysis done by EPA for 1960 through 1971, which shows no significant trend (up or down) in nonurban TSP levels. That analysis, based on 18 nonurban monitors, showed that annual TSP levels went up at 2, declined at 5, and stayed constant at 11 monitors. Aggregating the monitors resulted in no overall trend, since a decline in the 1960–68 period was offset by an increase in the 1968–71 period that may have been attributable to decreased rainfall[14] (the data set indicating no trend in nonurban TSP levels is not shown in Figure 3-1).

Regardless of which set of trend data is used for nonurban areas, average nonurban or rural levels were, at all times, substantially below the annual secondary (and, of course, primary) NAAQS promulgated in 1971. Most importantly, the worst areas were getting better long before the 1970 Clean Air Act was passed or became effective, while rural areas may or may not have been getting worse. Overall there should have been a decline in the adverse public health effects of TSP. The "national" average based on the 80 monitors indicated an improvement from 96 to 89 $\mu g/m^3$ between 1958 and 1970.[15] A second ensemble based on 95 monitors showed a more rapid improvement nationally: from 84 to 72 $\mu g/m^3$ between 1960 and 1970 and a further decline to 68 $\mu g/m^3$ the following year.[16] Those improvements apparently continued until 1975, about the time the federally enforceable state implementation plans were becoming more fully effective. Then, after a period of little change, TSP levels dropped sharply in 1981 and 1982, only to stabilize once again. The declines in 1980 and 1981 were due to "abnormally high" precipitation, reductions in economic activity, and, of course, additional controls.[17] The slope of the decline, however, may be exaggerated because in 1979 EPA had changed its supplier of filters used in the monitors to trap dust (particulates) and then reverted to the original supplier in 1982. The filters used in the interregnum were discovered to be more alkaline. Because that would have increased the likelihood of gases in the incoming air artificially forming sulfates, nitrates, and other secondary particulates on the filter, it may have inflated TSP readings.

In 1987, the TSP NAAQS were replaced by the PM-10 standards, which include only PM less than 10 micrometers (microns) in diameter. The change was necessitated by the recognition that PM-10 is a better indicator of health impact than is TSP, since smaller particles are more likely to be inhaled deeper into the lungs. The national composite annual average for PM-10 declined 25 percent from 32.4 to 24.0 $\mu g/m^3$ between 1988 and 1997.[18] For comparison, the primary annual NAAQS is 50 $\mu g/m^3$.

Sulfur Dioxide

Some data are available from 1962 to 1969 and from 1974 onward (Figure 3-2).[19] SO_2 concentrations declined dramatically in the 1960s. Earlier we noted that annual levels declined about 85 percent in New York City between 1964 and 1972, from 570 to 81 $\mu g/m^3$ (Figure 1-5). In 1997, measured levels were below 32 $\mu g/m^3$.[20] Other cities also showed substantial, though not as dramatic, improvements. Between 1962 and 1969, based on 21 urban monitors, the mean annual average dropped about 40 percent, from 69.4 to 42.5 $\mu g/m^3$.[21] The corresponding primary NAAQS is 80 $\mu g/m^3$.

An EPA trend analysis for 32 monitors also indicated a decline of over 50 percent (from 55 to 25 $\mu g/m^3$) between 1964 and 1971.[22] Finally, between 1974 and 1997, the national "average" dropped over 60 percent to about 14 $\mu g/m^3$, with over half of that drop occurring in the first 10 years.[23, 24]

Carbon Monoxide

Data on ambient CO air quality are sparse until the early 1970s. What few data there are suggest that CO air quality may have begun improving, at least in urban areas, in the mid-1960s, as indicated by the short segment of data for 1963–68 (Figure 3-3).[25] That segment was obtained from the federally operated six-city CAMP network, which began collecting data in 1962.[26] The six cities (Chicago, Cincinnati, Denver, Philadelphia, St. Louis, and Washington) were outside California, and the fact that declines apparently began before the Federal Motor Vehicle Control Program went into effect indicates that stationary source reductions played a role in the initial turnaround; those improvements then gathered momentum as an increasing number of vehicles became subject to federal tailpipe controls starting with the 1968 model year.[27]

An EPA trend analysis of CO data for five of the six CAMP cities from 1962 to 1971 also suggests a declining trend.[28] According to that analysis, the mean annual average concentrations dropped by 31 percent in the 1962–66 and 1967–71 periods.[29] However, because of changes in instrumentation and operating procedures in 1970 and 1971, the magnitude of the decline may have been overstated in the analysis.[30] Between these two time periods, there was about a 5 percent decline in the average of the annual second highest

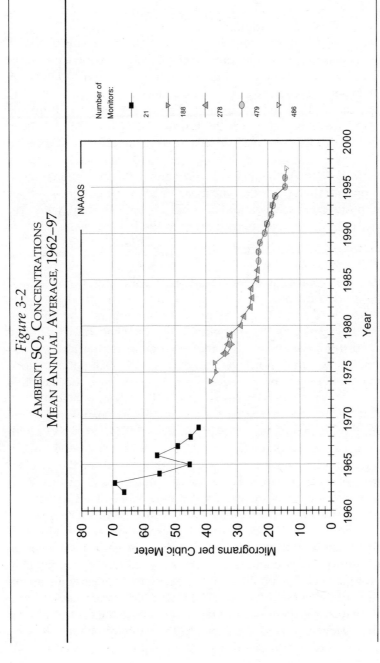

Figure 3-2
AMBIENT SO$_2$ CONCENTRATIONS
MEAN ANNUAL AVERAGE, 1962–97

SOURCES: *Environmental Quality* 1971; *Statistical Abstract* 1981; *AQ Trends* 1996, 1997.

one-hour value (which was expected to be less sensitive to the changes in instrumentation).[31]

Data from California also indicate that CO air quality, by and large, began to improve around 1965–67.[32] The frequency of days on which CO levels exceeded the future (1971) 8-hour CO NAAQS in, for instance, Lennox in the Los Angeles basin peaked at 99 to 100 percent in 1965 and declined to 42 percent in 1971.[33] In Burbank, the peak frequency at which the future NAAQS would have been exceeded dropped from 93 to 100 percent in 1966 to 34 percent in 1971.[34]

Figure 3-3 shows that between 1970 and 1997, the national mean CO concentration (based on the mean of the second highest 8-hour concentration at each location) decreased over 75 percent, with over 50 percent of that decrease occurring in the first 10 years.[35]

Ozone

Ozone, in contrast to other "traditional" pollutants, is not emitted directly. It is formed by a series of complex chemical reactions between VOC and NO_x in the presence of sunlight. The speed of those reactions and the movement and concentration of ozone depend upon meteorological factors such as temperature, wind speed, height of inversion layer, cloudiness, and precipitation. Ozone is one of the major components of Los Angeles smog. Because it is the product of a very complex set of reactions that are mediated by weather-related factors, it is difficult to predict changes in ozone levels due to reductions in their precursors (VOC and NO_x) with much accuracy. Another feature of ozone is that it can be formed and transported hundreds of kilometers away from the original sources of its precursors. To complicate matters still further, NO_x reductions may either increase or decrease ozone levels depending upon the ratio of NO_x to nonmethane hydrocarbons. So it is possible that ozone levels would decline in one place but increase in another.[36] The fact that NO_x was being reduced since the early 1970s even as VOC controls were instituted to attain the NAAQS for ozone may have aggravated that pollutant in some center-city areas while reducing it in outlying suburban areas.[37] Finally, for a long time EPA and other regulatory agencies have tended to ignore the contribution of natural (biogenic) VOC emissions to the ozone problem.[38] In fact, biogenic VOC emissions during the peak ozone season exceed

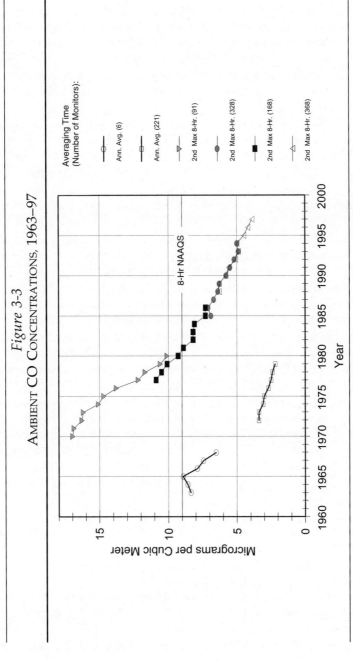

Figure 3-3
AMBIENT CO CONCENTRATIONS, 1963–97

SOURCES: *Environmental Quality 1971, 1981; Statistical Abstract 1981; AQ Trends 1994, 1996, 1997.*

anthropogenic emissions (19.2 million tons versus about 6.1 million tons, respectively, in 1990, based on preliminary estimates).[39] For those reasons, attaining the NAAQS for ozone has proved to be a difficult and expensive proposition. All this points to the futility of one-size-fits-all requirements for attaining ozone standards, which was finally—and grudgingly—acknowledged in the 1990 amendments to the Clean Air Act.

Most official data on ozone air quality are provided in terms of the statistic that is most readily compared with the NAAQS—that is, the magnitude of the second highest one-hour reading in the year (after eliminating the day with the highest one-hour number). Because this number is very sensitive to meteorological factors, it would be difficult to distinguish trends from year to year even if emissions were invariant. Figure 3-4 indicates the trend in the national mean for this statistic.[40] Those data became available only after 1974; before that there were not enough monitors outside of California to allow a reasonable "national" trend to be constructed.[41] This poor national coverage prior to 1974 only confirms that photochemical smog was not perceived by many to be a major air pollution problem nationally until the late 1960s, or even the 1970s.

Nevertheless, there are some pre-1974 data analyses available from areas outside California. An EPA analysis of oxidant trends at three sites on the East Coast (Bayonne, Newark, and Camden, New Jersey) showed improvements in oxidant air quality between 1966 and 1969 and once again between 1969 and 1972.[42] On the other hand, trend analysis using the six-city CAMP network data from 1964 through 1968 showed no definitive trends in oxidant ambient air quality.[43]

The California data in Figure 1-5 suggest that oxidant concentrations had begun declining there by the mid- to late 1950s. Those data indicate a secondary peak in the mid-1960s before the resumption of the long-term decline around 1966–67.[44] Azusa in the Los Angeles basin, for instance, registered 1,636 hours of exceedences of the future (1971) oxidant NAAQS in 1966; by 1972, that had declined to 1,082.[45] (For reference, there are 8,760 hours in a full year.) The hours of exceedence of the future standard in downtown Los Angeles also peaked in 1966 at 1,163, dropping to 516 in 1972.[46]

National trends shown in Figure 3-4 indicate a roughly 30 percent improvement between 1974 and 1997. Between 1985 and 1986, and 1993 and 1994, the two-year average for this statistic declined about 10 percent. There was more improvement, however,

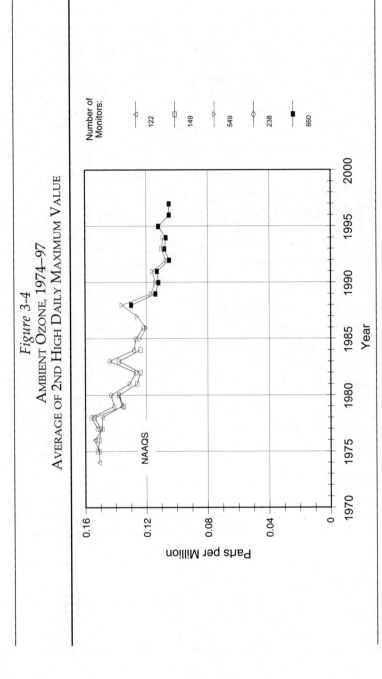

Figure 3-4
AMBIENT OZONE, 1974–97
AVERAGE OF 2ND HIGH DAILY MAXIMUM VALUE

SOURCES: *Environmental Quality 1981; AQ Trends 1994, 1996, 1997.*

in another statistic—the average number of exceedence-days, which has greater significance for public health. Based on two-year running averages at 352 nationwide trend sites, the number of exceedence-days decreased about 45 percent between 1985 and 1986 and between 1993 and 1994.[47] Clearly, trends in the statistic that better corresponds to the NAAQS do not tell the entire story regarding trends in the public health effects of ozone.

These national improvements are also evident in specific areas. It was noted earlier that one-hour ozone levels of 1,200 $\mu g/m^3$ were not unknown in the Los Angeles basin during the 1960s.[48] EPA's *AIRS Executive Data Base* indicates that in 1994 and 1995 the maximum one-hour ozone concentrations in Los Angeles County were about 510 and 425 $\mu g/m^3$, respectively.[49] One study indicated that the number of days in which the South Coast Air Basin (which includes Los Angeles) exceeded the NAAQS (235 $\mu g/m^3$, one-hour average) declined from 147 in 1976 to 111 in 1991, and stage I episode days (triggered at about 390 $\mu g/m^3$, one-hour average) declined from 91 to 36.[50] Adjusting the monitoring data to account for meteorological changes suggests a 22 percent decrease in exceedence-days (from 155 to 121) and a 64 percent decrease in stage I days (from 111 to 40). The annual number of exceedence-days for the Los Angeles-Long Beach area declined 68 percent between 1985 and 1986 and between 1996 and 1997,[51] in part due to El Niño. Most importantly, a National Research Council report on ozone control policy indicates that population exposure (per capita) declined 38 percent (from 42.1 to 26.1 ppm-hours) in the periods between 1976 and 1978, and 1985 and 1987.[52]

Nitrogen Dioxide

As noted previously, reliable NO_2 monitoring data are available only after the early 1970s. Figure 3-5 indicates that NO_2 peaked around 1978–1979 and has declined by about 25 percent since then.[53] Between 1985 and 1997, the mean annual average declined about 14 percent.[54] Currently there are no designated NO_x nonattainment areas in the United States [55]

Figure 3-5 indicates that NO_2 improved much more slowly than other pollutants. There are several reasons for this. First, its health effects are relatively minor. Second, very few areas were ever designated nonattainment areas for NO_2, so it was never viewed as a

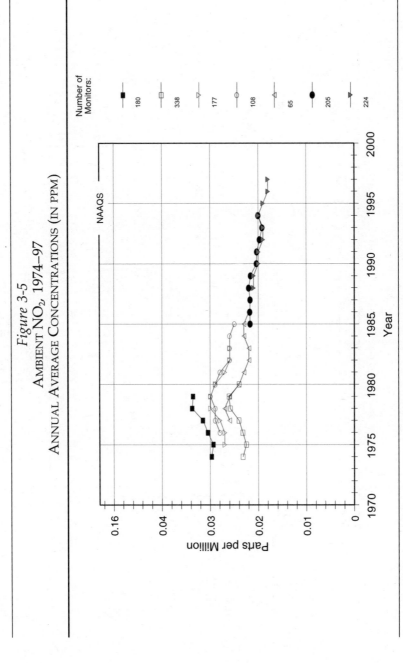

Figure 3-5
AMBIENT NO₂ 1974–97
ANNUAL AVERAGE CONCENTRATIONS (IN PPM)

SOURCES: *Environmental Quality* 1981, 1984; *Statistical Abstract* 1981, 1988; *AQ Trends* 1994, 1996, 1997.

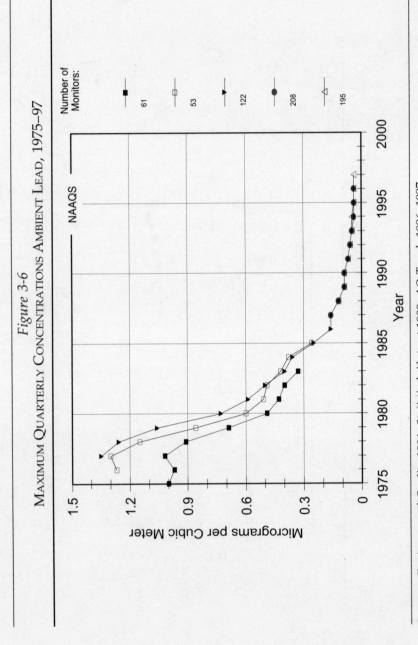

Figure 3-6

MAXIMUM QUARTERLY CONCENTRATIONS AMBIENT LEAD, 1975–97

Number of Monitors:

61
53
122
208
195

NAAQS

SOURCES: *Environmental Quality 1984; Statistical Abstract 1988; AQ Trends 1996, 1997.*

widespread problem. Once upon a time, EPA had projected that more than 40 areas could exceed the NO$_x$ NAAQS, but after discovering the flaws in the Jacobs-Hochheiser method that number dropped to two (Los Angeles and Chicago), and possibly three (Baltimore).[56] Third, many measures to increase combustion efficiency and reduce CO and VOC emissions increased the combustion temperature, which increased NO$_2$ emissions. Finally, although NO$_x$ was also implicated in ozone formation, the national emphasis for attaining NAAQS for ozone was on controlling VOC, not least because of the high control costs.[57]

Lead

Based on 92 urban and 16 rural sites, the national composite 50th percentile for lead increased from 1965 to 1971, probably because of the increased use of gasoline that contained lead additives to improve the octane rating, which improves the performance of vehicles.[58] It has dropped more or less continuously ever since. Since 1974, the national mean for the maximum quarterly average has declined over 95 percent (Figure 3-6).[59] Controls on lead in gasoline, paints, and point sources—for example, smelters and battery plants—have been the major causes of the improvement. In 1997, 10 areas exceeded the lead NAAQS, due mainly to point sources. Lead in blood samples, a far better indicator of the public health impact of lead than outdoor air quality, has also declined substantially.[60] Between the late 1970s and 1991, the proportions of people who had more than 10 micrograms of lead per deciliter of blood declined from 78 percent to 4.3 percent.[61]

4. Emissions Trends and Technological Change

Data Sources

Emissions Data. Unlike air quality data, emissions estimates are available for longer periods of time, going back to 1900 for SO_2, NO_x, and VOC; 1940 for PM-10 and CO; and 1970 for lead. These estimates, however—put together with great care by EPA—are not based on direct measurements as are air quality data. They are calculated by taking into consideration a number of factors that vary or evolve from year to year. Those factors include quantity and quality of fuels consumed by each end use category (i.e., residential, commercial, industrial, and utility), age structure of the vehicles in each category of motor vehicles (e.g., cars, light and heavy trucks), production from the various industrial, manufacturing, and other pollution-generating processes, control technologies and practices employed by the various emissions sources, and growth rates for the various economic and emissions sectors. To compile a long-term emissions inventory requires not only engineering knowledge of the processes and equipment contributing to emissions but also historical knowledge of the evolution of those processes and their controls and of operation and maintenance practices.

For any specific pollutant, different methodologies are used to derive estimates for different time periods. The methodologies used to estimate emissions for 1900–39 are different from those used for 1940–84 and for 1985 to the present. Every year EPA updates the latest set of emissions, and sometimes fine-tunes some of the earlier numbers as well. Although these estimates are currently the best available, because of the many assumptions that have to be made in developing emissions for each source category, uncertainties inevitably creep in. Accordingly, quantitative changes in emissions from one period to another should be viewed cautiously. Nevertheless, those estimates provide a good indication of the general trends in emissions.

The emissions estimates used in this chapter are based on EPA's emissions data used in the *1997 Update* of national emissions[1] (released in December 1998) and supplemented, as necessary, by the data used in the *1994 Trends Report*.[2] The national annual emissions estimates from the two data sets are, in general, essentially the same until 1969 for CO, NO_x, VOC, and PM-10, and until 1985 for SO_2.[3] Accordingly, for all pollutants I used the *1994 Trends Report* until the year 1969. For 1970 and later years, I used the *1997 Update* with the following exceptions for PM-10. First, the PM-10 data set in the *1997 Update* is incomplete for 1971 through 1974 since it only accounts for emissions from fuel combustion from electric utilities, on-road vehicles, and nonroad vehicles and engines for those years. Thus, annual PM-10 emissions in the *1997 Update* go from 13.1 million short tons (MST) in 1970 to 2.4 MST in 1971, then decline somewhat to 2.2 MST in 1974 before climbing back to 7.8 MST in 1975. Accordingly, for PM-10 I used the *1994 Trends Report* for 1940 through 1974 and the *1997 Update* for subsequent years. Nevertheless, the differences in national PM-10 estimates between the *1994 Trends Report* and *1997 Update* data sets are expected to be minor since the *1997 Update* estimates are higher by only 0.2 and 2.4 percent for the years 1970 and 1975, respectively.[4]

Second, PM-10 emissions in the *1997 Update* jump from 6.5 MST in 1984 to 45.6 MST in 1985, due to the introduction from 1985 onward of various fugitive dust sources (including wind erosion from natural sources, agriculture, forestry, cooling towers, paved and unpaved roads, and construction) into the emissions inventory. Accordingly, for 1985 and subsequent years, I eliminated these "new" source categories from the *1997 Update* inventory to ensure that the trend analysis in this chapter was based on comparable data sets. As a result of such a readjustment, the 1985 PM-10 emissions level from the *1997 Update* declined to 4.7 MST.

Economic Data. Emissions fluctuate with changes in the level of economic activity. For the measure of economic activity I will use gross national product (GNP) rather that the theoretically more appropriate gross domestic product (GDP) because it is easier to construct a time series for GNP going back to 1900, the first year for which I have emissions data. Moreover, the differences between GDP and GNP are slight for the United States. Using the recently constructed

Bureau of Economic Analysis (BEA) 1929–97 series, annual GNP, on average, is 0.54 percent greater than the corresponding year's GDP, with the maximum and minimum differences ranging from +1.21 to –0.05 percent.

To construct a data series for real annual GNP extending from 1900 to 1997, I used BEA's GNP series using chained 1992 dollars from 1929 to 1997.[5] The 1900–1928 GNP data were estimated by using the 1869–1970 GNP series (in 1958 dollars) from the Bureau of the Census's *Historical Statistics*.[6] This was accomplished by multiplying the 1900–28 GNP data by the ratio of the BEA's 1929 GNP (using chained 1992 dollars) to the 1929 GNP (using 1958 dollars) from the *Historical Statistics*.

Comparison of Trends in Emissions, Population, and Economic Activity

Figure 4-1 compares U.S. trends between 1900 and 1997 for SO_2, NO_x, and VOC emissions with population (P), affluence (A) as measured by GNP per capita, and total economic activity as measured by GNP, or the product of P and A. All values are normalized to 1900 levels—that is, 1900 levels = 1. By 1997, SO_2, VOC, and NO_x emissions grew, respectively, by 104, 126, and 803 percent (i.e., they went up to 2.04, 2.26, and 9.03, relative to unity for 1900), while population increased by 252 percent, affluence by 586 percent, and GNP (in constant dollars) by 2,314 percent.

Similarly, between 1940 and 1997, CO emissions decreased 7 percent and PM-10 declined 74 percent while population, affluence, and GNP increased 102, 281, and 673 percent, respectively (Figure 4-2). Between 1970 and 1997, lead emissions decreased 98 percent while population and GNP increased 31 and 113 percent, respectively.

These data show that over the long haul emissions for the criteria pollutants have generally increased far less rapidly than either P, A, or their product (GNP), with the exception of NO_x emissions, which grew faster between 1900 and 1997 than P or A but less than their product. This, coupled with the previous chapters' discussion on outdoor and indoor air quality, suggests that the notion advanced in some neo-Malthusian environmental literature that the environment is necessarily degraded with increasing population, affluence,

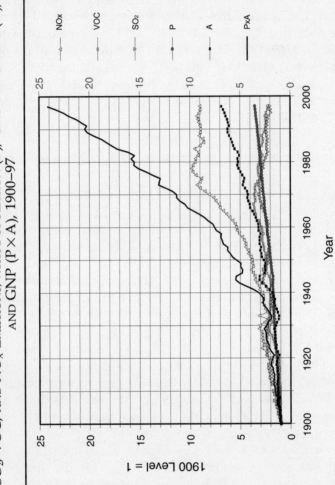

Figure 4-1

SO$_2$, VOC, AND NO$_X$ EMISSIONS, WITH POPULATION (P), GNP PER CAPITA (A), AND GNP (P × A), 1900–97

SOURCES: EPA 1995, 1998; USBOC 1975; BEA 1998.

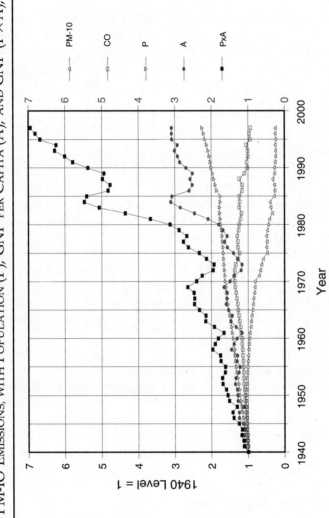

Figure 4-2

CO AND PM-IO EMISSIONS, WITH POPULATION (P), GNP PER CAPITA (A), AND GNP (P×A), 1940–97

SOURCES: EPA 1995, 1998; USBOC 1975; BEA 1998.

71

or new technology is not necessarily accurate.[7] These notions are often captured by the following identity:[8]

$$I = P \times A \times T$$

where I is the environmental impact; P and A, as noted above, are population and affluence, respectively; and T, denoting technology, is the environmental impact per unit of economic activity. Assuming that environmental impact is measured by emissions (E), then substituting emissions for impact and GNP per capita for affluence, the identity can be restated as

$$E = P \times (GNP/P) \times T = GNP \times T$$

Therefore,

$$T = E/GNP$$

Thus, E/GNP (or the T-factor) is a measure of the aggregate effect of technology on all of society's activities responsible for that pollutant's emissions, and the change in E/GNP is a measure of the net technological change.[9] A smaller T-factor means better technology and lower aggregate E/GNP. E/GNP may, for instance, increase if coal replaces natural gas, or decrease if old processes are replaced by new, more efficient technologies due to either economic factors or regulatory requirements. Alternatively, E/GNP may change with the structure of the economy (see Chapter 5).

Table 4-1, based on Figures 4-1 and 4-2, shows the extent to which technological change has helped reduce criteria air pollution emissions in the United States over the long term. The T-factor for SO_2 between 1900 and 1997 is 0.084, which means that \$1 of economic activity produced 0.084 times as much SO_2 in 1997 as it did in 1900. The corresponding figures for VOC and NO_x are 0.094 and 0.374, respectively. Similarly, \$1 of economic activity produced only 0.034 times as much PM-10 and 0.121 times as much CO as it did in 1940. And the change in the T-factor for lead, 0.008 in 1997 compared to 1 in 1970, is nothing less than spectacular.

Table 4-1 indicates that to estimate future environmental impacts, one must be able to project changes in the T-factor since, over the long term, environmental impacts have been more sensitive to technology than to population, affluence or, in most cases, aggregate economic activity. In fact, failure to account for the progressive lowering of

Table 4-1
CHANGES IN POPULATION (P), AFFLUENCE (A), ECONOMIC ACTIVITY (GNP = P × A), AND TECHNOLOGY (T) FOR CRITERIA POLLUTANTS, 1900–1997

Period	Population[a] (P)	Affluence[a] (A)	GNP[a] (P × A)	Pollutant	Emissions[a] (E)	Technology[a] (T = E/GNP)[b]
1900–97	3.52	6.86	24.14	SO_2	2.04	0.084
				VOC	2.26	0.094
				NO_x	9.03	0.374
1940–97	2.02	3.81	7.73	PM-10	0.26	0.034
				CO	0.93	0.121
1970–97	1.31	1.62	2.13	Lead	0.02	0.008

Calculated by the author using EPA 1995, 1998; Bureau of the Census 1975; BEA 1998.

NOTE: See notes 1, 2, 5, and 6.

[a]All values shown are the ratio of the value at the end of the period to the value at the beginning.

[b]The lower the T-factor, the more improved the technology and the lower the emissions per dollar of GNP.

the T-factor in the I = PAT identity is one of the major reasons why many neo-Malthusian predictions regarding population, food, natural resources, and the environment have so far failed to occur.[10] The other reason is in the assumption that many users of the identity have implicitly made—namely, that P, A, and T are independent of each other. As I have shown elsewhere, these are interdependent.[11] Affluence and technological change co-evolve, and both help create conditions to reduce total fertility rates, eventually contributing to reduced population growth rates.[12]

Trends in Emissions and Technology

In a society whose population and GNP have been growing contin-ually (as they have in the United States), unless there are sustained declines in E/GNP and emissions per capita (E/cap), there will be no eventual downturn in total emissions (though air quality may well improve). In other words, E/GNP and E/cap serve as *leading environmental indicators* rather than environmental indicators per se. Declines in these leading indicators may be the result of new—or greater penetration of less-polluting existing—technologies. Thus, technological change is a consequence of the acquisition of new knowledge and inventions as well as investments in new—as well as existing, but unused or underused—technologies.

Peaks in the leading environmental indicators help identify when "cleanup" efforts began, either consciously or unconsciously, due to economic and technological progress.

Figures 4-3 through 4-7 show U.S. trends in total emissions, E/cap, and E/GNP for SO_2, VOC, and NO_x from 1900 to 1997 and for PM-10 and CO from 1940 to 1997. Based on the recounting of historical developments in air pollution control in Chapter 1, these figures also indicate the t(F) and the p(P) for the various pollutants, unless those milestones fall outside the period covered by the time series.

In each of the figures, compared to the plots for the leading indicators, the plots for emissions have the largest year-to-year variability. This is due to the fact that fluctuations in emissions are determined largely by factors such as annual fuel use and industrial and manufacturing throughput, which, in turn, depend on economic output and weather conditions. Both can be highly variable.

E/cap plots show somewhat greater variability than E/GNP plots because E/cap is also influenced by the level of economic activity. The slope for E/cap also depends on the population growth rate, which too can fluctuate from year to year, though generally not as rapidly as economic growth.

Plots of E/GNP (or technological change) are the smoothest. First, by definition, annual fluctuations in economic activity are filtered out of those trends. Second, they depend on the capital stock held by industry, businesses, and households. That capital stock, which determines the fuel mix used by society, combustion efficiencies, the types of industrial and manufacturing processes used, age distribution and emissions profiles of vehicles, and the efficiency of any pollution control equipment, cannot be turned over rapidly. Third, E/GNP also depend on the structure of the economy—that is, the composition of the economy in terms of the agrarian, industrial, commercial, and service sectors—but this too evolves slowly. In unusual circumstances, E/GNP can vary rapidly, as during World War II, when GNP grew sharply but gas rationing was also in effect, or—to some extent—during the Great Depression, when the fuel mix changed rapidly.

In the following, I will use peaks in the E/GNP plots rather than E/cap to identify when cleanup began not only because the E/GNP

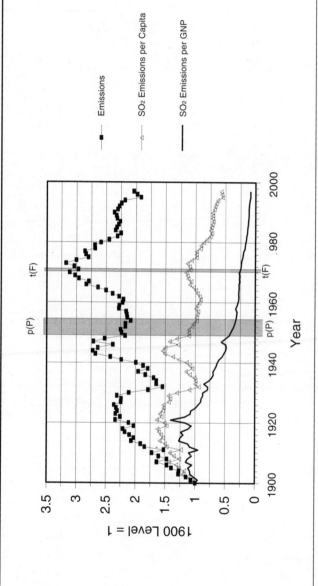

Figure 4-3

SULFUR DIOXIDE, 1900–97: EMISSIONS, EMISSIONS PER GNP, AND EMISSIONS PER CAPITA

SOURCES: EPA 1995, 1998; USBOC 1975; BEA 1998.

NOTES: p(P) = period of perception, t(F) = time of federalization.

Table 4-2
PROGRESSION OF T-FACTORS (OR E/GNP) AT VARIOUS
MILESTONES, 1900–97

	T-Factor at (year in parentheses)				
Pollutant	Beginning of Period	Peak Year	Beginning of p(P)	Time of Federalization	1997
SO$_2$	1	1.41	0.42	0.25	0.08
	(1900)	(1921)	(1950)	(1971)	
VOC	1	1.13	0.38–0.40	0.35	0.09
	(1900)	(1932)	(~1960)	(1967)	
NO$_x$	1	1.62	0.72	0.73	0.37
	(1900)	(1933)	(~1960)	(1971)	
PM-10	1	NA	NA	0.19	0.03
	(1940)	(<1940)	(<1940)	(1971)	
CO	1	NA	NA	0.39	0.12
	(1940)	(<1940)	(<1940)	(1967)	

NOTES: The lower the T-factor, the more improved the technology and the lower the environmental impact per dollar of GNP. See notes 1, 2, 5, and 6.

Calculated by the author using EPA 1995, 1998; Bureau of the Census 1975; BEA 1998.

plots are less prone to fluctuations but, as derived above, E/GNP corresponds to an easily grasped concept, namely, technology (or the T-factor).

Figures 4-3 through 4-7 show that with the exception of NO$_x$ emissions per capita, both sets of leading indicators for the original criteria pollutants (SO$_2$, VOC, NO$_x$, PM-10, and CO) had been declining for years, if not decades, before either total emissions began sustained downward trends or federal regulations were promulgated. Table 4-2, based on Figures 4-3 through 4-7, summarizes the magnitudes of T-factors and the year when peak values for the T-factors for SO$_2$, VOC, NO$_x$, PM-10, and CO were reached. It also indicates for each pollutant the magnitudes of the T-factors as different milestones [such as p(P) and t(F)] were reached. Clearly, by the time control for the five pollutants listed in this table was federalized, cleanup—using E/GNP as a measure—was well under way. In fact, using the data in Table 4-2, I estimate that 70 percent or more of the reductions in E/GNP between the peak years and 1997 had been achieved before federalization. In addition, for reasons explored in greater detail in Chapter 1, there were substantial improvements in the T-factors for SO_2, VOC, and NO_x between the peak years and the beginning of their respective periods of perception.

The following discusses the trends displayed in Figures 4-3 through 4-8 and Table 4-2 in greater detail.

Sulfur Dioxide, 1900–97. Currently, SO_2 emissions are at the same level as they were about 80 years ago (Figure 4-3).[13] The trend reflects the developments mentioned previously. In the first two decades of this century, industrialization and electrification drove up SO_2 emissions. Emissions stabilized in the 1920s because consumers increasingly favored gas and oil over coal and all sectors increased their efficiency of energy use. Thus, we see a rapid decline in E/ GNP (i.e., an improvement in the technology factor). During the depression, SO_2 emissions plunged. E/GNP also declined, suggesting that technological change was continuing, though at a slower rate. SO_2 emissions peaked again in the 1940s before postwar technological changes (e.g., further fuel switches and replacement of steam by diesel locomotives) turned them around. Following a rapid increase in the '60s, SO_2 emissions turned down in 1973 due to the triple forces of the Clean Air Act, oil shocks, and changes in the structure of the economy. After a period in the doldrums in the mid-1980s, SO_2 emissions began another descent, triggered initially by the recession in the Bush years but sustained by the acid rain reduction requirements in the 1990 Clean Air Act Amendments.

The long decline in E/GNP began in the early 1920s (see Table 4-2). The T-factor peaked in 1921 (at 1.41 relative to its 1900 level). In 1950 [i.e., at the beginning of the period of perception, p(P), for SO_2], it stood at 0.42. In 1970, at the threshold of the passage of the Clean Air Amendments of 1970, the T-factor had declined to 0.27. The following year it declined to 0.25, and in 1997 it was 0.08. Thus, about 87 percent of the reductions in E/GNP from the peak level had been obtained by t(F).

Clearly, SO_2 cleanup, while masked by economic and population growth, was in progress decades before SO_2 controls were federalized. The initial reductions—before the early 1960s—were in large part due to voluntary measures, many of which were taken to reduce smoke and particulate matter rather than SO_2 per se. The T-factor was more or less static in the late 50s and 60s; as a result, emissions went up. However, as discussed previously (Figure 3-2), despite these increases, urban ambient air quality improved in the 60s due to local and state requirements. The T-factor declined relatively sharply from 0.27 to 0.25 between 1970 and 1971. Some (but not too much) credit for this can go to the 1970 act, which was signed on the last day of 1970. The establishment of the SO_2 NAAQS (in early 1971) would no doubt have reinforced the need for state and local agencies to pursue SO_2 reductions already in the works, but the other provisions (such as state implementation plans based on the 1970 act, NSPS, PSD, and the disincentives for tall stacks) were, for practical purposes, not yet in place and deserve little, if any, credit for those reductions (see Chapter 1). In fact, the latter two sets of requirements would be litigated for several more years. Surprisingly, despite a few waivers, the oil shocks did not result in any backsliding on E/ GNP due to movement back to coal, partly because of the need to comply with primary NAAQS. Federal regulations and, to some extent, increased use of non–fossil fuel sources and changes in the structure of the economy are due credit for recent reductions commencing in the mid-1970s. However, it is debatable whether federal regulations were the only—or the most economical—method of obtaining those reductions.

Volatile Organic Compounds, 1900–97. Figure 4-4 indicates that VOC emissions are below their levels of half a century ago. They peaked in the mid- to late 1960s when California and federal auto emissions standards went into effect. Those declines were reinforced by the first oil shock in 1973. Any tendency to bounce back was arrested by the second oil shock and a recession. Most of the decline in emissions has been due to reductions from automobiles and other gasoline-fired on-road vehicles and, to a smaller extent, a variety of stationary sources (e.g., metal processing, refineries and other petroleum-related industries, and surface coating operations). However, emissions from waste disposal and recycling, which had dipped significantly, went up substantially after 1980.[14]

Remarkably, VOC E/GNP have been declining since the early 1930s despite the increased use of motor vehicles and air travel, both heavily dependent on hydrocarbon fuels. In 1932, the T-factor for VOC emissions stood at 1.13 relative to its 1900 level; it declined to 0.41 by 1955, around when p(P) commenced for VOC nationwide.

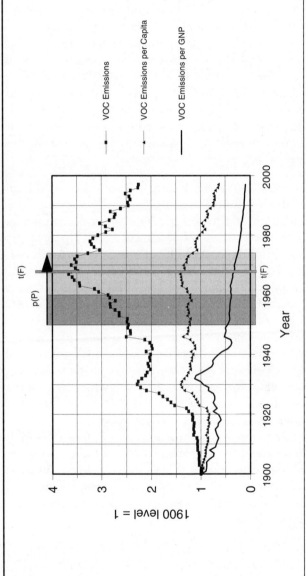

Figure 4-4

VOLATILE ORGANIC COMPOUNDS, 1900–97: EMISSIONS, EMISSIONS PER GNP, AND EMISSIONS PER CAPITA

SOURCES: EPA 1995, 1998; USBOC 1975; BEA 1998.

NOTES: p(P) = period of perception. California underwent its p(P) earlier than elsewhere. In fact, many areas were not aware they had a problem until the 1970s. See text, t(F) = time of federalization.

This, too, suggests that cleanup had started well before VOC got on the public agenda or its regulation was federalized, mainly due to market-driven forces.[15] In the mid- to late 1960s, emissions controls were imposed, first by California and then by the federal government. By 1967, when federal controls for VOC were instituted, the T-factor had declined to 0.35 (normalized to the 1900 level). By 1981, due to the two oil shocks and national emissions controls, the T-factor was reduced to 0.18. In 1997 it was 0.09. About 75 percent of the reductions in E/GNP since it peaked had been obtained by t(F).

A comparison of Figure 4-4 with Figure 3-4 indicates that emissions reductions may have preceded improvements in ozone ambient air quality, at least as measured by the second highest 1-hour maximum.

Nitrogen Oxides, 1900–97. Figure 4-5 shows that NO_x emissions increased steadily until the 1970s. Due to the combination of emissions regulations and the oil shocks, they peaked in the late 1970s. By 1997, NO_x emissions had declined about 8 percent from their 1978 peak—from 25.7 to 23.6 MST. Emissions were reduced 1.8 MST from natural gas–fired industrial combustion sources and 2.3 million tons from on-road motor vehicles, although the reductions were partially offset by increased emissions from other fuel combustion sources and nonroad vehicles and engines.[16]

NO_x emissions per GNP have been declining at least since the early 1930s. In 1933, the T-factor peaked at 1.62, normalized to 1900 levels. By 1955 it was about 0.67. It stayed more or less constant through the late '50s and '60s. In 1971, when NO_x controls were federalized, the T-factor for NO_x was 0.71. It commenced a steady decline after 1971–72, and by 1997 it stood at 0.37.

About 73 percent of the reductions in NO_x E/GNP since it peaked had been obtained by t(F). While some of the post-1972 reduction may have been due in part, at least initially, to the oil shocks, most of it was probably due to federal requirements. Some credit is also due to the increased reliance on non–fossil fuel energy sources, such as nuclear power.

Particulate Matter, 1940–97. Figure 4-6 shows trends in PM-10 emissions, E/CAP, and emissions per GNP. During this period, emissions peaked in 1950–51 at 1.07 (normalized to the 1940 level) and declined more or less continuously to 0.82 in 1970, 0.50 in 1977, and 0.26 in

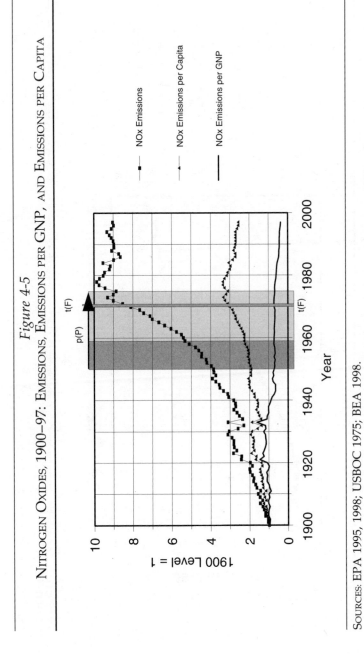

Figure 4-5

NITROGEN OXIDES, 1900–97: EMISSIONS, EMISSIONS PER GNP, AND EMISSIONS PER CAPITA

SOURCES: EPA 1995, 1998; USBOC 1975; BEA 1998.

NOTES: p(P) = period of perception. California underwent its p(P) earlier than elsewhere. In fact, many areas were not aware they had a problem until the 1970s. See text, t(F) = time of federalization.

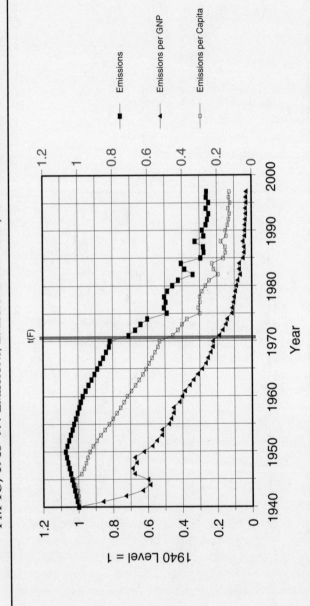

Figure 4-6

PM-1O, 1940–97: EMISSIONS, EMISSIONS PER GNP, AND EMISSIONS PER CAPITA

SOURCES: EPA 1995, 1998; USBOC 1975; BEA 1998.

NOTE: t(F) = time of federalization.

1994. The timing of these reductions indicates that a substantial portion of the initial reduction was due to voluntary measures, including, as noted previously, switching to cleaner energy sources and new technologies for combustion equipment in all sectors. Those measures were supplemented by regulations imposed by local and state jurisdictions for combustion sources, open burning, incinerators, and industrial sources in urban areas, regulations that in many cases preceded the 1970 Clean Air Act. The rapid decline in the last quarter-century, stimulated by regulations at all levels, was due to broader use of more efficient control technologies (e.g., electrostatic precipitators and baghouses), which were adapted from materials handling processes and smelters to a much broader spectrum of sources.[17]

Excluding the trough in the early 1940s (an artifact of the high GNP during the war years), E/GNP has declined almost continuously. In 1960, the T-factor was 0.40, relative to unity for 1940. By 1970, when PM control was federalized, this measure was at 0.23, and in the following 10 years it declined to 0.09. However, as for SO_2, it is not clear how much credit should go to federal requirements, particularly those beyond the NAAQS promulgation, for the first few years following the enactment of the 1970 act. In 1997 it was 0.03. Thus, more than 84 percent of the reductions in E/GNP had been obtained by t(F).

The trends in Figure 4-6 are, in general, consistent with the previous discussion regarding ambient TSP (and dustfall) air quality, for which continual improvements have been indicated at least since the end of World War II, particularly in urban areas. As for other cases, many of the improvements were driven by economics and adopted, more or less voluntarily, despite poorly written and badly enforced laws and regulations.

Carbon Monoxide. Figure 4-7 shows that CO emissions increased from 1940 to 1971, to 1.38 relative to the 1940 level, and then declined due to the Federal Motor Vehicle Emission Control Program and the oil shocks. In 1997 it was 0.93. Through the '50s and '60s, national CO emissions from stationary sources declined due mainly to continued reduction in the use of wood and coal in households and commercial establishments, and reduced emissions from refineries, carbon black plants, and wildfires. Railroad emissions also continued

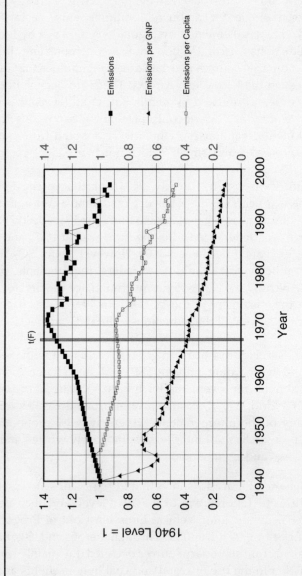

Figure 4-7

CARBON MONOXIDE, 1940–97: EMISSIONS, EMISSIONS PER GNP, AND EMISSIONS PER CAPITA

SOURCES: EPA 1995, 1998; USBOC 1975; BEA 1998.

NOTE: t(F) = time of federalization.

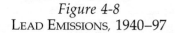

Figure 4-8
LEAD EMISSIONS, 1940–97

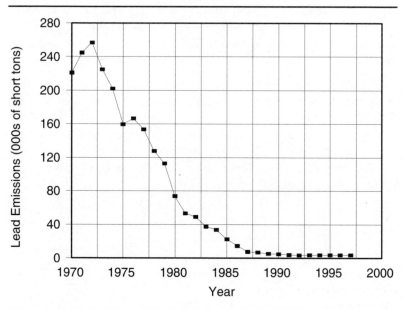

SOURCE: EPA 1998.

their decline. However, increased use of motor vehicles more than made up for all the reductions. Then, as noted, California and federal vehicle emissions standards helped turn around nationwide CO emissions in the mid- to late 1960s. In 1970, on-road and off-road vehicles and engines accounted for 98.7 million tons out of a total of 128.2 million tons (or 77 percent). In 1997, this share, accounting for 67.0 MST out of a total of 87.5 MST, was virtually unchanged. The major reductions during that period came from automobiles, followed by smaller reductions from a variety of sources—such as open burning, incineration, petroleum refineries and related industries, metals processing, and various chemical industries—while emissions increased from nonroad engines and vehicles.[18]

Emissions of CO per GNP have declined continuously since the war years. By 1960 the E/GNP had declined to 0.49, relative to the 1940 level. It declined to 0.39 in 1967, the year when federal motor vehicle emissions standards went into effect for the 1968 model year.

Due to federal standards and the 1973 oil shock, it went down further to 0.28 in 1977. In 1997, the T-factor was 0.12. Once again, we see that technological improvement, driven in large part by voluntary, market-driven forces, had begun well before federalization. More than 69 percent of the reductions in E/GNP for CO had been obtained by t(F).

Lead, 1970–97. Data for lead are available only from 1970 onward. Lead emissions broadly parallel trends in ambient air quality (Figure 4-8). In 1997, those emissions were less than 2 percent of their 1972 peak levels. Federal requirements, initially imposed to ensure that leaded gasoline did not poison catalytic converters used for tailpipe controls rather than to reduce public health impacts, were responsible for those spectacular improvements.[19]

5. The Environmental Transition

A common feature of the emissions trends for SO_2, VOC, NO_x, PM-10, and CO shown in Figures 4-3 through 4-7 is that although there may be substantial ups and downs from year to year before they were perceived to be problems—that is, p(P)—once those perceptions set in for a pollutant, its emissions went up for a while before finally coming down. In other words, once p(P) has been under way for some time, each emissions plot is shaped like a stylized inverted U (see Figure 5-1).

If affluence were plotted on the x-axis rather than time, then the plot of emissions versus affluence would also look like a stylized

---

Figure 5-1
THE ENVIRONMENTAL TRANSITION

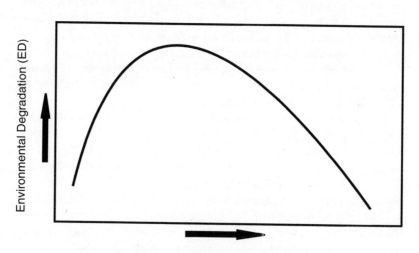

Time (or Technology or Affluence)

inverted U beyond the levels of affluence corresponding to p(P) because affluence has increased more or less steadily through this century; between 1900 and 1994, the correlation between affluence and time is 0.96.[1] A plot of environmental degradation against affluence that is shaped like an inverted U is known among economists as an environmental Kuznets curve, and is consistent with cross-country data for various short-range, primary air pollutants,[2] and with the theory of an environmental transition.[3] Under this theory, at low levels of affluence, environmental quality for a society is degraded as it becomes more affluent; however, as the society becomes wealthier, it goes through a transition so that additional wealth, instead of worsening environmental quality, actually helps improve it.[4]

An explanation offered for an environmental transition is that society is on a continual quest to improve its quality of life, which is determined by numerous social, economic, and environmental factors.[5] The weight given to each determinant varies constantly depending upon society's precise circumstances and perceptions. In the early stages of economic and technological development, which go hand in hand, a society attempts to improve its overall quality of life by placing a higher priority upon increasing affluence than on other determinants, even if that means tolerating some environmental degradation, because greater affluence provides the means for obtaining basic needs and amenities (such as food, shelter, water, and electricity) and reducing the most significant risks to public health and safety (risks such as malnutrition, infectious and parasitic diseases, and child and maternal mortality). However, as society becomes wealthier and tackles these problems, a number of factors come into play that tend to reinforce one another in helping to reduce environmental degradation.

First, as a nation becomes wealthier and progress is made on the higher-priority and more evident risks to public health and safety noted above, environmental problems automatically rise higher on society's priority list of unmet needs, even if environmental degradation does not worsen. Second, because of insufficient attention to environmental quality, added economic activity does, in fact, further degrade the environment, and that, by itself, moves environmental quality up on society's priority list. Thus, environmental quality becomes a more important determinant of the overall quality of life. Society, in effect, places a greater value on environmental quality.

Simultaneously, with increasing affluence, society is more able to afford improvements in its environmental quality. Because of the combination of these factors, greater affluence should ultimately result in improvements in environmental quality. And if cleanup does not come voluntarily or sufficiently rapidly, a democratic society will translate its desire for a less polluted environment into laws—and even if it comes voluntarily and rapidly, society may enshrine its environmental goals into laws for sheer symbolism, in order to make a statement about its priorities. The wealthier such a society, the more affordable—and more demanding—its laws.

This explanation of environmental transition is consistent with, but more complex than, Hays' explication of the evolution of environmental values.[6] Although this explanation is couched in terms of affluence, the air quality and emissions trends discussed in the previous chapters (and other analyses of long-term trends of water and land degradation) show that affluence is not the only time-dependent factor that helps bring about an environmental transition.[7] Technological change, which has also increased with time, is just as important. However, that may well be a distinction without much of a difference because affluence and technology are interdependent—that is, they co-evolve.[8] Affluence makes it possible to afford not only research and development of new or improved technologies but also their installation, particularly if the up-front costs of such technologies are higher. That is always the case for any add-on or end-of-pipe technology. It is often true for process changes, as well. Moreover, greater affordability leads to greater compliance and, arguably, more stringent regulations, which then result in further reductions in emissions per GNP—that is, greater technological change. In turn, broad technological change stimulates economic growth.[9]

The process of economic development, at least over the past century or more, involved a technology-mediated evolution in the structure of the economy that further buttressed the environmental transition in the United States. First, technological change was essential for the transformation of an agrarian to an industrial society. Without it, labor would not have been freed up from the farm, nor would there have been factories to absorb the surplus labor. Technological change was also the midwife for the metamorphosis of an industrial to a postindustrial society. The tools and products of that society—

whether hardware such as telephones, personal computers, or airplanes, or software such as e-mail, financial instruments (e.g., indexed mutual funds), or copyrighted music and books—are themselves products of, or dependent on, technology for their manufacture, distribution, and sale. And just as technology was responsible for the migration of labor from the farm to the factory, so was it instrumental in the movement of the housewife into the workplace. Technology such as the vacuum cleaner, the washing machine, and the microwave freed up the housewife's time, enabling her to go to the office to man the telephones, computers, and reservation desks. By reducing the premium on physical strength, it also expanded a woman's ability to participate in the broader work force—in assembly lines, in mines, and even in the military.

The evolution of the structure of the economy itself caused emissions per capita or per GNP to first increase, as society became more industrialized, and then decline as it moved into a postindustrial phase. Thus, plots of E/cap or E/GNP against affluence (i.e., GNP/cap) should also look like stylized inverted U's,[10] in that they, too, display an environmental transition of sorts.[11] And as Figures 4-3 through 4-5 show, they indeed follow such a pattern.

Demographic and economic factors further reinforce environmental transitions. Consider that in 1900 the mining and manufacturing sectors, traditionally associated with pollution, employed 40.2 percent of nonfarm labor.[12] After declining into the mid–30 percent range during the Depression, employment in those sectors rebounded into the 40(+) percent range during World War II before commencing a long-term decline that continues to this day.[13] Employment in the polluting sectors shrank to 28.2 percent in 1970 and 17.0 percent in 1997.[14] As the proportion of the population dependent on polluting industries for its livelihood declines, so does its economic and demographic clout, which only increases the likelihood of more stringent anti-pollution and environmental laws directed at those industries, particularly in a democratic society. Currently we see this principle in operation in the United States in the ranching, mining, and lumbering industries. Once those industries were kings in the West; today they are increasingly embattled, and will continue to be so in the future. The agricultural industry should also expect to see further moves to contain its environmental impacts or to control its demands on water use in water-short areas.

Plots of ambient air quality versus either affluence or time should also illustrate these environmental transitions. At first glance, some of the trends in air quality (e.g., Figure 3-1 for TSP) seem to lack a transition. But, as the historical account suggests, that is a consequence of the time series for those figures commencing after improvements in air quality had already begun. Accordingly, one sees only the posttransition downward slope for such pollutants. Thus, Figures 3-1 through 3-6 are consistent with the environmental transition hypothesis.

Figure 2-1, which is for proxy indicators of indoor air quality, is also consistent with the notion of an environmental transition, with the transition for each pollutant occurring in the 1940s if not earlier (except, possibly, for NO_x, which had a subsidiary peak around 1960). However, some of those transitions occurred fortuitously. When the transitions occurred, PM and CO were generally regarded as problems indoors but SO_2, VOC, and NO_x were not.[15] By the time the latter three substances gained recognition from the general public as problems, they had been reduced substantially indoors as a side effect of all the measures taken to reduce smoke (and CO). So it would be inappropriate to portray reductions in indoor air quality for SO_2, VOC, and NO_x as consequences of "true" transitions, even though they seem consistent with such an interpretation. The success of the inadvertent improvements in those three pollutants in households is, perhaps, one reason why there has never been any overt, concerted effort to reduce them indoors.

Deciphering Air Quality Trends for the United States

Table 5-1, based on the trends discussed in the previous chapters, shows the years or periods during which various "national" air quality indicators (indoor air quality, ambient air quality, national emissions, and emissions per GNP) were at their worst in the United States for each pollutant. This worst period, corresponding to the period during which each indicator is at or near its peak, is the "period of transition." The period of transition varies not only with the specific pollutant but also with the precise indicator or leading indicator (indoor or outdoor air quality, emissions, or emissions per GNP) used to characterize the environmental effect of that pollutant.

Table 5-1

MILESTONES AND TRANSITIONS FOR VARIOUS POLLUTANTS AND INDICATORS

Substance	Period or Year When Substance Was		Worst Year(s) or Period of Transition (Nationally, unless Noted Otherwise)			
	Recognized or Perceived as a Pollutant [p(P)]	First Federally Regulated [t(F)]	Indoor Air Quality	Outdoor Air Quality	Emissions (E)	E/GNP[a]
PM	Before 1900	1971[b]	<1940	<1957	1950[c]	1940s or earlier
SO$_2$	Approximately 1950	1971[b]	<1940[f]	Early to mid-1960s	1973	1920s
CO	Approximately late 1950s[d]	1967[e]	<1940	Mid-1960s (?) but not after 1970	1970–71	1940s or earlier
VOC/O$_3$	Calif., 1950s Elsewhere, 1960s or later	1971[g.a] 1967[e]	NE <1940[f]	Calif., 1966–67 Elsewhere, mid-to late 1970s	NE 1967	NE 1930s

NO$_x$	Calif., 1950s Elsewhere, 1960s or later	1971[b]	<1940, secondary peak around 1960[f]	1978–79	1978	1930s
Source	Table 1-1, Chapter 1		Fig. 2-1	Figs. 3-1 to 3-5		Figs. 4-3 to 4-7

NOTE: NE = not estimated.

[a]The peak in this leading indicator shows the latest time by which "cleanup" had begun either through deliberate actions or by happenstance (see text).

[b]The Clean Air Amendments of 1970 were signed on the last day of 1970, but most federal regulations went into effect later.

[c]For PM-10.

[d]CO: long known to be deadly indoors, but its status as an outdoor air pollutant was recognized much later.

[e]Model year 1968 for automobiles.

[f]Not generally recognized by the public or policymakers as needing remediation indoors.

[g]Because federal vehicle emissions were borrowed from, and went into effect after, California's, federalization did not have any effect until after the 1970 amendments were signed.

Table 5-1 compares the various periods of transition with their corresponding periods of perception, p(P), and times of federalization, t(F). The comparison shows that long before the federal government essentially took over air pollution control in the United States, matters had begun to improve, especially for the pollutants associated with excess mortality during the air pollution episodes of the 1940s, '50s, and '60s (TSP and SO_2). Moreover, we see that it is possible to improve air quality even while emissions may be increasing—for example, for SO_2 and CO.

Table 5-1 suggests that people and society dealt with air pollution almost as if driven by a relentless logic. Initially, the indicators of air pollution worsened as people and communities strove to improve their quality of life through jobs and economic growth. As the population became more prosperous and new technologies became available, the problems perceived to be the worst, and the easiest to address, were dealt with first. Families (and individuals) rid their personal environment—their households—of the most obvious problem—smoke and, to some extent, CO—before anything else. In so doing, they also improved the outside air in their neighborhoods. Fortunately, those measures also reduced indoor concentrations of other substances not generally deemed particularly harmful by the general public or policymakers at that time.

Next, attention turned to outdoor air. Once again, the first target was smoke because it was also the most obvious. New technologies and prosperity helped move the fuel mix from coal and wood toward oil and gas, and generally increased fuel efficiency across all economic sectors. As a result, soon after World War II if not earlier, most urban areas had gone through their environmental transitions for smoke.

With greater prosperity, better health, and reduced mortality, the risks of other outdoor air pollutants became easier to infer or spot. In the years following World War II, deadly air pollution episodes ascribed to PM, SO_2, or both occurred on both sides of the Atlantic. So transitions for PM and SO_2 air quality came next, followed in time by the transitions for CO and O_3 air quality. That the transition for NO_x air quality came last is fitting for a pollutant that was never ranked very high in terms of adverse effects at the levels it occurred in the outdoor air and that was also the most expensive to control.

For SO_2 and probably CO, both primary pollutants, the transitions for outdoor air quality occurred before those for aggregate national emissions. The data on PM are unclear as to which came first—the transition for air quality or for emissions—because the emissions data are for PM-10 but the national air quality data for PM-10 do not begin until 1988 (see Figure 3-1). With respect to O_3, a secondary pollutant, the transition for national emissions preceded that for air quality.

These progressions suggest that for a particular society the environmental transition for a pollutant is determined by the general level of affluence, the state of the technology, the effects of the pollutant relative to other societal risks, and the affordability of measures to reduce those effects. But those factors are not independent of each other. As noted, affluence and technology are interdependent. Moreover, knowledge of a pollutant's effects on society is itself a product of technology, and the affordability of control and· mitigation measures is a function of both affluence and technology. Thus, environmental transitions for a particular society are ultimately determined by affluence and technology.

Finally, since the timing of a transition depends upon the specific pollutant (or indicator) and the relative social, economic, and environmental costs and benefits of addressing that pollutant (or indicator), it is possible for a society, a group, or an individual to be simultaneously to the left of the environmental transition for one pollutant but to the right for another. Hence, it is quite rational to oppose, say, carbon dioxide (CO_2) controls on one hand while supporting stricter CO controls on the other. Nor would it be unusual to support VOC controls at refineries but oppose mandatory inspection and maintenance of one's own vehicle. However, there is a line beyond which such rationalizations mutate into hypocrisies: for example, bemoaning the environmental effects of sports utility vehicles while driving one, or decrying the buildup of greenhouse gases while opposing drilling for natural gas[16] or the construction and use of nuclear power plants.[17]

After the Transition: From a "Race to the Bottom" to "Not in My Back Yard"?

An examination of Figure 5-1 reveals that during the early phases of economic and technological development—or if the net costs of controlling a specific pollutant (or indicator) are perceived to be

Figure 5-2
AFTER THE TRANSITION

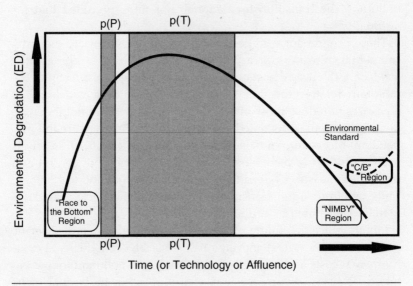

NOTE: p(P) = period of perception; p(T) = period of transition; NIMBY region = "not-in-my-back-yard" region (ED enters this region if benefits far exceed costs borne by beneficiaries); C/B region = ED enters this region if costs and benefits have to be more carefully balanced.

excessive—an affluence- and technology-driven environmental transition based upon a race to the top of the quality of life may superficially resemble a race to relax environmental standards for that pollutant (or indicator). But once a society (or group) gets past the transition and matters improve sufficiently—for instance, if environmental quality improves beyond the environmental standard—the race to the top of the quality of life may drive the environmental degradation trajectory in one of several different directions.

If the perceived benefits of control for the society (or group) are substantially less than its perceived costs, or if the costs are shifted to others while benefits are retained, society will move toward greater cleanup (as indicated by the solid posttransition curve in Figure 5-2), and environmental degradation (ED) will be driven down further.

In effect, under those circumstances the race to the top of the quality of life would look like a race to the top of environmental quality and masquerade as a not-in-my-back-yard (NIMBY) situation. Thus, the apparent race to the bottom and the NIMBY effect are, in fact, two aspects of the same phenomenon, but the former occurs prior to—while the latter occurs after—an affluence- and technology-driven environmental transition, and only if perceived benefits far exceed perceived costs.

However, if the perceived social and economic costs are in the same ballpark as the perceived benefits, which may occur if technological progress has been unable to substantially reduce costs or costs cannot be shifted to someone else, then the precise trajectory—whether it continues downward but not as steeply as in the NIMBY case, goes up, or stays more or less constant—will depend upon a more careful balancing of the perceived costs and benefits.[18] In a democracy, such a balancing is often done by legislators (or agencies authorized by them) and usually in a qualitative fashion. The dashed line in Figure 5-2 depicts a case in which at some point beyond the environmental transition the perceived additional benefits of further controlling that environmental problem are once again exceeded by the perceived additional costs. As a result, ED swings upward. I denote this region on the ED vs. affluence diagram as the "CB" region ("CB" is a handy mnemonic for "careful balancing of costs and benefits").

An upswing in ED could occur for a variety of reasons. First, society may decide that it has dealt with the particular environmental problem sufficiently and that scarce financial and human resources should now be turned toward addressing its other unmet needs. Second, based upon new information or changes in societal values and attitudes, society concludes that past control efforts, for whatever reason, went too far or were unnecessary. Third, limits of clean technologies have been reached for the activities that contribute to the environmental problem and there are no cleaner substitutes for those activities. Thus, additional activity would have to result in greater environmental impacts.[19] Fourth, as cleanup proceeds, additional cleanup becomes more expensive while its benefits diminish. Therefore, society (through its elected officials in a democracy) may judge that further cleanup may lessen rather than enhance the overall quality of life.

Having developed a rationale for an upswing in ED subsequent to an environmental transition, it is worth asking whether the long-term U.S. data for various indicators in fact show any recent upswings. An examination of the figures in the previous three chapters fails to reveal any such sustained upswings. The indicator that comes closest to having such an upswing is SO_2 emissions (Figure 4-3), for which national emissions went up in each of the last two years of the data series (1996 and 1997). Of course, two consecutive years do not a trend make. More significantly, the SO_2 ambient concentration continues to decline (Figure 3-2). Perhaps, it can be argued, it is only a matter of time before we see a sustained upswing, but that time apparently has not yet arrived for the United States.

The Environmental Transition and the Environmental Kuznets Curve

The environmental transition hypothesis (ETH) proposed above suggests that, in general, a plot of ED against time or affluence follows an inverted-U–shaped path except, possibly, at very high levels of affluence, where it may swing up under some circumstances. If the upswing were to continue, the plot would resemble the letter N. But despite the similarity in the pre-upswing region between a depiction of the environmental transition and an environmental Kuznets curve (EKC), there are fundamental differences between the environmental transition and the EKC hypothesis as the latter has usually been derived or proposed. First, the ETH applies to individual groups (usually countries), while the existence (or nonexistence) of EKCs is usually postulated based upon statistical analyses of data sets spanning several groups (also, usually countries). Second, under the ETH an environmental transition occurs over a period of time, which folds in both affluence and technological change. On the other hand, the EKC is usually based on a plot of ED against affluence. Ideally, its derivation ought to use a data set drawn from a narrow time period in order to exclude technological change as a confounding variable. Alternatively, analytical techniques have to be used to filter out the effects of technological change (as well as other confounding variables). However, separating out the effects of technological change and economic growth is easier said than done since, as discussed earlier, economic growth and technological change co-evolve.[20]

It is easy to see how a set of single-country environmental transitions followed by upswings (as indicated by the curve ending in the CB region in Figure 5-2) may lead to a similar N-shaped cross-country ED vs. affluence curve. However, I will show below that cross-country ED vs. affluence curves need not be inverted-U shaped even if the single-country ED curves are.

In order to demonstrate this, I will start from a set of single-country ED vs. affluence curves and use them to construct a cross-country ED vs. affluence curve. This approach is fundamentally different from the approach of other researchers who have started with cross-country curves and tried to use those to develop shapes for or derive conclusions or policies about the evolution of ED for single countries.[21]

For a given pollutant, one should expect that the shape of an environmental transition will vary from country to country depending upon its particular circumstances. For any given pollutant and any indicator used to characterize that pollutant's environmental impact, environmental transitions may be narrower for some countries, some may have steeper ascents, and others may have faster declines. The precise timing of a single-country environmental transition and the magnitude of ED at which that occurs will depend upon numerous interdependent factors in addition to the level of economic development and the availability and affordability of technology. Those factors include the distribution and quantities of its natural resource endowments; population density; climate; geography; level of knowledge (or, perhaps more importantly, perceptions) about the pollutant in question; cultural and religious attitudes toward the environment and the many other determinants of the aggregate quality of life; political and economic structures; and the precise nature and magnitude of the country's unmet social and economic needs.

Since no two countries are identical in all these respects, we should not, in general, expect their peaks for environmental degradation to be of the same magnitude or to occur at the same time or level of affluence. A divergence in just one of the several factors noted above could result in differences in the timing and the levels of affluence or ED at which their environmental transitions may occur. For example, if it is possible for two countries to be identical in every respect except that one's economic takeoff occurs later, then the lagging country's environmental transition is more likely to occur at a lower level of affluence, because it has the opportunity to benefit from technologies invented by the leading country (assuming trade in ideas and the willingness to learn on the part of the lagging country). For the same reason, the time between economic takeoff and the peak in the environmental degradation plot is more likely to be shorter for the lagging country.

Consider two countries, A and B. For the sake of simplicity, I will assume that both are past p(P), the period of perception. If country A is well endowed in coal, while B imports fossil fuels, then it should not be surprising if the former's economy is more dependent on coal and invests less in energy efficiency. (Compare, for example, the United States with Japan.) As a result, country A is more likely to have higher SO_2 emissions per capita and per GNP, and its environmental transition for ambient SO_2 air quality is likely to occur at a higher level of ED and when it is more affluent than country B.

A similar result could obtain if A and B were identical in every respect except that the latter has a higher population density. That would result in greater SO_2-related impacts on the population of country B, which, since all else is deemed equal, ought to result in an earlier and more drastic level of control. (Countries with greater population densities are also more likely to be able to justify mass transit and, hence, to have less intensive automobile use, which can be a major source of other fossil fuel–related emissions.)

Next, assume that country A, which is better endowed with coal and fossil fuels, launched on its economic growth path earlier. This could occur for a variety of reasons: Through an accident of history or conscious design, country A may have developed the appropriate institutions for stimulating economic growth and technological change sooner, or it may have been able to gain leverage from its natural resource endowments earlier. Thus, it could be past its environmental transition (which it reaches at time T_A) by the time country B reaches its point of transition at time T_B (with $T_B > T_A$).[22] At times beyond T_B the environmental degradation for country A could, nevertheless, exceed that for country B even after both have gone past their individual environmental transitions, despite country B's being less affluent. This is illustrated in Figure 5-3, in which both A and B have inverted-U–shaped curves for ED vs. affluence. That situation is clearly at odds with the general notion of an

Figure 5-3
EXAMPLES OF SINGLE-COUNTRY ENVIRONMENTAL TRANSITIONS

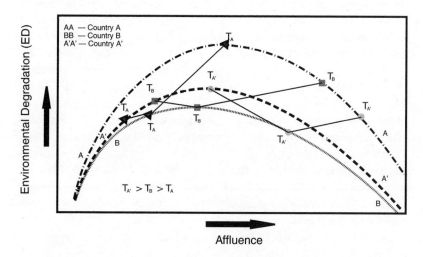

Affluence

inverted-U shape postulated by the EKC hypothesis (namely, that at high affluence levels, the more affluent country will also have a lower level of ED).

Now let us consider a third country, A', which is identical to A except that its economic takeoff occurred after A and B. A^1 would peak at a lower ED level than country A at time T_A^1 (with $T_A^1 > T_B > T_A$), but conceivably the peak could be higher than that for B, although A^1 was the last to take off economically and could avail itself of the technological changes devised by both the leaders (see Figure 5-3).

Figure 5-3 indicates the levels of ED and affluence for each country at times T_A, T_B, and T_A^1. We can construct cross-country ED vs. affluence plots by connecting the three points on the three country plots corresponding to each of those times. The three resulting cross-country plots do not look like inverted U's for any of those times. If anything, they look like upside-down EKCs.

Thus, it does not necessarily follow that an EKC will emerge from cross-country data even if each country has an environmental transition shaped like a Kuznets curve.

The second point illustrated by Figure 5-3 is that, given the numerous factors that govern the evolution of ED for any country, there is no reason why, left to their own devices, the "turning point" or peak ED for a particular pollutant should occur at the same level of affluence (or time) for all countries. (Of course, if each country is not left to its own devices, the timing and possibly the peak EDs may be interrelated—for instance, if they band together in an international agreement with similar obligations for each party.) Nor is there any reason, given the many factors that could determine the evolution of ED for any country, why the turning point in an EKC should be universally applicable to individual countries (in the absence of collective action or, perhaps, even then[23]). In fact, it is not clear what, if anything, is represented by the various inflection points in a cross-country ED vs. affluence curve, although with time the peak corresponding to the environmental transition is likely to move down and to the left because of technological change[24] and increased awareness (or perception) of the problems due to environmental degradation.

The above example is based on a very limited number of hypothetical countries. If we construct a cross-country curve from a much larger set of single-country curves covering the spectrum with respect to the many factors that could affect the shape, height, and timing of environmental transitions, then, based on the ETH, we should expect countries with very low and very high affluence levels to have generally low levels of ED and those with medium levels of affluence to have generally higher levels of ED. Hence, it is possible to obtain, in a very general sense, a stylized inverted-U–shaped cross-country curve from a set of single-country ET curves with, possibly, some peaks and troughs here and there, particularly toward the extremes of affluence, because the precise shape in those regions is necessarily determined by the few countries at those extreme reaches. As Figure 5-3 shows, these details can lead to some mighty peculiar shapes.

Does Greater Wealth Lead to Cleaner Environments?

Based on cross-country and single-country data for a variety of environmental indicators, it has been suggested that as a country gets richer it will, through some agency or the other, ultimately get cleaner.[25] One of the major arguments against that proposition is that some analyses of *cross-country* data indicate that at relatively high levels of affluence, a cross-country plot of ambient SO_2 concentrations vs. affluence may have an upswing—that is, the curve may be N-shaped.[26] I showed above that it was possible to have an N-shaped cross-country curve constructed from a hypothetical set of inverted-U–shaped single-country ET curves. Thus, the presence of an N-shaped cross-country curve is not, by itself, a persuasive argument against the hypothesis that as a country gets richer it is also likely, for whatever reason, to become cleaner. On the other hand, as the discussion accompanying Figure 5-2 suggests, richer is likely to be cleaner, but possibly only until the environment is sufficiently clean. Given the various possibilities, instead of speculating upon the direction of ED once a country is well past its environmental transition, I will examine empirical data on ambient SO_2 concentrations for countries with the highest levels of affluence.

The United States, the second most affluent country based on GDP per capita after adjusting for purchasing power parity (PPP),[27] so far shows no upswing in "national" ambient SO_2 concentrations (Figure 3-2). Figure 5-4 shows trends in "national" composite ambient SO_2 concentrations for the 13 countries for which such data were available from the Organization for Economic Cooperation and Development, whose membership includes, by and large, the richest industrialized nations.[28] The PPP-adjusted GDP per capita for 10 of those nations (among the world's richest and most industrialized) is above $18,000, and it is between $3,000 and $10,000 for the remaining 3 (the Czech Republic, Poland, and Slovakia).[29] The trends in Figure 5-4 suggest that single-country curves may be converging, that each of these countries is currently on the downhill side of the environmental transition, and that so far none of them has had a sustained upswing.

Based upon the previous discussion, one should not expect that the level of affluence is the sole determinant of the relative position of the tail of the ambient SO_2 concentration of a country. Indeed, a regression analysis of national SO_2 concentrations against PPP-adjusted GDP per capita for the richer set of countries using a single year (in this case, 1993)[30] shows no correlation between environmental degradation and affluence ($R^2 < 0.006$, $p >> 0.1$).[31] On the other hand, there is a much stronger correlation between national SO_2 concentrations and a country's dependence on solid fuels, as measured by the fraction of total fuel consumption due to solid fuel

Figure 5-4
AMBIENT SO$_2$ CONCENTRATIONS, VARIOUS OECD COUNTRIES, 1980–95

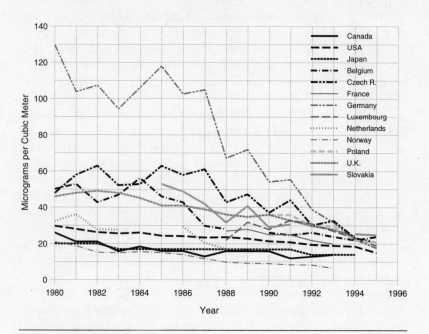

SOURCE: OECD 1997.

consumption (R^2 = 0.62, and the slope is significant at the 0.01 level). This is illustrated in Figure 5-5, which shows ambient concentrations increasing with dependence upon solid fuels.

In summary, as a country gets richer, ultimately it is also likely to be cleaner, at least until it is "clean enough." However, because of the many determinants of environmental transition that can vary from country to country, it does not follow that richer countries are necessarily always cleaner.

Determinants of Environmental Transition

In light of the above discussion and examination of empirical data from the United States and other richer nations, it is possible to list

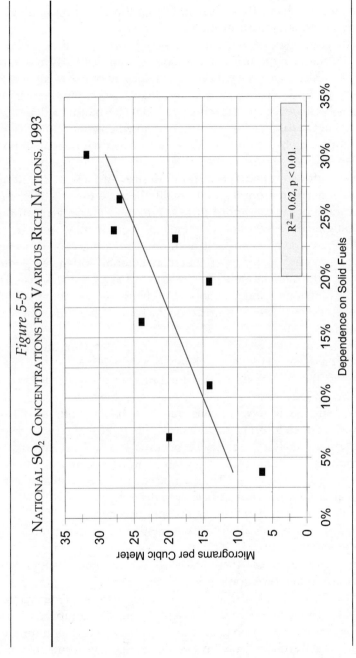

Figure 5-5

NATIONAL SO₂ CONCENTRATIONS FOR VARIOUS RICH NATIONS, 1993

$R^2 = 0.62, p < 0.01.$

Dependence on Solid Fuels

Micrograms per Cubic Meter

SOURCES: *OECD 1997; WRI 1998.*

105

several factors that affect the shape, height, and timing of single-country environmental transitions.

First, because society's quest for a better quality of life is fundamental to the ET hypothesis, that hypothesis implicitly assumes that society's desire to improve its collective quality of life is converted into actions. Such a conversion is more likely to occur in democratic societies.[32] However, the precise pace may be modulated by the attitudes of the ruling elites. Whether—and when—it occurs in non-democratic societies is entirely idiosyncratic, since it depends upon the ideologies or whims of their ruler(s) or ruling group(s).

Second, affluence helps convert our desires and needs, including that for a clean environment, into reality because the wealthier the nation the more it can afford to research, develop, and install the technologies necessary for a cleaner environment. Moreover, as countries become more affluent, additional economic growth seems to become more knowledge—rather than material—intensive, population growth rates moderate (as seems to have been the case for the richer nations), and technological change is sustained, if not accelerated.[33] All these trends tend to reinforce environmental transitions.

Third, regulations are likely to be an integral part of an ET in a democratic society. However, while more stringent regulation may be among the proximate causes for bringing about an ET, such regulation does not arise nor is its success achieved in a vacuum. Eventual success, in fact, is a consequence of having both the desire and the means to improve the quality of life (QoL). In other words, ETs are more likely to occur as democratic societies become richer and controls are made more affordable through economic growth and technological progress. Thus, while economic growth and technological progress are not sufficient, in the long run retarding them is also likely to retard environmental improvements.

Fourth, an ET comes about because neither economic growth nor environmental quality is identical to a society's aggregate quality of life (QoL) at all times. At an early stage of economic development, greater economic development is a better indicator of an improvement in QoL, while at later stages environmental quality is a better surrogate. However, once a sufficient level of cleanup has been achieved there is no reason to presume a priori that further improvements in environmental quality would necessarily result in a net improvement in the quality of life, since additional control is likely to be more expensive while benefits are likely to decline. Moreover, society presumably has other unmet needs on its agenda that it may want to address despite a less-than-total victory over environmental degradation. Some of the debate on the EKC hypothesis revolves around the concern that at very high levels of affluence there is, or may be, an upswing in ED.[34] But such a concern is only warranted if that also diminishes QoL. Whether that will occur at the relatively low posttransition levels of ED depends upon the marginal costs and marginal benefits of keeping ED in check (including forgone benefits due to unaddressed societal needs).

Fifth, the existence of p(P) is critical. In the absence of a general perception that a substance is a problem and therefore needs to be controlled, one ought not to expect any conscious actions to reduce ED. Consider, for example, the case of CO_2. Several analysts have noted that cross-country plots of several CO_2 emissions indicators vs. affluence do not follow inverted-U–shaped paths or, if they do, the turning points are at such high levels of affluence that many developing countries will, they claim, never reach that point.[35] There are a number of problems with this analysis:

- Although a number of environmentalists and scientists claimed in the 1980s (or even before) that CO_2 could be a major environmental problem, the p(P) extended at least until 1990, when the first report of the Intergovernmental Panel on Climate Change (IPCC) was published.[36] It is unreasonable to expect to see turning points for CO_2 so soon after that. First, despite the IPCC's reports, the basic issue of whether CO_2 is a major problem has not yet been fully settled among policymakers. Second, there has never been any showing that global warming is as important as the numerous other social, economic, and environmental problems facing humanity and the globe—including, for instance, indoor air pollution due to burning of solid fuels inside the home or sulfates outdoors, loss of habitat to agricultural uses, and water-related deaths and diseases. In the few studies in which this question has been raised, the answer seems to be in the negative, at least for the foreseeable future (50 to 100 years from now).[37] Third, energy systems need decades rather than years to be turned over. Such turnover has been retarded by the inability of proponents of control to show that accelerated turnover of the energy infrastructure is worth the benefits, by the added costs associated with non–fossil fuel energy alternatives, and by the lack of enthusiasm for a number of noncombustion alternatives to fossil fuels (such as nuclear or hydro) even among the most vociferous institutional supporters of greenhouse gas controls.

- The above CO_2 analysis assumes no technological change or technology transfer that would, in time, cause turning points to occur at lower levels of affluence for countries currently on the uphill segment of the EKC. But, as the long-term trends in emissions per GNP for various air pollutants (Table 4-1 and Table 4-2) indicate, ignoring technological changes can lead to serious errors in projections of the magnitude and impacts of emissions. That is also confirmed by analyses of long-term trends for land use, deaths due to water-related diseases, and indoor air quality.[38]

- Using cross-country CO_2 analyses to predict the evolution and timing of single-country environmental transitions is, as shown, an inherently risky exercise. For such analyses to succeed, the data will have to be filtered by using many more variables than have generally been tried, including variables that reflect the responsiveness of government to its population's perceptions of QoL; natural resource endowments; population densities; current level of economic development; structure of the economy; the type and magnitude of unmet needs, as well as the costs of meeting them; attitudes of peoples and ruling elites toward the environment; geography; and climate.

- Given the numerous variables that affect the timing, height, and width of an ET, it is just as risky to extrapolate from the experience of one country or a small set of countries to determine when and at what levels ETs may occur in others.

Finally, the choice of environmental indicator is critical (Table 5-1). Not all indicators are equal. Some are better measures of the environmental and public health impacts of a substance than others. In a democracy, public health impacts will generally be addressed before other environmental impacts. All else being equal, the more closely an indicator reflects public health impacts, the more likely is it to be addressed first. In addition, the cheaper it is to address an indicator, the more likely it is that that indicator will be addressed before others.

6. The States and Air Pollution: A Reassessment Based upon Empirical Evidence

Among the arguments for the federal takeover of air pollution control was that states had been dragging their feet on air pollution control and that federal control was necessary to ensure that interstate competition for jobs would not result in a race to the bottom and to excessive air pollution. This chapter examines whether the empirical evidence developed in previous chapters supports those arguments for federalization.

Did States Fail to Act Prior to Federalization?

Conventional wisdom is that federalization of air pollution control was necessary because "states had failed to act," that they "could not be trusted to adopt adequate environmental controls" because of interstate competition for business,[1] and that "Congress imposed national regulations to control pollution only after its efforts to prod states to act had failed."[2] Although such perceptions may well have been widely held, they are not supported by the empirical data presented in the previous chapters. That is particularly true for those pollutants that were generally known at the *time of federalization* to be the sources of public health problems, and especially in those areas where policymakers and the general public regarded them to be the worst problems.

Consider that PM and SO_2 were perceived to be the major air pollution problems in urban areas nationwide, responsible for outright deaths. The data indicate relatively rapid progress in urban air quality for those pollutants in the 1960s, or earlier (see Figures 1-2 and 1-7 for PM in various urban areas; Figure 3-1 for PM nationwide; Figure 1-6 for SO_2 in New York; and Figure 3-2 for SO_2 nationwide). Similarly, photochemical oxidants, although not generally regarded as deadly, were generally believed to be problems first

111

and foremost for California, particularly in the Los Angeles area; but oxidant air quality in that area too had been improving since at least 1965–67 (see Figure 1-5).

It can be argued that, because Figures 3-1 and 3-2 for PM and SO_2 are based upon trends in the average of several monitors around the country, some urban areas probably did have deteriorating air quality for one or another of the pollutants, as some rural areas did for TSP (see Figure 3-1 and accompanying text, Chapter 3).

However, the downward TSP trends were quite broad, particularly in urban areas. For instance, the average of the annual concentrations for TSP fell at 66 urban stations between 1960–1963 and 1968–1971, went up at 8, and showed no change at 42 (out of a total of 116 total stations).[3] Over the same periods, the number of urban stations exceeding the future annual primary NAAQS dropped from an average of 81 percent to 63 percent.[4] Moreover, with respect to nonurban areas, between 1960 and 1971, annual TSP concentrations increased at 2 locations, stayed the same at 11, and went down at 5 (out of a total of 18 monitors).[5]

Declines in the 1960s for SO_2 were similarly broad. Between 1964 and 1971, annual average SO_2 concentrations declined at 19 urban stations, went up at 1, and showed no change at 12, while between 1968 and 1971, the corresponding figures were 42, 3, and 17, respectively. In fact, at 33 stations the levels were "so low (less than 10 $\mu g/m^3$) that detection of trends is both statistically difficult and unrealistic."[6]

Is it possible that these trends were unduly influenced by the passage of the Clean Air Amendments of 1970—since, after all, the 1971 monitor data were collected after that? The answer to that is probably not. The 1970 act went into effect too late to influence trends in air quality until after the early 1970s. The act was signed on the last day of 1970, and it was not until early 1971 that the NAAQS were promulgated. By and large, control was based upon emissions control regulation of stationary sources. But, as noted in Chapters 1 and 4, federally enforceable state implementation plans and regulations affecting emissions from existing and new sources did not go into effect until much later. Finally, Figures 3-1 and 3-2 confirm that much of the reduction came prior to collection of the 1971 data. In fact, an EPA report on air quality trends released in 1973 noted: "[C]oncentrations of total suspended particulate matter experienced a general decline at many urban areas across the nation during the 1960s. In comparison, only a minor overall change has been observed thus far during the 1970s."[7]

CO air quality also improved substantially in California in the 1960s. Based upon what few data exist, Figure 3-3 indicates some improvement in urban areas outside of California even prior to the imposition of federal motor vehicle controls, although most CO came from motor vehicles (see Chapter 1). But the federal government already had taken over control of motor vehicle emissions (except for California) in the 1965 Motor Vehicle Air Pollution Control Act (P.L. 89-272). Therefore, the argument that the federalization of stationary source controls in the 1970 amendments was made necessary by the failure of states to do something about air pollution also rings hollow for CO.

Thus, in the period just preceding federalization, overall trends for the air pollutants responsible for the greatest effects on public health (namely, PM and SO_2 nationwide, oxidants in California, and possibly CO everywhere) were declining where they mattered most: in the most populated areas, which generally also had the worst air pollution problems. And despite conventional wisdom, there was—and is—no empirical basis for blanket statements that state and local agencies had failed or were failing to control air pollution at the time the Clean Air Amendments of 1970 were passed.[8]

Curiously, at least some of the pre-1970 trends developed in this book were essentially known at the highest levels of the National Air Pollution Control Administration, EPA's forerunner. One of its assistant commissioners coauthored a paper in 1969 that contained trends in urban air quality from the federal monitoring networks from the 1950s and 1960s.[9] In fact, a later version of that paper, published in April 1970, is the source of Figure 1-7, which plots dustfall data for various cities going back to the 1940s and earlier. It is worth noting, however, that it was—and is—necessary for proponents of federalization to believe in a "dismal failure"[10] in getting states and local agencies to improve air quality in order to justify nationalizing air pollution control beyond motor vehicles and interstate pollution.

With hindsight one might make an argument that oxidant pollution was not being addressed adequately in states outside of California. But few areas outside of California had realized that they had an oxidant problem until the late 1960s or, in some cases, later—after wider monitoring undertaken after federalization indicated that federal air quality standards (i.e., the NAAQS) promulgated in 1971 were being exceeded (see Chapter 1).[11] So it would hardly have been surprising if there had been little, if any, progress on oxidants in the rest of the nation, although, as suggested by the previously mentioned improvements in New Jersey, we do not really know if that was the case. Note that any progress on oxidant problems outside of California before federalization under the 1970 act would be due, in part, to the federal motor vehicle control program (which itself owed a lot to the state of California!). Such progress may be plausible justification for federal control of vehicle emissions, but it does not make the case for federalizing regulation of stationary sources that have only local impacts. As noted in Chapter 1, at the time of federalization the regional nature of the ozone problem was, by and large, unknown to the general public and decisionmakers.

It is no small irony that federalization was ostensibly imposed, in part, because state and local agencies were unable to improve air quality with sufficient rapidity in the three years following the Air Quality Act of 1967, but now, three decades later, many areas are still not attaining federal ambient air quality standards. As of December 8, 1998, 38 areas in the nation were designated "nonattainment areas" for the ozone NAAQS; 20 for CO; 38 for SO_2; 10 for lead; none for NO_2.[12] In addition, while the current PM-10, and the older TSP NAAQS that it replaced, are not strictly comparable, 78 areas were designated nonattainment for PM-10.[13] If the success of the 1970 federalization is judged by the same criterion that many of its proponents applied to state and local control and the 1967 act (namely, adherence to unrealistic schedules and timetables for the attainment of federal standards), federalization must also be judged to be a failure. And while this criterion for success (or failure) was, and remains, flawed, it does undermine the credibility of one of the major arguments advanced for the federalization effected by the 1970 amendments.

Race to the Bottom or to the Top?

Another rationale for federalization of air pollution control is that in its absence states would relax air pollution requirements, which would reduce net state well-being—in other words, federalization would eliminate any race to the bottom. As the term is used in this book, a race to the bottom is a race to relax, which also results in a net loss of well-being, consistent with academic articles on this topic.[14]

A corollary to the race-to-the-bottom or race-to-relax hypothesis is that if state and local agencies actually engaged in such races, there ought to have been no air pollution regulation in any jurisdiction before federalization, nor should there have been any improvements in air quality anywhere (except by accident or happy economic circumstance). But the empirical evidence presented in the previous chapters does not support the allegation that before federalization states were indulging in a race to the bottom. In fact, the race, if any, seems to be in the opposite direction.

First, Table 5-1 shows that for "national" air quality, TSP and SO_2 had gone through their environmental transitions and CO had either gone through, or was on the verge of, its own transition by the time the federal government began regulating those specific pollutants. Clearly, there is neither a race to the bottom nor a race to relax there.[15] Moreover, oxidants and O_3 had gone through a transition in California, an area where they were widely recognized to be a problem, before federalization had any real impact in that state. Outside California, few areas made any effort to reduce oxidants—not because they were racing to the bottom but because they were in no rush to solve problems they did not know they had. The inability to construct a national composite for ozone or oxidant air quality prior to the early 1970s because of insufficient monitor coverage is one of the best proofs of that. Another proof is the silence regarding ozone and oxidants in the 1968 and 1969 documents supporting the designations of interstate Air Quality Control Regions such as the metropolitan St. Louis area (covering portions of Missouri and Illinois); the Steubenville-Weirton-Wheeling area (Ohio and West Virginia); the metropolitan Providence area (Rhode Island and Massachusetts); the metropolitan Toledo area (Ohio and Michigan); the Washington, D.C., area; the metropolitan Chicago area (Indiana and Illinois); and the New Jersey-New York-Connecticut area.[16]

Second, in a trend that is inconsistent with any race to relax, local and state air programs grew significantly before the mid-1960s (Figure 1-3). Between 1960 and 1970, the number of county programs increased from 17 to 81, and state programs from 8 to 50. Even if those programs were established as sops to the public—national air quality trends for SO_2 and PM and oxidant air quality in California suggest they were not—their very presence would be at odds with the rationale for a race to the bottom, since that would send the wrong signal about the desire to attract industry.

Third, the progressive tightening of opacity standards nationwide before the 1970 Clean Air Act, mentioned in Chapter 1—in effect bidding standards up rather than down—is the antithesis of either a race to the bottom of environmental quality or a race to relax environmental quality. This was, unsurprisingly, accompanied by substantial improvements in efficiencies of dust collection, particularly in the most affected areas (see Figure 1-4), and those efficiencies, in turn, were reflected in improved air quality in those areas. In fact, a survey of the trends in air pollution control regulations undertaken by the National Air Pollution Control Administration and provided to Senator Muskie's subcommittee in 1970 noted that "[r]ecent trends in air-pollution-control regulations have been toward . . . required application of maximum emissions control technology."[17] The survey also suggested that one reason for the limited acceptance of the American Society of Mechanical Engineers' 1966 model air pollution control regulations for fuel burning equipment may have been because their "control requirements . . . are generally lenient compared to other modern regulations" and that "[m]any new industrial plants install equipment for purposes of eliminating all visible plumes, even if not required to do so" because they constituted good public relations and reduced complaints.[18]

Fourth, the federal preemption of motor vehicle emissions standards outside of California indicates that the automobile industry and Congress were concerned not about a race to the bottom or a race to relax but about a movement toward greater control. Partly to contain such movement, uniform standards were imposed to avoid a hodgepodge of requirements among the other 49 states.

There are other examples (not already discussed) in which states have imposed regulations going beyond, or despite the absence of, federal regulations. For instance, Dwyer notes that, while the federal government had been "notoriously slow" in establishing hazardous air pollutant and community right-to-know standards, some states and local governments had pushed ahead on their own.[19]

It could be argued that California was willing to regulate motor vehicles because they were manufactured elsewhere, thereby shifting its control costs to parties out of state. In essence, according to that argument, California was seeking to "externalize" its control costs. But even if the production, distribution, marketing, and selling of each automobile used in California were accomplished entirely out of state, the cost of living in California would still increase. The cost of labor in California would also increase, making the state somewhat less competitive in terms of jobs and economic growth. Thus, as a practical matter, it is impossible for a state to "externalize" its control costs so long as its inhabitants use the product and the producers pass on the added costs to their consumers in that state. And unless the consumer—which, in this particular case, is almost congruent with the general public—believes the trade-off is worth it, such externalization could cost politicians dearly at the next election. Indeed, many a politician has been turned out for less.[20]

Moreover, while some Californians may have thought they would be getting a free ride because new automobiles were built by Detroit, there is other evidence that California (and its jurisdictions) was doing much more than merely "externalizing" its control costs. In fact, they were more concerned about trying to improve their quality of life by seeking what, in their own estimate, were "reasonable" controls given their *particular* situation, and less concerned about on whom those costs might fall.

First, many of the California air pollution control districts, particularly the Los Angeles County district (LACAPCD), were pursuing stationary source controls with at least as much diligence as vehicle control. The LACAPCD, along with the Bay Area district in the San Francisco area, pioneered the so-called process-weight regulations for PM in the 1940s;[21] the LACAPCD established sulfur-in-fuel requirements for oil and gas by 1958; and its 1966 solvent emissions control regulations ("Rule 66") were stringent enough so that industry was quite concerned about their ability to comply with them.[22] Clearly, these stationary source controls would cost California's consumers and businesses directly.

Second, only after efforts to restore air quality through stringent controls of stationary sources in the 1940s and 1950s had failed did fresh research into smog formation convince Los Angeles and California to turn to motor vehicle controls to help solve their smog problem.[23] Thus, it seems cost shifting to out-of-state parties was not paramount in the minds of California's lawmakers, at least initially.

Third, in 1959–1960, California passed legislation, applicable to air pollution control districts that had not opted out of the program, that required crankcase and exhaust controls to be retrofitted in used vehicles after such devices had been certified by the Motor Vehicle Pollution Control Board.[24] The costs of the devices would have to be borne by the citizens of California. (However, while legislators were not thinking "cost shifting," their constituents were thinking about costs and convenience. Those concerns, aggravated by a series of bureaucratic mistakes combined with poor public relations, forced the state to back off and require used-car controls only when cars were resold.[25])

During the industrial era, when jobs and prosperity were better correlated with air pollution, the quest for a better quality of life may have seemed like a race to the bottom of environmental quality. But by the time the 1970 Clean Air Amendments were passed, the empirical data summarized above indicate that was no longer generally true. And in today's postindustrial era, the association between prosperity and pollution is even weaker. Today the service sectors (including the governmental sector) account for three out of every four nonfarm jobs.[26] That suggests that not only should the competition for polluting industries be less intense but—because success in attracting such industries may well serve to repel service-sector jobs—a jurisdiction might, in fact, maximize jobs by catering to the needs of the service sectors while actively discouraging polluting industries altogether. An example is Florida's ban on oil drilling off its Gulf coast, which, despite producing substantial revenues for the state and some jobs, could, according to its political leaders, "cause the economy to go bust by scaring off tourists and hurting commercial fishing."[27]

In particular, clean air, among other environmental amenities, can be used to attract low-polluting enterprises.[28] For instance, every year since 1987, *Money* magazine has published a ranking of "The Best Places to Live in America" that highly rated cities use to court new investments and businesses. The magazine's selections are based on a two-part process. First, the magazine conducts an annual poll of its readers to rank about 40 quality-of-life attributes (such as low crime rate, good schools, clean water, clean air, resistance of the local economy to recession, future job growth, and access to environmental amenities).[29] Then, having established the relative importance of the various determinants of quality of life to its readers, more objective data (on factors such as air quality and crime rate) are used to compare and rank the various cities. At least since 1991, readers have placed clean air among the top four attributes (predictably, always behind clean water).[30] Remarkably, clean air, which is ranked third in the latest (1998) poll, also placed third in 1991, a recession year.[31] Compared to the ordinary American, the average reader of *Money* is more affluent, perhaps more likely to be an employer or a high-level manager in the service sector, and possibly more confident about his or her future economic prospects.[32] Clearly, however, the days are long gone when *industrial* growth was equated with economic growth, which, in turn, was synonymous with quality of life (see Chapter 1). Pollution no longer signifies progress, and in the race to the top of the quality of life, it is possible to simultaneously enhance jobs, prosperity, and air quality.

The major reason why trends in air pollution estimates, air quality, and stringency of regulations before federalization are inconsistent with the race-to-the-bottom rationale is that the game-theoretic model on which it is based—the Prisoner's Dilemma model—is an overly simplistic depiction of human and societal behavior with respect to environmental quality.[33] It assumes that each society is composed of identical human beings with identical aspirations—specifically, that they all want to maximize jobs and incomes even at the expense of all the other determinants of the quality of life and, particularly, the quality of their environment.[34] There may be some individuals who are so inclined, just as there are those who would maximize environmental quality to the exclusion of anything else, but the majority of people, and the democratic societies of which they are part, are much more complex. In reality, as the prefederalization trends for the traditional air pollutants discussed in this book show, people will attempt to optimize their quality of life based upon what they perceive or know, no matter how imperfect their knowledge. The determinants of quality of life are weighted differently by each society at different times, depending upon a host of factors including the state-of-the-knowledge (itself a function of technology) and existing and expected levels of technology, affluence, pollution, mortality, morbidity, and so on, within the society's broader historical, social, and cultural context.

As noted in Chapter 5, all else being equal, poor societies (or individuals) are likely to weigh jobs and incomes more heavily than the environment because greater income and wealth provide them

119

the means to improve the quality of life at that stage of economic and technological development. Consequently, at that stage the race to the top of the quality of life may well look like a race to relax. On the other hand, as suggested by the various environmental transitions that predated federalization (and *Money* magazine's annual polls), affluent societies (or individuals) are more likely to tip the balance toward environmental quality (see Figure 5-1). And if individuals' actions cannot affect their environment sufficiently, they will attempt, in a democratic society, to persuade their political jurisdictions to take action in consonance with their perceived collective interests. That is precisely what leads to environmental transitions, and, as we have seen, governmental regulation is almost a natural part of that process in a democracy. Once society (and individuals) get past their transitions for a specific pollutant indicator, the race to the top of the quality of life could easily be mistaken for a race to the top of environmental quality for that indicator if the costs of controlling a specific environmental problem are particularly low relative to the benefits. As Figure 5-2 shows, that could result in NIMBY-like behavior.

Recently, Engel, who makes an interesting effort to bring some empirical information to bear on the validity of arguments for and against the race-to-the-bottom theory, has offered the opinion that there indeed is a race to the bottom.[35] The following is her rationale: Surveys of state environmental officers indicate that a "substantial minority of states relax environmental requirements" to attract industrial firms; on the other hand studies indicate that such relaxation has had little, if any, impact on industries' locational decisions. Hence, Engel argues, the loss of environmental benefits to the state in such instances is not offset by commensurate economic benefits and, therefore, the state's general welfare (and overall economic efficiency) is reduced.[36] That is, the ultimate outcome is suboptimal, so there is a race to the bottom.[37]

But there are several problems with this argument. First, any economic savings that accrue to a firm as a result of a relaxation of standards would end up as higher profits for the firm, higher salaries for employees, more jobs, reduced prices for consumers, or some combination of each of these. The first three of these outcomes would, through taxes, provide additional revenues to the state and the federal government. In turn, the additional revenues would redound to the taxpayers' benefit through improved services, lower taxes, or both. Moreover, the state's increased revenues could be diverted toward those programs that, in its collective wisdom, would most increase net societal welfare—and further air pollution control may not be in that category. The fourth outcome—reduced prices for consumers—provides direct economic benefits to the firm's consumers both within and outside the particular state. In addition, to the extent that additional jobs are created, either directly by the firm or indirectly because higher profits and salaries increase purchasing power, it could help the states (and the federal government) reduce taxes or welfare payments. Therefore, one cannot assume that a relaxation that does not modify a firm's locational decision would result in *no* economic benefits to the state, the federal government, or the consumer and would, therefore, necessarily reduce overall welfare.

Second, Engel's rationale assumes that the original requirements were either perfectly efficient or not tight enough. But how likely is that? EPA is required to promulgate primary NAAQS to protect public health "with an adequate margin of safety," and secondary standards to protect public welfare "from any known or anticipated adverse effects associated with the presence of . . . [pollutants] in the ambient air."[38] This has been its ostensible justification for not considering costs in setting standards. Thus, if EPA did its job as advertised, then for many, if not all, states, NAAQS requirements should by design result in "overregulation" compared to what it would have been had economic efficiency been the criterion for formulating those standards.[39] And if an overregulated state relaxes some requirements, it could well increase overall efficiency. Alternatively, assume that EPA, despite claims to the contrary or perhaps by sheer coincidence, devised NAAQS that were perfectly efficient from a *national* perspective. That would still mean some states would be overregulated while others would be underregulated. Once again, states falling in the overregulated category could relax their air pollution requirements while increasing the overall efficiency of their environmental requirements. Moreover, given the many location-specific factors that have to be considered in developing an efficient regulation, it would have taken a deus ex machina to devise a NAAQS which is perfectly efficient for each and every state. Even assuming such a miracle, the chances for overregulation are better than even because the Clean Air Act requires states (and sources) to comply with *additional* layers of regulation—for instance, NSPS, BACT, and other PSD requirements, which are only minimally constrained, if at all, by the requirement to balance economic, social, and environmental benefits and costs.

Third, the details of the relaxation are critical. Not all relaxations are equal. Perhaps the relaxation enabled the firm to informally use emissions trading, or perhaps it involved a more realistic calculation of a source's "potential to emit" than one based upon the assumption that the plant worked at 100 percent capacity for each moment of the year or a more site-specific determination of BACT. In any case, it cannot be assumed that in the larger scheme of things—with, for instance, several NSPs in the 99(+) percent range serving as the floor for BACT and "lowest achievable emission rate"—the relaxation had more than a trivial, if any, effect on air quality (to be offset by, possibly, equally trivial economic benefits), or that it led to an ultimate outcome which was less efficient.[40]

Note that the arguments advanced above in response to Engel's article as well as the dialectics on either side of the race-to-the-bottom debate indicate that in the absence of relevant data on environmental quality one can argue endlessly on either side of the question based upon claims of what "might" or "may" occur, which, in turn, could just as easily, and with equal validity, be countered by claims of what "might not" or "may not" occur. To avoid endless argument, it is best to examine real data on air quality and economic consequences to determine what effect, if any, states' behavior has had on air quality and societal well-being. That is what this book has attempted to do for air quality.

In summary, empirical data on emissions, air quality, and stringency of regulations from the period prior to federalization are at odds with any race-to-the-bottom explanation for the behavior of state and local authorities. In fact, if there is any race at all, it is to the top of the quality of life. As noted in Chapter 5, for a particular pollutant (or indicator), such a race may resemble a race to relax or a race to the bottom of environmental quality if society is to the left of its environmental transition (Figure 5-2); however, if it is to the right of that, the race to the top of the quality of life would seem more like a race to the top of environmental quality. And, if society is very far to the right, it could end up in NIMBY "territory," or decide that the environment is clean enough for it to focus on other priorities. Once upon a time, for a brief period in this nation's history, when pollution was almost synonymous with progress, the race-to-the-bottom rationale may well have seemed valid. But empirical evidence suggests that greater affluence and improved technology may have largely invalidated that argument for federalization by 1970. And that rationale is even less likely to be true today.

7. The Federal Role in Air Pollution Control and the Path to Reform

If the 1970 act, and subsequent amendments, were to be judged by adherence to mandated deadlines, they would have to be deemed failures. As noted, despite several extensions of the NAAQS deadlines, today—almost a quarter of a century after the original deadlines passed and after two major rewrites of the Clean Air Act—many areas still do not comply with the act's fundamental goals.[1] Although the repeated inability to deliver on the deadlines undercuts the rationale offered for the 1970 federalization (namely, federalization was necessary because progress by states was not sufficiently rapid), that should not be interpreted as lack of progress in improving the nation's air quality. In fact, as shown earlier, air quality in the United States is much better today than it has been for decades, in part due to federal regulations.

Among the most effective features of federalization are the NAAQS, which established an objective yardstick for people to gauge whether their air quality was "healthful." Just as the existence of the Toxics Release Inventory has helped reduce the amounts of those emissions (yet another refutation of the race-to-the-bottom rationale as well as confirmation that by and large the nation is on the downward slope of an environmental transition for air toxics), the very existence of NAAQS created pressures to improve air quality. In fact, since it would be a few years before other features of federalization would become effective, the mere existence of the NAAQS may have been the major federal contribution to the emissions reductions at *existing stationary sources* and associated improvements in air quality immediately following federalization (until the 1973 oil shock). The increases in energy prices led to substantial energy conservation efforts on one hand and, on the other, a greater reliance on coal, particularly in the utility sector. Those responses helped accelerate VOC and CO emissions reductions and would have helped increase SO_2 and, possibly, TSP emissions. The existence of the *primary* NAAQS probably had much to do with the fact that SO_2 emissions did not rise dramatically.

The air quality monitoring program instituted in response to the 1970 amendments also aided cleanup in the long term because it accelerated recognition of the oxidant pollution problem outside California. However, full-scale federalization is not a prerequisite for deploying a comprehensive network of monitors.

Federal intervention was, on the whole, quite effective in reducing motor vehicle emissions. It helped establish an orderliness regarding vehicle controls, without which, in many areas, it would have been difficult—but, as California has shown, not impossible—to make as much progress as has been made for VOC, O_3, and CO. In addition, motor vehicle emissions controls were instrumental in bringing about the dramatic improvements in air quality for lead. Federalization of new source requirements (including NSPS and PSD requirements), although slow to bear fruit, also helped ensure that gains from existing source controls would not be lost due to population and economic growth.

Long-term trends show that even prior to federalization, air quality was improving for the deadliest pollutants in the areas where they were known to be problems. By then, killer air pollution episodes were, for practical purposes, things of the past. In most urban areas, air quality for PM and SO_2 had already peaked, and they were about to peak for CO, if they had not already done so. Emissions per unit of GNP, a leading environmental indicator as well as a surrogate for technological change, had been dropping for all traditional pollutants for decades—since the 1920s for SO_2, the '30s for VOC and NO_x, and at least the '40s for PM and CO. California, the state with the worst oxidant (or ozone) problem and one of the worst CO problems, was setting the pace for controlling both mobile and stationary sources. In fact, not only did the federal government borrow California's emissions standards for motor vehicles, it also used the latter's stationary source requirements for guidance on "technology-forcing" determinations such as best available control technology and lowest achievable emission rates. Moreover, during the late 1960s and 1970s, the standard reference on air pollution control technology and the bible for many a permit engineer in state and local agencies, the *Air Pollution Engineering Manual* (which was published and distributed by EPA and its forerunners), was written by and based upon the expertise of the engineers of the Los Angeles County Air Pollution Control District.[2] With respect to VOC and O_3, the lack of progress in jurisdictions outside California before federalization was due to the fact that, like New York, few areas realized the magnitude of their oxidant or ozone problem until after wider air quality monitoring was instituted in the early 1970s. When they did, many turned to Los Angeles' Rule 66 for inspiration on regulations, as this author did while he was working on Michigan's state implementation plan for photochemical oxidants and hydrocarbons in the mid-1970s.[3]

Given these underlying trends, the absence of any real race to the bottom and the fact that democratic societies—no less than private individuals—hope to maximize their quality of life, one should expect that there would have been continued improvements in air quality even in the absence of federalization. However, federalization is due some credit for the amount and pace of the post-1970 cleanup.

EPA's Study of the Benefits and Costs of the 1970 and 1977 Amendments

A recent EPA report to Congress, *The Benefits and Costs of the Clean Air Act: 1970 to 1990* (referred to here as the "EPA Benefit-Cost Study"), estimates that the mean cumulative benefits (in 1990 dollars) amounted to $22.2 trillion (with a range from $5.6 to $49.4 trillion) while the direct costs totaled $0.5 trillion.[4] Ninety percent of the benefits were of reductions in premature mortality and cases of chronic bronchitis due to improvements in PM air quality. According to the study's mean estimates, but for the improvements in PM levels due to the 1970 and 1977 amendments, there would have been 184,000 more cases of premature mortality and 674,000 more cases of chronic bronchitis in 1990. Aggregated over the 1970–90 period, those two categories of benefits equaled $16.6 trillion and $3.3 trillion, respectively. Ironically, emissions controls for lead (which were originally promulgated to avoid fouling up catalytic converters used to control auto emissions rather than directly to improve public health[5]) were estimated to provide another $1.3 trillion worth of benefits because fewer people would die prematurely (22,000 fewer premature deaths were estimated in 1990 alone). The benefits of reductions in premature mortality were based upon an estimate that society would be willing to pay $4.8 million (in 1990 dollars) for postponing a single premature death. The benefits of reducing one case of chronic bronchitis were pegged by EPA at $260,000 (in 1990 dollars).

The EPA Benefit-Cost Study estimated costs of the Clean Air Act Amendments using compliance cost data through the years. Benefits were estimated by using four major sets of models connected in series, with the outputs of one set serving as the inputs for the next. The first set of models was used to estimate emissions in the absence of EPA's regulations. That set alone consisted of at least 11 separate models or modeling approaches.[6] Their outputs were then employed to estimate changes in air quality for the various criteria pollutants. At least six different types of models were used in this set, ranging from simple-minded models (such as "roll-up" or linear scaling for CO, SO_2, and TSP) to complex photochemical models for modeling urban O_3. The outputs from this set of air quality models then were used to estimate the physical and medical impacts due to the additional pollution. Finally, those impacts were used to estimate benefits in terms of dollars.

Numerous uncertainties are associated with these models, and a variety of assumptions have to be made prior to their execution. Lutter, a risk analyst with the AEI-Brookings Joint Center for Regulatory Studies, in a critique of the EPA Benefit-Cost Study notes that it is possible to reduce the benefit estimates by a factor of five by using alternate, but plausible, assumptions regarding the likelihood of a causal relationship between PM concentrations and premature mortality, whether the concentration-response function is linear and has a threshold, latency periods for mortality and onset of chronic bronchitis, and the valuation of society's willingness to pay to avoid a case of chronic bronchitis, and by using the value of a life-year saved rather than the so-called "value of a statistical life" as the appropriate measure of the mortality-related benefit (or cost) of air pollution.[7] Lutter also notes that the EPA study's estimates translate into mean annual benefits of $1.25 trillion in 1990 or about 20 percent of GDP (with an upper bound of 50 percent of GDP).

Given society's other unmet needs and real-world budget constraints, it is implausible that society would pay that much to garnish the magnitude of benefits estimated in the EPA Benefit-Cost Study. First, 99 percent ($22 trillion) of the benefits estimated by the EPA study were health related.[8] Thus, according to that study, society would (and, the study implies, should) have been willing to pay 20 percent of the GDP in 1990 for those health-related benefits. That is disproportionately high in light of the fact that in 1990 the total national expenditures on health (not including sums spent to reduce pollution hazards) amounted to 12 percent of GDP![9]

Second, the enormous estimate of benefits is directly traceable to the value of $4.8 million placed on postponing a single death. That, according to EPA, translates into a willingness to pay $293,000 per year of life saved.[10] But there are numerous other interventions that would save a life-year much more cheaply. A study of hundreds of life-saving interventions undertaken by the Harvard School of Public Health's Center for Risk Analysis shows that there are many under-utilized interventions that could save a life-year at a fraction of the $293,000 the EPA Benefit-Cost Study claims society should be or is willing to pay. Those include procedures such as annual mammograms for women aged 40 to 64 (supplemented by breast exams), which is estimated to cost about $17,000 per life-year saved in 1993 dollars,[11] pap smears every four years for women between 20 and 75 (as much as $16,000 per life-year in 1995 dollars[12]); and annual colorectal screening for men between 50 and 75 (as much as $18,000 per life-year in 1995 dollars[13]). See Table 7-1. So long as society forgoes opportunities to save a life-year for tens of thousands of dollars, it is impossible to sustain the notion that it will or should pay hundreds of thousands of dollars to do the same, which is what is implied by the EPA study's valuation of a life-year. By its real-world allocation of resources, society has proved otherwise.

How much ought society to pay to save a life-year? In 1992, about 2.2 million people died in the United States, which translates to about 36.7 million life-years lost.[14] Let us assume, arbitrarily, that the nation would have been willing in 1992 to devote 33.3 percent of its GDP ($6.2 trillion in 1992 dollars) to eliminating those life-years lost (*beyond* the 14 percent it was already devoting to other health expenditures).[15] Accordingly, the nation would be paying as much as $57,000 per life-year saved (on average). That is probably an overestimate given that society will need funds for other priorities— such as food, education, housing, clothing, heating and cooling, and national defense—needed to improve the quality (and not just the quantity) of life for everyone, including those whose lives would be extended. Nevertheless, the $57,000 per life-year estimate is much below the $313,000 (corrected to 1992 dollars) per life-year used by

Table 7-1
COST PER LIFE-YEAR SAVED USING VARIOUS INTERVENTIONS

Procedure	Cost per Life-Year Saved[a]
Medical interventions (various, n = 310)	$19,000 (median cost)
Fatal injury reductions (various, n = 133)	$48,000 (median cost)
One-time mass screening for cervical cancer for women aged 38	$1,200
Hypertension screening for black men aged 55–64 and blood pressure ≥ 90 mm of mercury	$5,000
Influenza vaccination for people aged 5+	$1,300
Comprehensive (vs. fragmented) health care services for mothers and children	$11,000
Pneumonia vaccination for people aged 65+	$1,800–2,200
Annual mammograms and breast exams for women aged 40–64 (compared with just exams)	$17,000
Pap smears every four years for women aged 20–75	$16,000[b]
Annual colorectal screening for men aged 50–75	$18,000[b]

SOURCES: Tengs et al. 1995; Tengs and Graham 1996; Graham 1999.

[a] 1993 dollars, unless specified.

[b] 1995 dollars, based on quality-adjusted life-years; hence, the specified value is an upper bound.

EPA. Note also that national health expenditures in 1992, which ran at 14 percent of GDP,[16] were considered by many to be excessive—spawning, for instance, President and Mrs. Clinton's aborted health policy initiative.

The EPA Benefit-Cost Study values each case of chronic bronchitis avoided at $260,000 (in 1990 dollars). Using its methodology for valuing chronic bronchitis (that is, multiplying the number of cases by $260,000), we can calculate what according to the EPA study ought to be society's willingness to pay for avoiding or eliminating cases of chronic bronchitis. In 1995, an estimated 14.53 million people

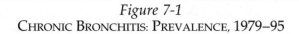

Figure 7-1
CHRONIC BRONCHITIS: PREVALENCE, 1979–95

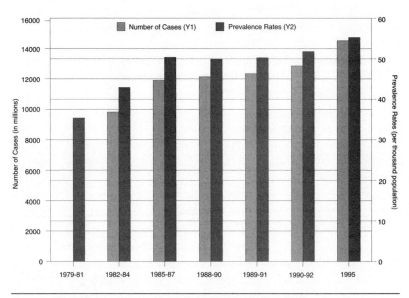

SOURCES: Cohen and Van Norstrand 1994; Collins 1997.

were affected by chronic bronchitis.[17] Thus, according to the study methodology, to avoid these chronic bronchitic cases society ought to be willing to pay at least $4.0 trillion (in 1992 dollars), which amounts to 60 percent of U.S. GDP ($6.7 trillion in 1995 in 1992 dollars).[18] That is patently absurd since society has quite a few other unmet needs on its agenda.

Curiously, the number of people afflicted with chronic bronchitis increased 31 percent between 1982–84 and 1995, from 9.83 million[19] to 14.53 million.[20] The prevalence rates increased from 35.4 per 1,000 population in 1979–81 to 55.3 in 1995, an increase of about 55 percent.[21] See Figure 7-1. In other words, the benefits of cleaner outdoor air in terms of reducing chronic bronchitis have been overwhelmed by other factors, whatever they may be.

Asthma, another condition often associated with air pollution, poses another conundrum for public health.[22] Despite the improvements in air quality, the number of asthma cases and deaths attributed to asthma have been increasing relatively rapidly since having bottomed out in the 1970s.[23] See Box 7-1. According to the EPA Benefit-Cost Study, as a result of the 1970 and 1977 amendments the number of asthma attacks in 1990 was reduced by 850,000. It has been estimated, however, that annual office visits attributed to asthma, which are about ten times larger, increased about 50 percent between 1975 and 1990–92.[24]

A fundamental assumption of the EPA analysis is that there would have been no additional controls imposed beyond 1970 levels in the absence of the 1970 and 1977 amendments to the Clean Air Act. Because of that assumption, EPA estimates that but for the amendments, air quality in several U.S. urban areas in 1990 would have exceeded levels in some of the most polluted cities in the world— namely, Moscow, Bangkok, Bombay, Manila, and Delhi.[25] That too is implausible.

The historical evidence prior to federalization shows that in democratic societies local communities and states will act to deal with real or perceived threats to public health, and the greater the perceived threat, the quicker the action. First, as the data presented in this book show, before federalization air quality was improving rapidly in the areas that were perceived to have the greatest problems during the 1950s and 1960s (see, for example, Figures 1-2, 1-5 through 1-7, and 3-1 through 3-3 for PM, SO_2, and CO). There is no reason to believe that the behavior that drove those trends would have been suspended in 1971, particularly since the factors driving that behavior were only gathering strength. Specifically, knowledge of pollutant impacts was increasing and, most importantly, the country was becoming richer and less dependent upon the pollution-producing sectors. Between 1970 and 1990, per capita GDP in real dollars increased 47 percent, and the share of the workforce employed in manufacturing and mining declined from 28.2 to 18.0 percent. Accordingly, one should expect that the improving trends in air quality would have continued even in the absence of the 1970 amendments. In the parlance of the environmental transition hypothesis, by the time the 1970 amendments were enacted, the nation was going through or had gone past its transitions for those pollutants (for PM, SO_2, and possibly CO, nationwide and for oxidants in California), and greater wealth and structural changes in the economy would only serve to strengthen any posttransition downward trends in environmental degradation.

Similarly, there is no reason to believe that the downward trends in the leading indicators (emissions per capita and emissions per unit of GNP) that commenced in the early decades of this century (and that were due to a combination of changes in technology, structure of the economy, and local and state regulatory efforts) would have ended but for federalization. Figures 4-3 through 4-7 show that those declines accelerated during the early 1970s. But the 1970 amendments cannot get all the credit for the accelerations. First, as pre-1970 trends in air quality and the leading indicators suggest, a number of state and local regulatory efforts had not fully run their course. Neither had the benefits of the federal motor vehicle emissions standards for the 1968 (and subsequent) model years been fully captured. Arguably, the 1971 promulgation of the NAAQS made it easier for state and local agencies to insist upon compliance with their own regulations, making their jobs somewhat easier, although, as noted previously, a few years would pass before most federally enforceable state implementation plans would go into effect. Fourth, the oil shock of 1973 helped reduce oil and natural gas combustion and stimulated investments in more efficient equipment (see Figure 1-1). On the other hand, increases in the price of petroleum led to increased use of coal and could have increased SO_2 emissions were it not for the primary NAAQS. Fifth, as Figures 4-4 and 4-5 for VOC and NO_x indicate, many areas that would subsequently be designated nonattainment for O_3 had not recognized that *they* had an O_3 problem until after the 1970 amendments went into effect. One would expect that once those areas recognized their O_3 problem they would have taken steps to address it, just as (history tells us) they were addressing PM and SO_2 problems.

Figure 4-6 for PM-10 indicates that emissions per unit of GNP declined more or less linearly between 1950 and 1970. The best linear fit for this segment of the curve for PM E/GNP curve is given by the following equation:

$$E/GNP = 0.595 - 0.0197 (YEAR - 1950).$$

R^2 for this equation is 0.99, and the slope is significant at the 0.001 level (i.e., $p < 0.001$). Noting that in Figure 4-6 E/GNP is normalized to be 1 in 1940, this equation tells us that relative to its 1940 level, E/GNP had declined to 0.595 units in 1950 (a reduction of 40.5 percent) and was decreasing another 0.0197 units each year between 1950 and 1970.

Box 7-1: Asthma and Air Pollution

Asthma, which many people tend to associate with polluted air, has more than doubled since 1980 despite the fact that outdoor air is cleaner today than it was then. The estimated annual rate of self-reported asthma increased from 31 per 1,000 in 1980 to about 64 per 1,000 in 1998. As a result the estimated number of people with self-reported asthma increased 2½-fold over this period, from 6.8 million to 17.3 million. Similarly, adjusted for age, the average rate of office visits for asthma increased from 21.4 per thousand population in 1975 to 39.0 in 1993–95. Most importantly, the death rates attributed to asthma as the underlying cause declined rapidly in the 1960s (from 28.2 per million population in 1960–62 to 11.8 in 1968–71) before bottoming out in the late 1970s (at 8.2 per million in 1975–78) and climbing back to 17.9 in 1993–95. The annual numbers of deaths attributed to asthma are now higher than they were in the early 1960s.

Why is asthma—and deaths related to it—going up now after having been reduced from the early 1960s to the mid-1970s?

One theory holds that people, and children in particular, are spending more time indoors because of TV, which has increased their exposure to household allergens such as dust mites or cockroaches. We do know that since the mid-1970s, in response to the 1973 oil shock, houses began to be sealed more tightly in order to save energy (see Chapter 2). Since most people spend most of their time indoors, exposure to such allergens could well have increased due to the two oil shocks of the 1970s, and interestingly enough the troughs in deaths and death rates occurred in the mid- to late 1970s.

Another theory is that improvements in public health are to blame for the rise in asthma! Because of these improvements, goes this theory, children are exposed to fewer infections and hence have not built up their immune system to combat allergic reactions. Studies have shown that people who have had early exposure to tuberculosis and hepatitis A virus seem to be less prone to allergic reactions.

Nonetheless, no matter what may have caused the resurgence in asthma, it has more than neutralized the asthma-related benefits as estimated by EPA's Benefit-Cost Study of the 1970 and 1977 amendments.

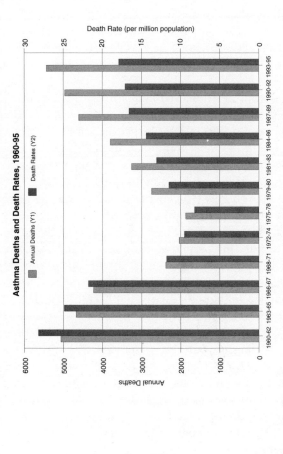

Asthma Deaths and Death Rates, 1960-95

SOURCES: Rappaport and Boodram, "Forecasted State-Specific Estimates of Self-Reported Asthma Prevalence"; Mannino et al., "Surveillance for Asthma—United States, 1960–1995"; Vogel, "Why the Rise in Asthma Cases?"

The 1971–90 segment can also be fitted with a downwardly sloping straight line. However, that slope is not as steep (-0.0072, $R^2 = 0.93$) but it too is significant at the 0.001 level (i.e., $p < 0.001$). Thus, it seems that for PM-10 this simple mechanistic analysis suggests that the 1970 and 1977 acts did not necessarily improve matters. In fact, extending the 1950–70 straight line to 1990 results in negative emissions after 1981![26] Although such an outcome is implausible (because it would take an infinite amount of money to eliminate PM-10 emissions), it suggests that the EPA Benefit-Cost Study's estimate that TSP emissions in the absence of the 1970 and 1977 amendments would have been 68 percent higher is a substantial overestimate.[27]

The notion of negative PM-10 emissions is just as implausible as the notion that society would be willing to pay \$4.8 million for each of 184,000 lives (or \$293,000 per life-year) that EPA estimates would have been lost in 1990 absent the 1970 and 1977 acts. Such absurdities should serve as warnings that mechanistic analyses are poor substitutes for common sense in coming to conclusions and devising policies, and that is equally true for mechanistic analyses as complex as those used in the EPA Benefit-Cost Study.

A similar analysis for SO_2, which because of its potential to be transformed into fine particulate sulfates is also a major contributor to the EPA study's benefits associated with postponing mortality,[28] shows that the slope for SO_2 emissions per unit of GNP declined at a rate of 0.0062 units per year from 1950 to 1970 ($R^2 = 0.83$, $p < 0.001$) and at 0.0079 units per year between 1971 and 1990 ($R^2 = 0.96$, $p < 0.001$).[29] Thus, the 1970 and 1977 amendments may have improved matters for SO_2. However, these results suggest only a modest effect, since extending the 1950–70 linear regression line to 1990 gives an SO_2 emissions estimate that is only 5 percent higher than the 1990 level specified in EPA's *1997 Update* (for emissions). By comparison, the EPA study estimated that in the absence of the 1970 and 1977 amendments, SO_2 emissions would have been 40 percent higher.[30]

NO_x is a third contributor to fine PM, although some analysts have noted that there seems to be little or no evidence linking fine particulate nitrates to health effects.[31] The 1950–70 data plotted in Figure 4-5 show no trend ($R^2 = 0.02$, $p > 0.1$). According to those data, however, there is a significant downward trend (0.01674 per year) for NO_x emissions per unit of GNP for the 1971–90 period (R^2 = 0.97, p < 0.001). This suggests that in the absence of the 1970 and 1977 amendments, NO_x emissions would have been 60 percent higher, rather than 29 percent as estimated in the EPA study.[32]

This result is driven by the absence of a downward trend between 1950 and 1970 for NO_x. That lack of trend, however, is hardly surprising considering that the nation was still in the midst of its period of perception for NO_x in 1970 (see Figure 4-5), and many of the technological changes that improved energy efficiency (thereby reducing emissions for the other traditional pollutants) also increased NO_x emissions. If societies revert to type, increased information regarding the various environmental effects of NO_x (and changes in the structure of employment and the economy) would probably have turned this into a downward trend from 1971 to 1990 even in the absence of the 1970 and 1977 amendments.

There are other problems with the EPA Benefit-Cost Study. First, the federal Clean Air Act cannot claim much credit for the vast majority of benefits obtained (and costs incurred) in California, which comprised 12 percent of the U.S. population in 1990, since that state's control requirements by and large preceded federal requirements.

Second, the EPA analysis assumes that increases in emissions must lead to increases in ambient air concentrations. But that is true only if new plants and new equipment are not located in areas or built to specifications that favor greater dispersion of pollutants and if the dispersion characteristics of existing equipment (e.g., height and diameter of chimneys and temperature and volume of exhaust gases) do not change with time. More importantly, we have seen that the peaks in ambient concentrations and emissions do not generally coincide (see Table 5-1). In other words, there is a less than one-to-one correspondence between emissions and ambient concentrations.[33] In fact, during the 1960s, SO_2 air quality improved vastly in the urban areas of the United States although national emissions went up.

The EPA Benefit-Cost Study's estimates of premature mortality have also been criticized on the grounds that despite statistical association between outdoor PM concentrations, no plausible biological mechanism has been identified as the cause for that association, or for EPA's assumption of a linear relationship between concentrations and premature mortality.[34]

EPA's major defense against these criticisms is that its study has been extensively peer-reviewed by various EPA-selected panels and passed muster with them.[35] However, that is less a defense of EPA's analysis than an indictment of its peer review, considering the implausibility of the study's final results (namely, that the nation would be willing in 1990 to pay 20 percent of its GDP—more than the sum of all health expenditures—for what, by EPA's own estimates, are relatively modest gains in comparison with other outstanding public health needs), the logical consequences of its valuation of premature mortality and chronic bronchitis cases for the allocation of society's scarce resources (and particularly resources devoted to public health and medicine), and the unsupportable and counterhistorical assumption that states and local agencies in democracies would not have acted to reduce risks to public health absent federalization despite increasing wealth and the movement away from polluting industries. The peer-review process seems to have been more concerned with the plausibility of individual models than with that of the whole enterprise (essentially focusing on individual gains rather than the full picture).

On the cost side, while it is not a criticism of the EPA study, there is little doubt that because of the Clean Air Act's command-and-control regime, the nation has paid excessively for the emissions reductions and air quality improvements obtained (even if aggregate or, for that matter, marginal benefits may have exceeded aggregate, or marginal, benefits).[36] That is particularly true for federal new source requirements.[37] The effectiveness of emissions trading in reducing the costs of acidic deposition controls instituted under Title IV of the 1990 Amendments compared to what they would have been under a command-and-control regime hints at the inefficiencies and excessive costs of the latter system.[38] As an EPA official notes, "Not only are emissions reductions greater than expected, but compliance costs are now expected to be half that originally projected. The flexibility offered by the SO_2 allowance trading system deserves much of the credit."[39]

Finally, regardless of whether or not the benefits of the 1970 and 1977 amendments to the Clean Air Act exceed its costs, some of the recent expenditures on air pollution control could well have purchased greater improvements in public health and welfare if they had been diverted elsewhere (see Table 7-1), or even through

138

redistribution of efforts (and dollars) within the realm of air pollution control.[40] Consider, for instance, that there may be situations in which certain combinations of VOC and NO_x controls may reduce O_3 concentrations at the expense of aggravating fine PM, and vice versa (see Box 7-2, which describes such a case for California's South Coast Air Basin, which includes metropolitan Los Angeles).[41] Yet, studies suggest that the benefit-cost ratio for ozone per se is relatively low, while that of controlling fine PM is much higher.[42] Thus, society would be better off if the former were deemphasized and at least some of the resulting savings were applied to the latter. As the example in Box 7-2[43] indicates, "risk-risk" trade-offs are best studied and implemented at the state or regional level rather than the national level because the relative risk-reduction-to-cost ratios for the various risks depend upon numerous local factors, such as the magnitude and mix of emissions, population density, geography, weather, and various socioeconomic factors such as income, education, and access to health care.

The Path of Reform

The previous discussion suggests several improvements that would increase the efficiency and effectiveness of air pollution control in the United States without giving up the improvements in air quality that have occurred over the last several decades.

Given how far along states (and the average individual in the United States) are in their environmental transitions, states are unlikely to indulge in a race to the bottom today. If they do, the powers that be will hear from their citizens. Therefore, for intrastate pollutants—that is, relatively short-range, primary pollutants—the federal government's role should be limited to undertaking research, providing scientific and technical information about benefits and costs of controls to the states and the public, and establishing guidelines for NAAQS. The states would then be responsible for adopting their own ambient air quality standards and attaining those standards at a pace dictated by their own political processes and their knowledge and perception of what balances need to be struck to optimize their quality of life. This is preferable to having such decisions made by those who do not directly bear either the costs or the benefits of attainment.

Box 7-2: Risk-Risk Analysis—Improvements in Ozone vs. Fine Particulate Matter

An analysis by atmospheric chemists at Caltech and the University of California, Irvine, illustrates some of the complexities and potential risks of ignoring risk-risk trade-offs between ozone and fine particulate matter (FPM, that is, PM less than 2.5 micrometers in diameter). Using an urban and regional atmospheric model, they modeled the changes in concentrations of various gases and aerosols in California's South Coast Air Basin (which includes Los Angeles and Riverside) due to changes in VOC and NO_x emissions using meteorological conditions that occurred during a two-day episode on August 27 and 28, 1987.

Maximum one-hour concentrations modeled at Riverside showed that a 50 percent basinwide reduction in NO_x alone would reduce O_3 by only 6 percent and FPM by 18 percent. On the other hand, a 50 percent reduction in VOC alone would reduce O_3 by a larger amount (34 percent) but *increase* FPM (19 percent). Given the relative health impacts of FPM compared to those of O_3, this suggests that a 50 percent reduction in VOC alone could actually aggravate public health problems. Finally, a simultaneous reduction of 50 percent in both NO_x and VOC would reduce O_3 by 25 percent and FPM by 15 percent.

So which is the best control strategy for protecting public health from pollution in Riverside—reducing only NO_x by 50 percent or both VOC and NO_x by 50 percent?

To make matters more complex, a 1991 National Research Council study, *Rethinking the Ozone Problem in Urban and Regional Air Pollution*, notes that reducing NO_x emissions would reduce O_3 concentrations in outlying, downwind areas (where O_3 concentrations are the highest) at the expense of increasing concentrations in downtown and midbasin areas. So whether what is best for Riverside in terms of reducing O_3-related health impacts is also best for the South Coast Air Basin will depend upon the relationship between O_3 concentrations and health response. A linear, no-threshold function may give one answer, while a nonlinear relationship may give another. And the final result will depend upon the distribution and socioeconomic characteristics of the population in the downtown, midbasin, and outlying areas. (Why socioeconomic characteristics? Poorer and richer populations may be more susceptible to air pollution–related health effects than others.)

Finally, one must ask whether the cost of the best strategy to protect public health from air pollution is also the best use of money to reduce health problems in general for that area. It is not sufficient that benefits exceed costs; one must also get those benefits at the cheapest price.

Such questions can only be addressed location by location because the answer depends upon the precise details of meteorology, geography, population density, socioeconomic character of the population, and chemical composition of the emissions in the area, as well as the ratios of NO_x-to-VOC emissions. Given these complexities, a one-size-fits-all approach may improve matters in some areas while making them worse in others.

SOURCES: Meng, Dabdub, and Seinfeld 1997; National Research Council 1991.

Emissions trading for a given pollutant should be allowed between all sources—new and old. That would significantly reduce the costs of air pollution control.[44] In addition, because of diminishing returns from further tightening of federal new-source emissions standards, those standards should be frozen at current levels. States, however, would be free to make them more stringent in their own jurisdictions if they so chose.

For regional and interstate problems, such as ozone transport or acidic deposition, there are no easy answers. Interstate problems were an important part of the original rationale for federal intervention. The success of the European nations in negotiating SO_2 and NO_x reductions and that of the world community in reducing chlorofluorocarbons prove that states can come to negotiated solutions that do not need to be imposed by a "higher" political authority.[45]

In the United States, most observers have claimed that federalization, in fact, has had little impact on interstate pollution.[46] That analysis may have been valid until the early 1990s, but since then the pace has picked up for control of pollutants that ostensibly contribute to cross-boundary impacts. It is worth noting that the federal government has been much maligned for its inaction through the 1980s, the argument being that it had the authority and discretion to address these issues and chose not to do so. To its credit, the federal government did not act precipitously because, based upon the knowledge that existed at that time, as a 1984 acid rain study by the congressional Office of Technology Assessment noted, it was unclear whether the national costs could be justified by the national benefits.[47] Similarly, a 1989 study by the same office laments the lack of sufficient information to formulate additional control strategies to further reduce ozone and ozone transport in a manner scientists could be confident would result in net benefits to society.[48]

The 1990 amendments to the Clean Air Act established, under Title IV, an acid deposition control program that some may view as a success story because its control costs are less than many anticipated,[49] compliance occurred faster than expected,[50] and the concentration of sulfate ions in acidic deposition has declined substantially.[51] Whether sulfate emissions trading met its original environmental goals, however, is a matter of debate (see Box 7-3).[52] In fact, based upon the premise that both EPA and industry had projected higher compliance costs for the acidic deposition program prior to the passage of Title IV, proponents of tighter air quality standards argue that preregulation cost estimates are "each and every time . . . grossly overestimated" in the words of EPA administrator Carol Browner.[53] And hence, goes this argument, compliance with tighter standards will necessarily be cheaper than anticipated. However, the underlying premise that acid rain compliance costs had been overestimated has been disputed by some energy and environmental economists,[54] who also note that it is premature to estimate costs since not all the elements of Title IV are in place.[55] More importantly, the success of the acidic deposition control program with respect to meeting its original environmental goals is a matter of debate.

A Resources for the Future analysis of the expected costs and benefits of the Title IV program from 1995 to 2030 suggests that if the program is a success (in terms of benefits exceeding costs), it may be for reasons other than those for which it was enacted.[56] They estimate "negligible benefits in the areas that were the focus of attention in the 1980s—namely, the effects of air pollution and acid rain on soils, forests and aquatic systems."[57] However, their analysis indicates substantial benefits from reduced risks of premature mortality because of reductions in secondary particles formed from the precursors of acidic deposition—namely, SO_2 and NO_x. Benefits from reduced morbidity and improved visibility were also estimated to be significant.

Interestingly, Resources for the Future reports that the majority of expected benefits will accrue to the very states that incur the largest costs, that is, the states that are heavy users of coal in their utilities because, the analysis suggests, most of the SO_2-related pollution generated by such a state will be deposited within its own borders. Thus, if one accepts this benefit-cost analysis, the acidic deposition problem in the eastern United States no longer fits the classic mold of an interstate problem in which the upwind states export their pollution to downwind states because their pollution does not have a significant effect on themselves. In other words, according to this analysis, much of the success of the acid rain control program would be because of the intrastate (rather than interstate) nature of the problem.

Another reason why heavy coal-burning states may also be the major beneficiaries of the expenditures on controls could be that each such state imports approximately as much pollution from other

**Box 7-3: How Successful Is the Acidic
Deposition Control Program?**

Despite the SO$_2$ emissions trading program's success in reducing control costs, it is unclear whether the acidic deposition control program enacted by Title IV of the 1990 amendments is meeting the environmental goals that prompted its existence.

When the 1990 amendments were passed, the major goals of the Title IV program, which was by and large focused on the eastern United States, included improving visibility, reducing material damage, and, most of all, restoring the acidified aquatic systems, soils, and high-elevation spruce forests, particularly in the Adirondacks and the mid-Atlantic highlands.

Between 1985 and 1995, sulfate ion concentration in precipitation in the eastern United States declined from 2.02 to 1.47 mg per liter, nitrate ion concentration was essentially unchanged, and hydrogen ion concentration declined from 37.6 to 28.2 mg per liter. Overall, precipitation became slightly more basic, with hydrogen-ion concentration (pH) increasing from 4.43 to 4.55 units. The modest change in pH is partly due to the fact that pH is measured on a logarithmic scale, so that a tenfold change in hydrogen-ion concentration changes pH by 1 unit.

About 30 to 50 percent of all acidic deposition is deposited as "dry deposition" in the form of particles or gases. Dry deposition in the rural eastern United States has declined 35 percent for SO$_2$ and 26 percent for sulfates between 1989 and 1995, a period during which Ohio River Valley regional SO$_2$ emissions declined about 8 percent. Over the same period, nitrates in dry deposition declined about 8 percent.

Have all these improvements in physical measures of the components of deposition reduced environmental impacts? Are the environmental goals envisioned for the program being achieved?

EPA's 1997 *AQ Trends Report* notes that visibility in the eastern United States declined between 1970 and 1980 but increased from 1980 to 1990. However, 1988–97 data show that although visibility has improved during days with moderate haziness, it may have worsened a little during the haziest days. On the other hand, in the western United States, where visibility is already better than in the East, visibility has improved steadily.

With respect to restoring acidified aquatic systems, the National Acid Precipitation Assessment Program's (NAPAP) 1990 Integrated Assessment reported that a 50 percent reduction in SO_2 emissions in the eastern United States would after 50 years only marginally increase (from 88 to 97 percent) the number of streams in the Adirondacks with chemistry suitable for sensitive fish species (e.g., rainbow trout). "Suitable" streams in the mid-Atlantic highlands would be unchanged at 79 percent after 50 years of reductions. With respect to lakes, the NAPAP report estimated the percentage of lakes suitable for brook trout would increase in the Adirondacks from 76–87 percent to 86–96 percent. Data are unavailable at this time to confirm the NAPAP's prognostications, but some researchers note that "the expected recovery of natural ecosystems has not been observed," adding that there has been no significant change since 1983 in the pH of precipitation in the Hubbard Brook Experimental Forest, which has the longest precipitation chemistry record in the United States.

Interestingly, a preliminary Resources for the Future study estimates that in 2010 estimated benefits of the acid rain control program may exceed its expected costs, not because of the reasons the program was enacted in 1990 (namely, effects upon soils, forests, and aquatic systems) but because of health-related impacts that more recent studies suggest accompany fine PM (formed by the transformation and transport of SO_2 and NO_x in the atmosphere). This study uses a value of a statistical life that is two-thirds of that used by the EPA Benefit-Cost Study. However, the Resources for the Future analysis suffers from some of the same problems associated with the EPA study.

SOURCES: NAPAP 1991; Burtraw et al. 1997; 1997 Air Quality Trends Report; Likens et al. 1998; CEQ 1999.

states as it exports. In such a case we have a collective problem amenable to collective action of which federalization does not have to be a part. That is more or less how Europe dealt with its long-range transboundary problems related to SO_2 and NO_x, for instance.

The reason why states had not worked on reducing sulfates of their own volition earlier was that much of this information was not available until relatively recently. Certainly, it was not available prior to federalization, so states should not have been expected to launch such efforts before that. The period of perception for sulfates per se (rather than PM in general) probably did not start until the mid- to late 1970s.[58] It was under way in 1979, when EPA produced a report to Congress on protecting visibility,[59] and in 1980 when the NAPAP was established to study the causes and effects of acidic deposition.[60] This period of perception extended until 1990, when the Clean Air Act was amended to establish the acid rain control program under Title IV. Moreover, when information did become available, it was subject to differing interpretations, many of which still persist. As the Office of Technology Assessment's 1984 study noted, it was far from clear in the 1980s whether additional SO_2 control was justifiable. However, there is no fundamental logic as to why the federal government should be expected to have the corner on "correct" interpretations. In fact, the danger of federalization is precisely that—if the federal entity's interpretation is incorrect, all 50 states are saddled with its consequences. As all centrally directed economies have discovered, centralized structures have a tendency to magnify even small errors or incorrect assumptions into major blunders. That does not mean that central authorities are always wrong, only that when they are, they are *very* wrong. For instance, the asbestos removal program, which reputedly cost over $50 billion, produced very little improvement in public health.[61] Similarly, the median cost for avoiding a cancer case caused by the Superfund program was in excess of $418 million according to an EPA-supported study by researchers at Harvard and Duke Universities.[62]

The pace of change with respect to interstate transport of ozone or its precursors has been slower than for acidic deposition. Recently, based upon the recommendations of the Ozone Transport Assessment Group and, including a formal petition, pressure from the northeastern states, EPA promulgated rules for NO_x state implementation plans covering 22 states in the East and the Midwest.[63] Under those rules, states had a September 1999 deadline for submitting plans and final implementation of NO_x rules was slated for May 2003. However, in May 1999, a U.S. District Court Appeals panel put those EPA rules on hold pending a further order.[64] In response, EPA is attempting to sidestep this ruling by proposing to regulate 10 of the 22 states on the strength of the northeastern states' earlier petition.[65]

That may ultimately help reduce interstate pollution, but it is unlikely to help reduce risks to public health and welfare efficiently or raise the overall quality of life, except by chance, because by design these rules exclude consideration of the broader factors that constitute the overall quality of life. Instead, they are designed to fulfill an overly narrow objective—ensuring compliance with O_3 NAAQS—rather than a reduction in overall risks to public health and welfare in a region. It would be preferable for the downwind states, the putative beneficiaries of control measures undertaken in the upwind states, to decide whether they would rather divert the money that would otherwise be spent on upwind ozone controls to, say, PM control or, possibly, purchasing health insurance for the indigent, immunization programs, broad cancer screening, or whatever public health and welfare measure they agree would provide the largest benefits in their jurisdiction(s). As Table 7-1 indicates, there is no shortage of worthy and underutilized substitutes for reducing risks to public health more efficiently.

8. Conclusion

Once prosperity and technology were responsible for air pollution. Today they are necessary for its cleanup. Their transformation—from problems to solutions—began toward the latter part of the last century. The advent of new, clean energy sources and more efficient combustion technologies made it possible to reduce pollution and to prosper in the bargain. Those technological changes propelled by—and in turn propelling—prosperity gathered steam through the past century. And through the decades, one by one, the various pollutants were brought under control, by force of an affluence- and technology-driven environmental transition. As if in accordance with a grand design, the problems that were the most obvious and the easiest to control were addressed before others, and each pollutant's transition was determined by factors dependent ultimately on prosperity and technology—namely, knowledge regarding its causes and effects, its risks relative to other societal risks, the availability and affordability of measures to reduce those risks, the mix of energy sources used by society, the structure of the economy, and, of course, the general level of affluence. Improvements were achieved indoors before outdoors; in primary pollutants, in air quality before total emissions; and for primary pollutants before secondary pollutants.

Declines in emissions per GNP—measures of technological change which also serve as leading environmental indicators in a growing economy—indicate that cleanup had begun no later than the 1920s for SO_2, the '30s for VOC and NO_x, and the '40s for PM and CO. The first improvements came from voluntary, market-driven measures. People of their own accord cleaned up their households of the most obvious problem, smoke. That also improved air quality in their neighborhoods. Then the focus turned to outdoor air. Outdoor smoke went through a transition in urban areas shortly after World War II, if not earlier. With greater prosperity, better health, and reduced mortality, the risks of PM and SO_2 became more evident.

They were implicated in a series of deadly post–World War II air pollution episodes on both sides of the Atlantic. Local and state governments became more active in controlling these pollutants. Transitions for PM and SO_2 air quality came next. In the meantime, California had discovered the dark side of the automobile and instituted motor vehicle emissions controls that were later adopted by the federal government for the rest of the nation. Federalization of air pollution control—bolstered by the 1970s oil shocks, greater use of nonfossil fuels, and changes in the structure of the economy—helped bring about transitions for CO and O_3 air quality and SO_2 emissions. NO_x went through its transition last because it was much less of a public health problem and the most expensive to control. As a result, the nation's air is far cleaner now than it has been in several decades.

Conventional wisdom gives most, if not all, the credit for the remarkable improvements in air quality to the federalization of air pollution control effected by the Clean Air Amendments of 1970. Before that, conventional wisdom asserts, the state laws that did exist were poorly written and badly enforced, and there was little or no improvement in air quality. That foot-dragging, it is claimed, was the inevitable result of a race to the bottom. The notion that states participate in such a race to the bottom, relaxing environmental requirements and reducing overall state well-being, is critical to any justification for federalizing control of pollutants that have no significant interstate effects. A corollary to the race-to-the-bottom hypothesis is that before Washington intervened, there should have been no improvements in air quality anywhere, except by chance.

But, in fact, there were broad improvements in air quality before federalization. The race, if any, seems to be in the opposite direction, particularly for those pollutants associated with—and in the areas where they were most likely to create—the greatest public health risks. Ambient air quality for TSP and SO_2, the pollutants associated with the killer episodes of the 1940s, '50s, and '60s, had gone through their environmental transitions nationally before the federal government began regulating those pollutants. The improvements were especially noticeable in urban—that is, the most populated and highest risk—areas. Similarly, CO had either gone through, or was on the verge of its own, transition prior to federalization. In addition, oxidants and ozone had also gone through a transition in California, the area where they were widely recognized to be a problem. Outside California, few areas made much effort to reduce oxidants (or their precursors) because most people were unaware that those pollutants posed a problem in their jurisdictions until just before—or, in many cases, after—federalization. Perhaps the best evidence for this is the inability to construct a national composite for ozone or oxidant air quality prior to the early 1970s because of insufficient monitor coverage outside California. Thus, the relatively tardy response to ozone and oxidants outside California was attributable not to a race to the bottom but to the fact that states were not racing to solve problems they did not know they had.

The historical account reveals several other discrepancies between what did transpire and what ought to have transpired had there been a race to the bottom. County and state air programs grew significantly during the 1960s. Their very presence is, at the least, akin to adopting a self-imposed handicap in what is supposed to be a race for jobs and economic growth (since that is a fair characterization of the race to the bottom). Second, prior to the 1970 amendments many emissions standards were progressively tightened in numerous jurisdictions nationwide, in effect bidding standards up rather than down—the very antithesis of either a race to the bottom or a race to relax. Moreover, the efficiencies of dust collection rose steadily throughout the century. Third, the federal preemption of motor vehicle emission standards outside California was an effort by the automobile industry and Congress to thwart any race to the top by individual states because they were opposed to the hodge-podge of control requirements that otherwise could have resulted.

The contradictions between the race-to-the-bottom rationale for federalization on one hand and historical events and empirical trends on the other indicate that the race-to-the-bottom rationale is intrinsically flawed. If there is any race, it is not to the bottom of environmental quality but to the top of the quality of life.

The rise and fall of air pollution in this country are entirely consistent with the hypothesis of an environmental transition driven by society's race to improve its quality of life. In that race, society harnesses both economic and technological development (the two, in fact, co-evolve).

In the early phases of economic and technological development, during the industrial era when jobs and prosperity often signified

151

air pollution, the race for a better quality of life may have seemed like a race to the bottom of environmental quality. But once the society goes through its environmental transition, that race increasingly favors environmental quality, at least until the environment is sufficiently clean. Thus, in today's postindustrial era, prosperity is often inversely correlated with pollution. Today the service sectors account for three out of every four nonfarm jobs. Accordingly, many jurisdictions maximize jobs by catering to the needs of the service sectors (and their employees) while actively discouraging polluting industries altogether.

In the absence of federalization, air quality might well have continued to improve, but probably not as rapidly in some areas. Nevertheless, because command-and-control has been the norm for EPA regulations, the additional improvements have come at a higher price than necessary. The total current risk to public health would have been lower had there been a conscious effort to maximize risk reduction for the total costs incurred by society.

Another question related to the usefulness of the federalization regime imposed on the nation by the 1970 and subsequent amendments to the Clean Air Act is whether the marginal benefits exceed their marginal costs. Although no study has made such estimates, EPA undertook a very ambitious, multiyear benefit-cost study in an effort to compare aggregate benefits with aggregate costs and found that the former exceeded the latter by about 40 to 1. About 90 percent of those benefits were due to PM-10 reductions that would not, according to the study, have occurred without the amendments. In addition, 90 percent of the benefits were attributed to fewer premature deaths (mainly due to improvements in PM-10 and lead air quality).

But that study is seriously flawed. It makes the fatal assumption that without the 1970 (and subsequent) amendments, controls would have been frozen at the 1970 level. The historical experience, as summarized by the prefederalization trends in air quality compiled in this book, shows that before the 1970 amendments were passed air quality was improving remarkably in the areas where the criteria pollutants were recognized to be problems. Emissions per GNP had been declining for decades prior to that. In fact, for the original criteria pollutants, about three-quarters (or more) of the reductions in emissions per GNP between their peaks and 1990 had occurred by 1970. Assuming, in the absence of the 1970 federalization, that the 1950–70 trends in emissions per GNP had continued through 1990, NO_x emissions would have been 60 percent higher than "actual" 1990 emissions; more importantly, PM-10 emissions would have been lower and SO_2 emissions would have been only 5 percent higher.

There is no reason to think that the factors driving the prefederalization improvements in air quality and emissions per GNP would have come to an abrupt halt in 1970 but for federalization. If anything, the underlying forces driving those improvements—greater knowledge, greater wealth, and less economic dependence upon the traditional polluting sectors—were only gathering strength.

Moreover, putting aside the issues related to the EPA study's estimations of public health impacts in the absence of federalization, accepting its analysis as valid forces one to embrace a number of wildly implausible implications. One such implication is that in 1990 the nation would have been willing to pay 20 percent of its GDP for just the health-related benefits of air pollution control despite the fact that it spent only 12 percent of GDP on *all* health care that year—an amount many thought excessive. Another implication is that the nation is or should have been willing in 1995 to spend 60 percent of its GDP on eliminating all existing cases of chronic bronchitis. A third implication is that the nation should pay hundreds of thousands of dollars to eliminate the loss of one life-year because of air pollution even though there are many underused medical procedures that could provide the same benefit at a tenth or a hundredth of that cost. That would be a recipe for poor public policy and wasteful spending.

Today the nation is well into its postenvironmental transition period for the traditional air pollutants. Air quality continues to improve, and politicians, no matter what their partisan stripe, have by and large embraced the environment. For instance, it figured prominently in the campaign rhetoric of President Clinton in his successful reelection bid in 1996. Therefore, the devolution of air pollution control to the states is unlikely to result in rollback of the air quality improvements of the past few decades. However, in light of the progress made, and given that the easy—and several tough— reductions have already been made, further improvements in air quality may not be sustainable if they come at the expense of the broader quality of life.

To ensure that the improvements in environmental quality and quality of life go hand in hand in this posttransition period, emissions trading should be expanded to allow trades between old and new sources, and the pollutant-by-pollutant approach should be replaced by one that focuses on reducing overall risks to public health and welfare at local and regional levels. Control of interstate pollution should be negotiated between affected states, with the downwind states being free to accept, in lieu of additional control of specific air pollutants, other reductions in risk to public health and welfare funded by the upwind (polluting) states if the downwind states deem that such measures would provide greater benefits to their populations. For intrastate pollution, the federal government should step back from its role as the micromanager of air pollution control and instead enter into a more equal partnership with the states. Under such a federalist approach, the federal government would set idealized goals, and states would determine their own attainment schedules and control measures for pollutants produced within, and affecting, their own jurisdictions. That is only appropriate, because the trade-offs that have to be made to improve their overall quality of life, of which environmental quality is only one facet, necessarily depend upon numerous location-specific factors, and states will be the major winners or losers from their own actions (or inaction). Because many of the determinants of the quality of life are unquantifiable, optimizing the quality of life should be left to each state's political process. To paraphrase Winston Churchill, in a democracy it may be the worst method, until you consider all the others.

There are lessons for other countries in the rise and fall of air pollution in the United States. According to the environmental transition hypothesis, the transitions result from continually increasing levels of affluence and technology. Once past the transition, as a country gets richer it is also likely to be cleaner, at least until it becomes "clean enough." So far, the U.S. experience with air pollution has been consistent with that. Similarly, many of the world's developed nations have gone through environmental transitions for various air pollutants over the past several years.[1]

However, the seemingly logical progression in the environmental transitions that have occurred so far for air pollution in the richer countries should not be mistaken for predestination. History indicates that neither economic nor technological development is inevitable. Various societies have suffered long periods of economic and technological stagnation—and, sometimes, even retrenchment. The richer nations, which have gone through some, if not all, of the environmental transitions for air pollution, were fortunate that their political and legal systems by and large supported the institutions that fostered economic growth and technological change. Other nations, such as those with erstwhile centrally planned economies, which lacked such institutions, have had the worst of all worlds— they are poorer and their environment is wretched. Their problems were further aggravated by the absence of democracy, which provides a powerful incentive to decisionmakers to constantly monitor and improve the quality of the ordinary citizen's life.

There has been some debate in the academic literature regarding whether economic development is sufficient to bring about environmental improvements, or whether environmental policies have to be imposed.[2] But that is a false choice, since although such policies may be among the proximate causes for bringing about an environmental transition, such policies do not arise in a vacuum. What factors impel a society to adopt such policies? More importantly, once having adopted such policies, which may extend from general statements of good intentions to economic incentives to detailed command-and-control dictates, what converts them into realities?

The environmental transition hypothesis provides an explanation for both these questions. Essentially, as a country becomes more economically and technologically developed, in order to improve its quality of life it first addresses immediate needs such as food, running water, basic medical services, electricity, and education. Once those needs are met satisfactorily, the country turns its attention to the other determinants of its quality of life, such as air pollution and other environmental matters. Accordingly, it specifies its desires for a clean environment in various policies. Then, greater economic and technological development helps convert those policies into reality. The wealthier the country, the more it can afford to research, develop, and install cleaner or cleanup technologies. Moreover, the structure of the economy changes as it becomes wealthier. The economy becomes more knowledge—rather than material—intensive. And, with increasing wealth, the population growth rate eventually moderates, and technological change is sustained, if not accelerated.[3] All of these trends tend to reinforce environmental transitions.

As this progression of events suggests, policies and regulations are likely to be an integral part of environmental transitions in a democratic society, and such transitions are more likely to occur as a democratic society becomes richer and controls become more affordable through economic growth and technological progress. However, although a country is ultimately more likely to be cleaner as it becomes richer, it does not follow that a richer country is necessarily always cleaner than one that is poorer (because of the numerous determinants of environmental transition, which can vary from country to country).

It has often been noted that economic growth and technological progress are not panaceas.[4] They may not be panaceas, but they increase the likelihood of, first, purchasing the medicine and, then, making it more palatable. Thus, while economic growth and technological progress may not be sufficient, in the long run retarding them is also likely to retard environmental improvements.

Often disdaining economic growth and sometimes rejecting new technologies, many environmentalists hold that lifestyle changes are essential to a cleaner environment.[5] Perhaps—but, as this recounting of the 20th-century history of air pollution in the United States shows, economic growth and new technologies were indispensable to bringing about the various environmental transitions without which air quality (and the quality of life) would have been even poorer than it was a generation or more ago. And the need for fiscal resources and new technologies is not diminished either in the United States or worldwide. A recent (April 1997) United Nations Development Programme study estimates that between $300 billion and $600 billion will be needed worldwide for pollution control projects by the year 2000.[6] As the world's future environmental problems become more challenging, there will be an even greater demand for fiscal resources to research, develop, and implement new technologies in order to bring about environmental transitions for those problems.[7] Thus, one of the keys to environmental progress is to nurture the institutions that bolster economic growth and technological change in order to move societies further to the right toward—and beyond—their environmental transitions.

Notes

Introduction

1. Indur M. Goklany, "Richer Is Cleaner: Long Term Trends in Global Air Quality," in Ronald Bailey, ed., *The True State of the Planet* (New York: Free Press, 1995), pp. 339–77; Indur M. Goklany, "Factors Affecting Environmental Impacts: The Effects of Technology on Long-Term Trends in Cropland, Air Pollution and Water-Related Diseases," *Ambio* 25 (1996): 497–503.

2. Frederick W. Lipfert, "Sulfur Oxides, Particulates, and Human Mortality: Synopsis of Statistical Correlations," *Journal of the Air of the Pollution Control Association* 30 (1980): 366–71.

3. See, for example, John P. Dwyer, "The Practice of Federalism under the Clean Air Act," *Maryland Law Review* 54 (1995): 1183–225; Robert V. Percival, "Environmental Federalism: Historical Roots and Contemporary Models," *Maryland Law Review* 54 (1995): 1141–82.

4. Richard B. Stewart, "Pyramids of Sacrifice? Problems of Federalism in Mandating State Implementation of National Environmental Policy," *Yale Law Journal* 86 (1977): 1196–272.

5. Ibid.; Robert L. Rabin, "Federal Regulation in Historical Perspective," *Stanford Law Review* 38 (1986): 1189–326; Edmund S. Muskie, "Role of the Federal Government in Air Pollution Control," *Arizona Law Review* 10 (1968): 17–24.

6. Ibid.; Stewart.

7. Richard L. Revesz, "Rehabilitating Interstate Competition: Rethinking the 'Race to the Bottom' Rationale for Federal Environmental Regulation," *New York University Law Review* 67 (December 1992): 1210–54; Henry N. Butler and Jonathan R. Macey, "Externalities and the Matching Principle: The Case for Reallocating Environmental Regulatory Authority," *Yale Law Policy Review, Yale Journal on Regulation, Symposium Issue: Constructing a New Federalism: Jurisdictional Competence and Competition* 14, no. 2 (Symposium) (1996): 23–66; David Schoenbrod, "Why States, Not EPA, Should Set Pollution Standards," *Regulation* 19, no. 4 (1996), available at http://www.cato.org/pubs/regulation/reg19n4a.html; Stewart.

8. Kirsten H. Engel, "State Environmental Standard Setting: Is There a 'Race' and Is It 'to the Bottom'?" *Hastings Law Journal* 48 (1997): 271–377; Joshua D. Sarnoff, "The Continuing Imperative (But Only from a National Perspective) for Federal Environmental Protection," *Duke Environmental Law and Public Policy Forum,* 7 (1997): 225–319; Gary D. Libecap, "Environmental Regulation and Federalism," *Arizona Law Review* 38 (1996): 901–7; Daniel C. Esty, "Revitalizing Environmental Federalism," *Michigan Law Review* 95 (1996): 570–653; Peter P. Swire, "The Race to Laxity and the Race to Undesirability: Explaining Failures in Competition among Jurisdictions in Environmental Law," *Yale Law Policy Review, Yale Journal on Regulation, Symposium Issue: Constructing a New Federalism: Jurisdictional Competence and Competition* 14, no. 2 (Symposium) (1996): 67–110.

9. See notes 2 through 8.

10. See, for example, Swire; Butler and Macey.

11. Of all the references cited in notes 2 through 8, Schoenbrod's is an exception to this statement. Based apparently upon particulate matter and sulfur dioxide air quality data from Robert W. Crandall, *Controlling Industrial Pollution: The Economics and Politics of Clean Air* (Washington: Brookings Institution, 1983), pp. 18–19, he estimates that air pollution declined three times faster before federalization than just after it, concluding that "it was the federal government, not the states, that had been the laggard" in air pollution control. While he is right about the states, he may be overly harsh on the federal government, perhaps reading more into the data than they can deliver. For the several reasons articulated in Chapter 3, trends from such data are best seen to be qualitative rather than quantitative. Moreover, one would expect that the rate of improvement would decline since, in a rational world, once the easiest and cheapest reductions are obtained, additional reductions are harder to achieve. Furthermore, despite having caused economic slowdowns and increased pressures to conserve energy, the oil shocks of the 1970s also increased the pressure to reduce controls and use higher sulfur fuels, particularly coal (see Chapter 1). Any head-to-head quantitative comparison of air quality trends before and after federalization should take such factors into consideration. Discretion being the better part of valor, this book will not attempt such a quantitative comparison, but it will examine long-term trends in air quality, emissions and emissions per unit of gross national product to determine whether the 1970 act made much, if any, difference in their pre-1970 long-term trends.

12. Goklany, "Factors Affecting Environmental Impacts."

13. Ibid.; Goklany, "Richer Is Cleaner."

14. Ibid.; Goklany, "Factors Affecting Environmental Impacts."

15. *Encyclopædia Britannica* (1959), "Smoke and Smoke Prevention," Vol. 20, pp. 841–43.

16. SO_2 and CO are examples of primary pollutants; they are emitted as SO_2 and CO from various combustion processes. On the other hand, O_3 and sulfates, which are the transformation products of various primary pollutants, would be classified as secondary pollutants. Previously, prior to current levels of control, PM used to be regarded mainly as a primary pollutant; however, at current control levels, a significant portion of the remaining PM in the air is made up of sulfates, a secondary pollutant.

17. Stewart, p. 1197: "The failure of prior efforts (heavily dependant on state initiatives) to check air pollution prompted Congress to enact the 1970 Clean Air Amendments." Also see, for example, Dwyer, pp. 1191, 1193 (footnotes 32, 37); Percival, pp. 1160–61; Swire, p. 68.

18. See, for example, Stewart, pp. 1211–12; Revesz, pp. 1210–11, 1224–27; Swire, pp. 71–78.

Chapter 1

1. Peter Brimblecombe, *The Big Smoke* (New York: Methuen, 1987), pp. 16–18; Peter Brimblecombe, "Attitudes and Responses towards Air Pollution in Medieval England," *Journal of the Air Pollution Control Association* 26 (1976): 941–45.

2. Brimblecombe, "Attitudes and Responses towards Air Pollution in Medieval England"; *Encyclopædia Britannica* (1959), "Smoke and Smoke Prevention," in Vol. 20, pp. 841–43.

3. Brimblecombe, "Attitudes and Responses towards Air Pollution in Medieval England"; *Encyclopædia Britannica*, "Smoke and Smoke Prevention."

4. A. R. Meetham, *Atmospheric Pollution: Its Origins and Prevention*, 3rd (rev.) ed. (New York: Macmillan, 1964); Howard R. Lewis, *With Every Breath You Take* (New York: Crown, 1965).

5. Brimblecombe, "Attitudes and Responses towards Air Pollution in Medieval England"; Brimblecombe, *The Big Smoke*, p. 9.

6. John Evelyn, *Fumifugium or the Inconvenience of the Aer and Smoake of London Dissipated* (1661) in James P. Lodge, *The Smoke of London: Two Prophecies* (Elmsford, N.Y.: Maxwell Reprint, 1969), p. 25.

7. Ibid., pp. 5–6.

8. Ibid., pp. 28–31, 40.

9. Ibid., p. 34.

10. John Graunt, *Natural and Political Observations . . . Upon the Bills of Mortality* (1662), available at http://rowlf.cc.wwu.edu:8080/~stephan/Graunt/graunt.html (8 January 1997).

11. Graunt, p. 70.

12. Brimblecombe, *The Big Smoke*, p. 34.

13. Daniel Defoe, *A Journal of the Plague Year* (1712), available at ftp://uiarchive.cso.uiuc.edu/pub/text/gutenberg/etext95/jplag10.txt (8 January 1997).

14. B. A. Cohoe, "The Relationship of Atmospheric Pollution to Health" in Oskar Klotz and William C. White, eds., *Papers on the Influence of Smoke on Health*, Smoke Investigation Bulletin No. 9, Mellon Institute of Industrial Research and School of Specific Industries (Pittsburgh: University of Pittsburgh, 1914), pp. 7–53.

15. Cliff I. Davidson, "Air Pollution in Pittsburgh: A Historical Perspective," *Journal of the Air Pollution Control Association* 29 (1979): 1035–41.

16. Bureau of the Census, *Historical Statistics of the United States, Colonial Times to 1970* (Washington: Government Printing Office, 1975), pp. 587–88.

17. Raymond R. Tucker, "The St. Louis Code and Its Operation," in *Air Pollution: Proceedings of the United States Technical Conference on Air Pollution* (New York: McGraw-Hill, 1952), pp. 726–28.

18. *Encyclopedia Britannica*, "Smoke and Smoke Prevention."

19. Raymond R. Tucker and J. H. Carter, "Some Legal Foundations for Air Pollution Control," in *Proceedings of the Third National Air Pollution Control Symposium* (Los Angeles: National Air Pollution Symposium, 1955), pp. 211–15.

20. Bureau of the Census, pp. 587–88.

21. Brimblecombe, "Air Pollution in Industrializing England," *Journal of the Air Pollution Control Association* 28 (1978): 115–18; R. Dale Grinder, "The Battle for Clean Air: The Smoke Problem in Post-Civil War America," in Martin V. Melosi, ed., *Pollution and Reform in American Cities, 1870–1930* (Austin: University of Texas, 1980), pp. 83–103; Davidson; Cohoe, p. 10. The quote is from Cohoe.

22. Tucker and Carter.

23. Cohoe.

24. Davidson.

25. *New York Times*, January 9, 1902, p.1; January 13, 1902, p. 5.

26. Ibid.; *New York Times*, January 10, 1902, p. 2; January 25, 1902, pp. 1, 2; Z. A. Willard, "The Smoke Problem in the United States of America," in *Papers Read at the Smoke Abatement Conference, March 26, 27 & 28, 1912* (Westminster: Coal Smoke Abatement Society, 1912), pp. 59–61.

27. Ellwood H. McClelland, *Bibliography of Smoke and Smoke Prevention*, Smoke Investigation Bulletin No. 2, Mellon Institute of Industrial Research and School of Specific Industries (Pittsburgh: University of Pittsburgh, 1913), p. 45.

28. Rudolf Kudlich, *Ringelmann Smoke Chart*, Department of the Interior, Bureau of Mines, Information Circular 6888, June 1936.

29. Ibid.

30. See, for example, *Manual of Smoke and Boiler Ordinances and Requirements, etc.* (Chicago: Smoke Prevention Association, 1940), pp. 100–101; John A. Danielson, ed., *Air Pollution Engineering Manual, 2d ed.*, Publication AP–40 (Research Triangle Park, N.C.: Environmental Protection Agency, Office of Air Quality Standards and Planning, 1973).

31. *Power*, March 14, 1916, p. 384; R. G. Johansen, "The Law as Applied to Air Pollution," in *Manual of Smoke and Boiler Ordinances and Requirements, etc.* (Chicago: Smoke Prevention Association, 1940), pp. 24–28.

32. Arnold W. Reitze Jr., "A Century of Air Pollution Control Laws: What's Worked, What's Failed, What Might Work," *Environmental Law* 21 (1991): 1549–1646.

33. *New York Times*, February 11, 1903, p. 3; February 12, 1903, p. 8; April 22, 1903, p. 3.

34. *New York Times*, July 21, 1906, p. 1.

35. Thomas E. Donnelly, "Smoke Abatement in Chicago," in *Papers Read at the Smoke Abatement Conference, March 26, 27 & 28, 1912*, pp. 51–58.

36. Samuel B. Flagg, *City Smoke Ordinances and Smoke Abatement*, Department of the Interior, Bureau of Mines, Bulletin 49 (Washington: Government Printing Office, 1912).

37. Joel A. Tarr, *The Search for the Ultimate Sink: Urban Pollution in Historical Perspective* (Akron, Ohio: University of Akron, 1996), pp. 323–33.

38. Bureau of the Census, pp. 41, 716.

39. Pittsburgh Bureau of Smoke Regulation, *Handbook for Nineteen-Seventeen* (Pittsburgh: Department of Public Health, 1917).

40. Osborn Monnett, *Smoke Abatement*, Department of the Interior, Bureau of Mines, Technical Paper 273 (Washington: Government Printing Office, 1923), p. 1.

41. Grinder.

42. George H. Perkins, *The International Smoke Abatement Exhibition Held in London, March and April 1912* (New York: American Society of Mechanical Engineers, 1912), pp. 1543–56.

43. R. G. K. Lempfert, "Sunshine Records: A Comparison of Sunshine Statistics for Urban and Rural Stations," in *Papers Read at the Smoke Abatement Conference, March 26, 27 & 28, 1912*, pp. 22–28; Perkins.

44. W. J. Bean, "A Note on Recent Observations of the Smoke Nuisance at Kew Gardens," in *Papers Read at the Smoke Abatement Conference, March 26, 27 & 28, 1912*, p. 29.

45. Rollo Russell, "Smoke and Fog," in *Papers Read at the Smoke Abatement Conference, March 26, 27 & 28, 1912*, pp. 21–22.

46. Pittsburgh Bureau of Smoke Regulation, p. 11.

47. Pittsburgh Bureau of Smoke Regulation.

48. Donnelly.

49. Bureau of the Census, pp. 646 and 832.

50. Ibid., p. 591.

51. Samuel H. Schurr et al., *Electricity in the American Economy: Agent of Technological Progress* (New York: Greenwood, 1990), p. 386.

52. F. A. Chambers, A. D. Singh, and I. A. Deutch, "Atmospheric Pollution in Chicago," in *Proceedings of the Thirty-First Annual Convention of the Smoke Prevention Association, May 31st–June 5th, 1937, Pennsylvania Hotel, New York*, typewritten copy, p. 149.

53. Davidson.

54. Figure 1-2 is based on Davidson's paper, but it is also consistent with information provided in John H. Ludwig, George B. Morgan, and Thomas B. McMullen, "Trends in Urban Air Quality," *EOS* 51 (1970): 468–75. The dustfall method is one of the most rudimentary methods for measuring ambient particulate matter concentrations. It essentially consists of collecting dust in an open bucket. That method has now been abandoned partly because, except in unusual circumstances, it now takes a much longer time to collect measurable quantities of dust.

55. Grinder.

56. Bureau of the Census, pp. 41 and 716.

57. *Manual of Smoke and Boiler Ordinances and Requirements, Etc.* (Chicago: Smoke Prevention Association, 1936).

58. Flagg.

59. *Manual of Smoke and Boiler Ordinances and Requirements*, pp. 114–15.

60. Pittsburgh Bureau of Smoke Prevention, *1995 Report* (Pittsburgh: Department of Public Health, 1955); Joel A. Tarr and Carl Zimring, "The Struggle for Smoke Control in St. Louis: Achievement and Emulation," in Andrew Hurley, ed., *Common Fields: An Environmental History of St. Louis* (St. Louis: Missouri Historical Society Press, 1997), pp. 199–220; Tarr, pp. 233–35.

61. Davidson.

62. The Smoke Abatement League of Cincinnati and Hamilton County, Ohio, *Smoke and Dust Pollution Analysis, July 1, 1948 to June 30, 1949*, Charles N. Howison, Executive Secretary, December 1, 1949.

63. J. Cholak, L. J. Schafer, and R. F. Hoffer, "Results of a Five Year Investigation of Air Pollution in Cincinnati," *Archives of Industrial Hygiene and Occupational Medicine* 4 (1952): 314–25.

64. Davidson.

65. Pittsburgh Bureau of Smoke Prevention.

66. Tarr, p. 17.

67. Pittsburgh Bureau of Smoke Prevention.

68. Tarr, p. 229.

69. Arthur C. Stern, "History of Air Pollution Legislation in the United States," *Journal of the Air Pollution Control Association* 32 (1982): 44–61.

70. Stern.

71. Tarr, p. 70. This chapter is based on a paper originally written with Robert U. Ayres; see p. xvii.

72. Ibid., p. 69. Note that while an increase in control efficiency from 93 to 95 percent between 1940 and 1950 may seem trivial, that would, all else being equal, reduce emissions by about 30 percent by mass. Moreover, that would reduce the number of smaller particles by a greater amount, which ought to result in a disproportionately larger reduction in any public health–related impacts.

73. William W. Moore, "Reduction in Ambient Air Concentration of Fly Ash—Present and Future Prospects," in *Proceedings: The Third National Conference on Air Pollution*, PHS Publication No. 1649 (Washington: Government Printing Office, 1966), pp. 170–78.

74. James E. Krier and Edmund Ursin, *Pollution and Policy: A Case Essay on California and Federal Experience with Motor Vehicle Emission Control 1940–1977* (Berkeley, Calif.: University of California Press, 1977), p. 58.

75. Ibid., p. 65.

76. Ibid.; George H. Hagevik, *Decision-Making in Air Pollution Control: A Review of Theory and Practice, with Emphasis on Selected Los Angeles and New York Management Experiences* (New York: Praeger, 1970), pp. 81–127.

77. *Air Conservation: The Report of the Air Conservation Commission of the American Association for the Advancement of Science* (Washington: AAAS, 1965), pp. 119–120. However, Krier and Ursin, p. 72, note that many sources of emissions were not in the district's inventory.

78. Krier and Ursin, pp. 77–86; Hagevik, pp. 82–87, 121–22.

79. H. H. Schrenk, et al., *Air Pollution in Donora, Pa.: Epidemiology of the Unusual Smog Episode of October 1948, Preliminary Report*, PHS Bulletin No. 306 (Washington: Public Health Service, 1949).

80. Standards for air quality are normally established in terms of air pollutant concentrations at a fixed point in the outdoors over a specified period of time. One method of specifying air quality is based upon measuring the weight of pollutant, generally in micrograms (μg), in a fixed volume of air [1 cubic meter (m^3)]—that is, in terms of $\mu g/m^3$. An alternative approach is to specify the number of molecules of the pollutant in a million molecules of air—that is, parts per million (ppm). For instance, in the United States, the annual public health–related (or primary) air quality standard for sulfur dioxide is a never-to-be-exceeded average of 80 $\mu g/m^3$ or 0.03 ppm at any point outdoors. Similarly, the short-term public health and welfare standards for SO_2 are 365 $\mu g/m^3$ (0.14 ppm) for 24 hours and 1300 $\mu g/m^3$ (0.5 ppm) for 3 hours, respectively. Short-term standards are not to be exceeded more than once a year for any single outdoor point.

81. R. E. Waller and B. T. Cummins, "Episodes of High Pollution in London 1952–1966," in *Proceedings: Part I. International Clean Air Congress, London, 4–7 October 1966*, International Union of Air Pollution Prevention Association (London: National Society for Clean Air, 1966), pp. 228–31.

82. F. Pearce, "Back to the Days of Deadly Smogs," *New Scientist*, December 5, 1992, pp. 25–28.

83. Indur M. Goklany, "Factors Affecting Environmental Impacts: The Effects of Technology on Long-Term Trends in Cropland, Air Pollution and Water-Related Diseases," *Ambio* 25 (1996): 497–503.

84. Frederick W. Lipfert, "Sulfur Oxides, Particulates, and Human Mortality: Synopsis of Statistical Correlations," *Journal of the Air Pollution Control Association* 30 (1980), pp. 366–71; F. W. Lipfert, *Air Pollution and Community Health* (New York: Van Nostrand Reinhold, 1994).

85. Bureau of the Census, p. 60.

86. Samuel B. Hays, *Beauty, Health, and Permanence: Environmental Politics in the United States, 1955–1985* (Cambridge, U.K.: Cambridge University Press, 1987), pp. 34–35.

87. Lipfert, "Sulfur Oxides, Particulates, and Human Mortality"; Lipfert, *Air Pollution and Community Health*.

88. Jack C. Fensterstock and Robert K. Fankhauser, *Thanksgiving 1966 Air Pollution Episode in the Eastern United States*, National Air Pollution Control Administration, Publication AP-45 (Durham, N.C.: NAPCA, 1968), p. 35.

89. Jean J. Scheuneman, "A Roll Call of the Communities—Where Do We Stand in Local or Regional Air Pollution Control?" in *Proceedings: The Third National Conference on Air Pollution*, PHS Publication 1649 (Washington: Government Printing Office, 1966), pp. 386–99.

90. Charles D. Yaffe, "A Roll Call of the States—Where Do We Stand in State and Interstate Air Pollution Control?" in *Proceedings: The Third National Conference on Air Pollution*, pp. 359–63.

91. Sidney Edelman, "Air Pollution Abatement Procedures under the Clean Air Act," *Arizona Law Review* 10 (1968): 30–36; Department of Health, Education and Welfare, *Progress in the Prevention and Control of Air Pollution, First Report of the Secretary of Health, Education and Welfare to the United States Congress*, 90th Congress, 2d Session, Document 92 (Washington: Government Printing Office, 1968).

92. See, for example, Robert W. Crandall, *Controlling Industrial Pollution: The Economics and Politics of Clean Air* (Washington: Brookings Institution, 1983), p. 7; Reitze, p. 199; and Stern.

93. John T. Middleton, "Future Air Quality Standards and Motor Vehicle Emission Restrictions," in *Proceedings: The Third National Conference on Air Pollution*, pp. 45–54.

94. Krier and Ursin, pp. 146–47.

95. Ibid.

96. Ibid.

97. Krier and Ursin, pp. 146–51.

98. Ibid., pp. 150–53; Middleton.

99. World Health Organization/United Nations Environment Programme (WHO/UNEP), *Urban Air Pollution in the Megacities of the World*, published for Global Environment Monitoring System (GEMS), WHO, and UNEP (Cambridge, Mass.: Blackwell Reference, 1992).

100. Hugh W. Ellsaesser, "Trends in Air Pollution in the United States," in Julian L. Simon, ed., *The State of Humanity* (Oxford, U.K.: Blackwell, 1995), pp. 491–98.

101. Environmental Protection Agency, Office of Air and Water Programs, *Monitoring and Air Quality Trends Report, 1972*, EPA-450/1-73-004, pp. 4-23–4-26.

102. EPA, *Monitoring and Air Quality Trends Report, 1972*, 4–21.

103. See, for example, E. Donald Elliott, Bruce A. Ackerman, and John C. Millian, "Toward a Theory of Statutory Evolution: The Federalization of Environmental Law," *Journal of Law, Economics and Organization* 1 (1985): 313–40; *New York Times*, March 29, 1965, p. 39; September 11, 1965, p. 10.

104. John T. Middleton and Arie J. Haagen-Smit, "The Occurrence, Distribution, and Significance of Photochemical Air Pollution in the United States, Canada, and Mexico," *Journal of the Air Pollution Control Association* 11 (1961): 129–34. See also J. Cholak, L. J. Schafer, and D. W. Yeager, "The Concentration of Ozone in the Atmosphere of Certain American Cities," *Journal of the Air Pollution Control Association* 6 (1956): 227–32.

105. Herbert C. McKee, "What's in the Air?" in *Proceedings, National Conference on Air Pollution, Washington, DC, November 18–20, 1958*, Public Health Service Publication 654 (Washington: Government Printing Office, 1959), pp. 33–34.

106. S. Smith Griswold, "Regulation of New Motor Vehicles," in *Proceedings: The Third National Conference on Air Pollution*, PHS Publication 1649 (Washington: Government Printing Office, 1966), pp. 57–60.

107. National Air Pollution Control Administration, *Report for Consultation on the Metropolitan St. Louis Interstate Air Quality Control Region (Missouri–Illinois)*, December

1968; *Report for Consultation on the Metropolitan San Antonio Intrastate Air Quality Control Region (Texas)*, October 1969; *Report for Consultation on the San Francisco Bay Area Air Quality Control Region*, December 1968; *Report for Consultation on the Steubenville-Weirton-Wheeling Air Quality Control Region (Ohio, West Virginia)*, August 1969; *Report for Consultation on the Metropolitan Providence Interstate Air Quality Control Region (Rhode Island–Massachusetts)*, July 1969; *Report for Consultation on the Metropolitan Toledo Interstate Air Quality Control Region (Ohio–Michigan)*, November 1969; *Report for Consultation on the Phoenix–Tucson Intrastate Air Quality Control Region (Arizona)*, September 1969; *Report for Consultation on the Washington, D.C. National Capital Inter-state Air Quality Control Region*, July 1968; *Report for Consultation on the Metropolitan Chicago Interstate Air Quality Control Region (Indiana–Illinois)*, September 1968; *Report for Consultation on the Air Quality Control Region for the New Jersey–New York–Connecticut Interstate Area*, August 30, 1968.

108. *New York Times*, July 28, 1970, p. 33. See also Hagevik, who notes on p. 156 of *Decision-Making in Air Pollution Control*, written in 1970, that "the air pollution problems in Los Angeles and New York City are in some senses fundamentally different."

109. *New York Times*, July 28, 1970, p. 33. See also the discussion by Alexander Rihm, Assistant Commissioner of Health, New York State, "Regulation of New Motor Vehicles," in *Proceedings: The Third National Conference on Air Pollution*, pp. 61–63, which focuses on CO emissions from motor vehicles.

110. EPA, *Monitoring and Air Quality Trends Report, 1973*, EPA/450/R-93-032, Office of Air Quality Planning and Standards, October 1974, pp. 117–25.

111. Jan Gordon Laitos, *A Legal-Economic History of Air Pollution Controls* (Arlington, Va.: Carrollton Press, 1980), pp. 360–61, 368.

112. Senate Committee on Public Works, *A Legislative History of the Clean Air Act Amendments of 1970* (Washington: Government Printing Office, 1974), pp. 244–45.

113. Ibid.; Edmund S. Muskie, quoted in Senate Committee on Public Works, p. 228.

114. Edmund S. Muskie, "Role of the Federal Government in Air Pollution Control," *Arizona Law Review*, Vol. 10, 1968, pp. 17–24.

115. See, for example, David Schoenbrod, "Why States, Not EPA, Should Set Pollution Standards," *Regulation* 19 (No. 4), 1966, available at http://wwato.org/pubs/regulation/reg19n4a.html; Elliott, Ackerman, and Millian.

116. Frederick W. Bowditch, "Introductory Statement," in *Proceedings: The Third National Conference on Air Pollution*, pp. 76–77.

117. Rihm.

118. Senate Committee on Public Works, pp. 1104, 1126–36.

119. Council on Environmental Quality, *Environmental Quality 1970* (Washington: CEQ, 1970), p. 75.

120. See, for example, Elliott, Ackerman, and Millian, "Toward a Theory of Statutory Evolution"; Reitze, p. 1590.

121. See, for example, Conrad Simon and Edward F. Ferrand, "The Impact of Low Sulfur Fuel on Air Quality in New York City," in *Proceedings of the Second International Clean Air Congress* (New York: Academic Press, 1971), pp. 41–50.

122. Goklany, "Factors Affecting Environmental Impacts."

123. "In the last fifteen years the high stack has become almost symbolic of good industrial air pollution practice, and its use as an effective and economical device for reducing ground-level air pollution has become widespread." Thus started a paper by Maynard E. Smith, "Reduction of Ambient Air Concentrations of Pollutants

by Dispersion from High Stacks," in *Proceedings: The Third National Conference on Air Pollution*, pp. 151–60. That conference, held in December 1966 just after the Thanksgiving 1966 episode in New York City and other parts of the Northeast, was a major event that helped set the stage for the Air Quality Act of 1967; see Stern, p. 53. The conference, which occurred every four years, also heard from Vice President Humphrey, Senators Muskie, Nelson, and Boggs, Representatives Daddario, Dingell, and Ryan, and Secretaries Udall and Gardner, as well as other luminaries from federal, state, and local governments and agencies, industry and universities, and conservationists.

124. Baghouse technology came to utility boilers after 1970.

125. Environmental Protection Agency, data underpinning *National Air Pollutant Emission Trends, 1900–1994*, EPA/450/R-93-032, Office of Air Quality Planning and Standards, 1995, provided by Sharon Nizich.

126. H. Schimmel and T. J. Murawski, "SO$_2$—Harmful Pollutant or Air Quality Indicator?" *Journal of the Air Pollution Control Association*, 25 (1975): 739–40.

127. The 1972 level is based on the highest one-day reading reported in the city in EPA's data summary for 1972. See EPA, *Monitoring and Air Quality Trends Report 1972*, p. A-13.

128. Davidson; Environmental Protection Agency, AIRS Database, available electronically, 1994.

129. Allen V. Kneese, "Air Pollution—General Background and Economic Aspects," in Harold Wolozin, ed., *The Economics of Air Pollution* (New York: W. W. Norton), p. 23.

130. Ludwig, Morgan, and McMullen.

131. Reitze, p. 1589.

132. Paul R. Portney, ed., *Public Policies for Environmental Protection* (Washington: Resources for the Future, 1990), pp. 50–51.

133. Crandall, pp.16–31.

134. See, for example, Richard L. Revesz, "Rehabilitating Interstate Competition: Rethinking the'Race to the Bottom' Rationale for Federal Environmental Regulation," *New York University Law Review* 67 (December 1972); Henry N. Butler and Jonathan R. Macey, "Externalities and the Matching Principle: The Case for Reallocating Environmental Regulatory Authority," *Yale Law Policy Review, Yale Journal on Regulation, Symposium Issue: Constructing a New Federalism: Jurisdictional Competence and Competition* 14, no. 2 (Symposium) (1996): 23–66.

135. "So-called" because this "academic" definition of "race to the bottom," the one used in this book, conjures, for the nonspecialist, visions of uncontrolled chimneys and vehicles belching forth smoke and toxic fumes and episodes of killer smogs. In fact, as defined by academics, the end result of such a race does not have to be zero environmental safeguards but any level below what would be "optimal" from the point of view of net societal welfare, and a race to relax becomes a race to the bottom if, and only if, net societal welfare also declines. See, for example, Revesz, p. 1210; Peter P. Swire, "The Race to Laxity and the Race to Undesirability: Explaining Failures in Competition among Jurisdictions in Environmental Law," *Yale Law Policy Review, Yale Journal on Regulation, Symposium Issue: Constructing a New Federalism: Jurisdictional Competence and Competition* 14, no. 2 (Symposium) (1996): 67–110.

136. Schoenbrod.

137. *New York Times*, August 4, 1970, p. 61; see also *Congressional Record*, August 3, 1970, p. 26392.

138. Hubert H. Humphrey, "The Problem of Air Pollution," in *Proceedings: The Third National Conference on Air Pollution*, p. 10. See also note 123 above on that conference.

139. *New York Times*, January 11, 1969, p. 1. Seven minor companies were named as coconspirators.

140. *New York Times*, September 12, 1969, p. 1.

141. *New York Times*, February 22, 1970, p. 49; April 17, 1970, p. 43; September 9, 1970, p. 1.

142. *New York Times*, August 6, 1970, p. 54.

143. *New York Times*, February 8, 1970, p. 44; February 22, 1970, p. 49.

144. *New York Times*, August 4, 1970, p. 61.

145. In a mirror image of the jockeying for power at the national level, in New York the incumbents, Governor Rockefeller and Mayor Lindsay, were battling an array of potential contenders from other parties to establish their environmental records. *The New York Times Index* 1970 alone has a redoubtable four pages devoted just to stories on air pollution in the city and the associated politics. See *The New York Times Index 1970* (New York: New York Times Co., 1971), pp. 29–33.

146. CEQ, *Environmental Quality 1970*.

147. A detailed chronological account of the developments leading to the passage of this legislation can be found in Stern.

148. *New York Times*, May 13, 1970, p. 6; May 14, 1970, p. 10; May 16, 1970, p. 24; June 12, 1970, p. 38.

149. Edmund S. Muskie, September 21, 1970, quoted in Senate Committee on Public Works, Vol. 1, p. 225. The same quote can be found on p. 124, made on December 18, 1970.

150. Ibid., p. 226.

151. Indur M. Goklany, *The Federal Role in Improving Environmental Quality in the United States: Evidence from Long-Term Trends in Air Pollution*, presented at the American Society of Environmental History Conference on Government, Science and the Environment, Baltimore, Md., March 6–9, 1997. See also Portney, p. 92, footnote 12, which suggests 1973 or 1974.

152. Council on Environmental Quality, *Environmental Quality 1972* (Washington: CEQ, 1972), p. 111.

153. Council on Environmental Quality, *Environmental Quality 1973* (Washington: CEQ, 1973), pp. 157–59.

154. Office of Energy, Minerals, and Industry, Review of New Source Performance Standards for Coal-Fired Utility Boilers, Vol. I, EPA-600/7-78-155a (Washington: EPA, 1978), pp. vi, 2–9.

155. Council on Environmental Quality, *Environmental Quality 1975* (Washington: CEQ, 1975), p. 53.

156. Christopher J. Bailey, *Congress and Air Pollution* (Manchester, U.K.: Manchester University Press, 1998), p. 78.

157. Howard K. Gruenspecht, "Differentiated Regulations: The Case of Auto Emissions Standards," *American Economic Review* 72, no. 2 (1982): 328–31.

158. *Annual Energy Review 1995* (Washington: DOE/Energy Information Administration, 1996).

159. CEQ, *Environmental Quality, 1975*, pp. 123–24.

160. Reitze, pp. 1594–95.

161. Bailey, pp. 176–83.

162. The short time frames for developing, analyzing, and executing state implementation plans precluded any real analysis, particularly with the threat of sanctions. It led to widespread paper showings of attainment, and many states adopted technology-based standards for broad source categories as a substitute for credible analysis showing attainment. See Pacific Environmental Services, Inc., *An Overview of the SIP Review Process at the State Level and the SIP for Particulate Matter, Sulfur Dioxide and Ozone*, Report to the National Commission on Air Quality, NTIS no. PB81 1127573 (1980).

Chapter 2

1. Environmental Protection Agency, *Report to Congress on Indoor Air Quality Volume II: Assessment and Control of Air Pollution*, Office of Air and Radiation, EPA/400/1-89/001C, 1989.

2. GEOMET, Inc., *Comparison of Indoor and Outdoor Air Quality* (Palo Alto, Calif.: Electric Power Research Institute, 1981), p. ES-5.

3. Environmental Protective Agency, *Air Quality Criteria for Carbon Monoxide*, EPA/600/890/045F, 1991.

4. Environmental Protective Agency, *Air Quality Criteria for Oxides of Nitrogen: Volume 1*, Office of Research and Development, EPA/600/8-91-049aF, 1993.

5. Lance Wallace, "A Decade of Studies of Human Exposure: What Have We Learned?" *Risk Analysis* 13 (April 1993): 135–39; and Wayne Ott and John Roberts, "Everyday Exposure to Toxic Pollutants," *Scientific American* (February 1998): 86–91, both cited in Peter VanDoren, *Chemicals, Cancer, and Choices* (Washington: Cato Institute, 1999), p. 17.

6. Kirk R. Smith, "Fuel Combustion, Air Pollution Exposure, and Health: The Situation in Developing Countries," *Annual Review of Energy and the Environment* 18 (1993): 529–66.

7. Indur M. Goklany, "Factors Affecting Environmental Impacts: The Effects of Technology on Long-Term Trends in Cropland, Air Pollution and Water-Related Diseases," *Ambio* 25 (1996): 497–503. Indur M. Goklany, "Richer Is Cleaner: Long Term Trends in Global Air Quality," in Ronald Bailey, ed., *The True State of the Planet* (New York: Free Press, 1995), pp. 339–77. The emissions data used to construct this proxy are obtained from Sharon Nizich of EPA's Office of Air Quality Planning and Standards and were used in Environmental Protection Agency, *National Air Pollutant Emissions Trends, 1900–1994*, EPA-454/R-95-011, 1995. The demographic data were obtained from Bureau of the Census, *Historical Statistics of the United States: Colonial Times to 1970* (Washington: Government Printing Office, 1975); and Bureau of the Census, *Statistical Abstract of the United States 1992*.

8. EPA, *Report to Congress on Indoor Air Quality Volume II*.

9. Bureau of the Census, *Statistical Abstract of the United States 1992*.

Chapter 3

1. Environmental Protection Agency, *Air Quality Data for 1968 from the National Air Surveillance Networks and Contributing State and Local Networks*, Office of Air Programs, August 1972, p. 1-3.

2. See, for example, Environmental Protection Agency, *National Air Quality and Emissions Trends Report, 1994. Data Appendix*, Office of Air Quality Planning and Standards, EPA 454/R-95-XXX, (1995) (cited hereafter as *AQ Trends 1994*).

3. See, for example, National Academy of Sciences, *Air Quality and Stationary Emission Control*, prepared for the Committee on Public Works, U.S. Senate, Serial No. 94-4 (Washington: Government Printing Office, 1974).

4. Warren Freas, Office of Air Quality Planning and Standards, Environmental Protection Agency, personal communication, 1994.

5. See, for example, Environmental Protection Agency, *National Air Quality and Emissions Trends Report, 1992*, EPA 454/R-93-031, OAQPS 1993; A. Davidson, "Update on Ozone Trends in California's South Coast Air Basin," *Air & Waste*, vol. 43 (1993): 226–27.

6. Environmental Protection Agency, *National Air Quality and Emissions Trends Report, 1992*, EPA 454/R-93-031, OAQPS, 1993.

7. Environmental Protection Agency, *National Air Quality Levels and Trends in Total Suspended Particulate and Sulfur Dioxide Determined by Data in the National Air Sampling Network*, U.S. EPA, Office of Air Quality Planning and Standards, NTIS PB 227059, April 1973.

8. Cliff I. Davidson, "Air Pollution in Pittsburgh: A Historical Perspective," *Journal of the Air Pollution Control Association* 29 (1979): 1035–41. Figure 1-2 does not have any data from the war years.

9. J. H. Ludwig, G. B. Morgan, and T. B. McMullen, "Trends in Urban Air Quality," E0551 (1970).

10. Council on Environmental Quality, *Environmental Quality 1971* (p. 242), *1981* (p. 243), *1991* (Washington: CEQ); Council on Environmental Quality, *Environmental Statistics 1978* (Washington: Government Printing Office, 1979), p. 245 (cited hereafter as *Environmental Statistics 1978*); Environmental Protection Agency, *National Air Quality and Emissions Trends Report, 1990* (cited hereafter as *AQ Trends 1990*); EPA, *AQ Trends 1994, Data Appendix*, 1995; Environmental Protection Agency, *National Air Quality and Emissions Trends Report, 1996*, OAQPS, EPA 454/R-97-013, 1998, p. 88 (cited hereafter as *AQ Trends 1996*); Environmental Protection Agency, *National Air Quality and Emissions Trends Report, 1997*, OAQPS, EPA 454/R-98-016, 1999, p. 118 (cited hereafter as *AQ Trends 1997*).

11. CEQ, *Environmental Quality 1971*, p. 242.

12. Ibid.

13. Ibid.

14. Environmental Protection Agency, *The National Air Monitoring Program: Air Quality and Emissions Trends Annual Report, Volume 1*. OAQPS, EPA-450/1-73-001-a, 1973, Figure 4-4, pp. 4-8, 4-9, 4-11.

15. This average is based on the data from CEQ's *Environmental Quality 1971*, p. 242.

16. CEQ, *Environmental Quality 1981*, 243.

17. Environmental Protection Agency, *National Air Quality and Emissions Trends Report 1983*, OAQPS, EPA-450-4-84-029 1985, pp. 3-5–3-10.

18. EPA, *AQ Trends 1994*.

19. CEQ, *Environmental Quality 1971*; Bureau of the Census, *Statistical Abstract 1981*; EPA, *AQ Trends 1996, 1997*.

20. Environmental Protection Agency, *AIRSData Monitor Values Report*, available at http://www.epa.gov/airsdata/monvals.htm, March 7, 1999.

21. CEQ, *Environmental Quality 1981*, p. 243.

22. Environmental Protection Agency, *The National Air Monitoring Program: Air Quality and Emissions Trends Annual Report, Volume 1*. EPA-450/1-73-001-a 1973, pp. 1-8–1-10. Note that these data are not plotted in Figure 3-2 since the data for each year were not provided. See also p. 1-11.

23. EPA, *National Air Quality and Emissions Trend Report, 1992*.

24. EPA, *AQ Trends 1996; AQ Trends 1997;* Bureau of the Census, *Statistical Abstract 1981*, p. 204.

25. EPA, *Environmental Quality 1971* (p. 242), *1981* (p. 243), *1984* (p. 583); Bureau of the Census, *Statistical Abstract 1981*, p. 204; Freas; EPA, *AQ Trends 1997*.

26. CEQ, *Environmental Quality 1971, p. 242; Environmental Protection Agency, Air Quality Data for 1968* from the National Air Surveillance Networks, p. 1-3.

27. CEQ, *Environmental Quality 1971*, pp. 214 and 242.

28. This analysis excluded data from Washington, D.C., since that station was relocated in 1969. See Environmental Protection Agency, *The National Air Monitoring Program: Air Quality and Emissions Trends Annual Report, Volume 1*, p. 4-21.

29. Ibid., pp. 4-22–4-27.

30. Ibid., pp. 4-21, 4-23.

31. Ibid., pp. 4-21–4-29.

32. Environmental Protection Agency, *Monitoring and Air Quality Trends Report, 1972*, EPA-450/1-73-004, Office of Air and Water Programs, pp. 4-14–4-23.

33. Ibid. p. 4-23. The range in the frequency of these "would-be" exceedences in the peak year is attributable to the fact that Los Angeles County modified its instruments in 1968; the specified range accounts for uncertainties in converting pre-1968 readings into ones consistent with post-1968 instrumentation.

34. Ibid.

35. CEQ, *Environmental Quality 1971, 1981;* Bureau of the Census, *Statistical Abstract 1981; AQ Trends 1994, 1996, 1997*.

36. National Research Council, *Rethinking the Ozone Problem in Urban and Regional Air Pollution* (Washington: National Academy Press, 1991).

37. Indur M. Goklany et al., *Critique of Air Quality Analysis Methods Used to Establish Motor Vehicle Emission Standards*, Environmental Research and Technology, Concord, Mass., prepared for Volkswagen of America, Warren, Mich. (Concord, Mass.: Environmental Research and Technology, 1981); E. L. Meyer, Jr., *Review of Control Strategies for Ozone and Their Effects on Other Environmental Issues*, EPA-450/4-85-001, OAQPS, (Research Triangle Park, N.C.: Environmental Protection Agency, 1986); J. B. Milford, A. G. Russell, and G. J. McRae, "A New Approach to Photochemical Pollution Control: Implications of Spatial Patterns in Pollutant Responses to Reductions in Nitrogen Oxides and Reactive Organic Gas Emissions," *Environmental Science and Technology* 23 (1989): 1290–1301; National Research Council; J. S. Roselle, T. E. Pierce, and K. L. Schere, "The Sensitivity of Regional Ozone Modeling to Biogenic Hydrocarbons," *Journal of Geophysical Research* 96 (D4) (1991): 7371–94.

38. Goklany et al.; National Research Council; Roselle, Pierce, and Schere.

39. Based on data from Environmental Protection Agency, *National Air Pollutant Emissions Trends 1900–1992*, 6-14, 7-1, 7-11.

40. CEQ, *Environmental Quality 1981; AQ Trends 1994, 1996, 1997*.

41. EPA, *Monitoring and Air Quality Trends Report, 1972*, pp. 1-11–1-12.

42. Ibid., pp. 4-27–4-28.

43. J. H. Ludwig, G. B. Morgan, and T. B. McMullen, "Trends in Urban Air Quality."

44. See also EPA, *Monitoring and Air Quality Trends Report, 1972*, pp. 4-23–4-26.

45. Ibid., p. 4-26.

46. Ibid.

47. EPA, *AQ Trends 1994*.

48. World Health Organization/United Nations Environment Programme (WHO/UNEP), *Urban Air Pollution in the Megacities of the World* (Cambridge, Mass.: Blackwell Reference, 1992).

49. Environmental Protection Agency, *AIRS Executive Data Base*, January 3, 1997.

50. A. Davidson.

51. EPA, *AQ Trends 1994; AQ Trends 1997*, p. 173.

52. National Research Council.

53. CEQ, *Environmental Quality 1981, 1984;* Bureau of the Census, *Statistical Abstract 1981, 1988; AQ Trends 1994, 1996, 1997*.

54. EPA, *AQ Trends 1997*.

55. Ibid.

56. CEQ, *Environmental Quality*.

57. Indur M. Goklany, "Richer Is Cleaner: Long Term Trends in Global Air Quality," in Ronald Bailey, ed., *The True State of the Planet* (New York: Free Press, 1995). Indur M. Goklany, *Do We Need the Federal Government to Improve Air Quality?* Policy Study 150 (St. Louis, Mo.: Center for the Study of American Business, Washington University, December 1998).

58. R. B. Faoro and T. B. McMullen, *National Trends in Trace Metals in Ambient Air, 1965–1974*, OAQPS, EPA-450/1-77-003, NTIS PB 264906, 1977; Environmental Protection Agency, *National Air Quality and Emissions Trends Report 1992*, EPA, 454/R-93-031, 1993. EPA, *National Air Quality and Emissions Trends Report, 1983, 1985;* Bureau of the Census, *Statistical Abstract 1986, 1988;* Freas.

59. CEQ, *Environmental Quality 1984;* Bureau of the Census, *Statistical Abstract 1988;* EPA, *AQ Trends 1996, 1997*.

60. EPA, *National Air Quality and Emissions Trends Report, 1997*.

61. D. Brown, "Lead Level in Americans' Blood Has Fallen 75% since the Late '70s," *Washington Post*, July 27, 1994.

Chapter 4

1. EPA, *National Air Pollutant Emission Trends Update, 1970–1997*, Office of Air Quality Planning and Standards, EPA 454/E-98-007 1998 (cited hereafter as *1997 Trends Update* or *1997 Update*). The data used in these reports were furnished by Sharon Nizich and Thomas McMullen of OAQPS in e-mails sent on January 1, 1999, and February 2, 1999.

2. These data were obtained from Sharon Nizich by e-mail, April 1996, and served as the basis for *National Air Pollutant Emissions Trends, 1900–1994*, OAQPS, EPA-454/R-95-011, 1995 (cited hereafter as *1994 Trends Report*). Chapter 6 of that report describes methodologies used to derive these emissions.

3. One exception seems to be the PM-10 estimate for 1940, which was lowered from 15,946,000 to 15,747,000 short tons between the *1994 Trends Report* and the *1997 Update*, a difference of 1.25 percent.

4. Notably, compared to the *1994 Emissions Trends Report*, the 1970 national emissions data from the *1997 Trends Update* for CO, NOx, VOC, and PM-10 emissions are 0.1, 2.7, 0.3, and 0.2 percent higher, respectively. While this may result in minor discontinuities going from 1969 to 1970, the differences are relatively minor given the various sources of uncertainties.

5. Bureau of Economic Analysis, "Summary Data, 1929–97," from the *Survey of Current Business*, August 1998, available at http://www.bea.doc.gov/bea/dn/0898nip3/maintext.htm, March 10, 1999.

6. *Historical Statistics*, 224.

7. Indur M. Goklany, "Factors Affecting Environmental Impacts: The Effects of Technology on Long-Term Trends in Cropland, Air Pollution and Water-Related Diseases," *Ambio* 25 (1996): 497–503.

8. Barry Commoner, "The Environmental Cost of Economic Growth," *Chemistry in Britain* 8 (1972): 52–65; Paul R. Ehrlich and John R. Holdren, "Impact of Population Growth," *Science* 171 (1971): 1212–17; Paul R. Ehrlich and Anne H. Ehrlich, *Healing the Planet* (New York: Simon and Schuster, 1991), p. 7.

9. Goklany, "Factors Affecting Environmental Impacts"; Indur M. Goklany, *The Federal Role in Improving Environmental Quality in the United States: Evidence from Long Term Trends in Air Pollution,* presented at the American Society of Environmental History Conference on Government, Science and the Environment, Baltimore, Md., March 6–9, 1997.

10. Goklany, "Factors Affecting Environmental Impacts."

11. Indur M. Goklany, "Strategies to Enhance Adaptability: Technological Change, Economic Growth and Free Trade," *Climatic Change* 30 (1995): 427–49; Indur M. Goklany, "Saving Habitat and Conserving Biodiversity on a Crowded Planet," *BioScience* 48 (1998): 941–53; Indur M. Goklany, "Meeting Global Food Needs: The Environmental Trade-Offs between Increasing Land Conversion and Land Productivity," *Technology* (formerly *Journal of the Franklin Institute, Part A*) 6 (1999): 107–30.

12. Ibid.

13. EPA, *1994 Trends Report; 1997 Update.*

14. Ibid.

15. The trough during the war years was probably due to gasoline rationing at a time when the GNP grew rapidly. Similar troughs are evident for both NO_x and CO (see Figures 4-5 and 4-7).

16. EPA, *1997 Update.*

17. Goklany, "Factors Affecting Environmental Impacts"; Indur M. Goklany, "Richer Is Cleaner: Long Term Trends in Global Air Quality," in Ronald Bailey, ed., *The True State of the Planet* (New York: Free Press, 1995).

18. EPA, *1997 Update.*

19. David Schoenbrod, *Power without Responsibility: How Congress Abuses the People through Delegation* (New Haven, Conn.: Yale University Press, 1993): p. 78; and David Schoenbrod, testimony, Subcommittee on Commercial and Administrative Law, Judiciary Committee, U.S. House of Representatives, September 12, 1996, available at ⟨http://www.cato.org/testimony/ct-ds091296.html⟩.

Chapter 5

1. Calculated from data on GNP and population from Bureau of the Census, *Historical Statistics of the United States: Colonial Times to 1970* (Washington: Government Printing Office, 1975); and Bureau of the Census, *Statistical Abstract of the United States 1996.*

2. Thomas M. Selden and Daqing Song, "Environmental Quality and Development: Is There a Kuznets Curve for Air Pollution?" *Journal of Environmental Economics and Management* 27 (1994): 147–62; Gene Grossman and Alan Krueger, *Environmental Impacts of a North American Free Trade Agreement,* Discussion Paper No. 158 (Princeton, N.J.: Woodrow Wilson School, Princeton University, 1991).

3. Indur M. Goklany, *Air and Inland Surface Water Quality: Long Term Trends and Relationship to Affluence* (Washington: U.S. Department of the Interior / Office of Policy Analysis, 1994); Indur M. Goklany, "Strategies to Enhance Adaptability: Technological Change, Sustainable Growth and Free Trade,"*Climatic Change* 30 (1995): 427–49; Indur M. Goklany, "Saving Habitat and Conserving Biodiversity on a Crowded Planet," *BioScience* 48 (1998): 941–53; Goklany, "Richer Is Cleaner: Long-Term Trends in Global Air Quality," in Ronald Bailey, ed., *The True State of the Planet* (New York: Free Press, 1995).

4. In Goklany, "Strategies to Enhance Adaptability," it is noted that there are points of similarity between the theories of demographic transition and environmental transition.

5. Goklany, *Air and Inland Surface Water Quality*; Goklany, "Strategies to Enhance Adaptability"; Goklany, "Saving Habitat and Conserving Biodiversity"; Goklany, "Richer Is Cleaner."

6. Hays, *Beauty, Health, and Permanence, Environmental Politics in the United States, 1955–1985* (Cambridge, U.K.: Cambridge University Press, 1987), pp. 34–35.

7. Indur M. Goklany, "Factors Affecting Environmental Impacts: The Effects of Technology on Long-Term trends in Cropland, Air Pollution and Water-Related Diseases," *Ambio* 25 (1996): 497–503; Goklany, "Strategies to Enhance Adaptability."

8. Goklany, "Strategies to Enhance Adaptability."

9. Ibid.; Goklany, *Air and Inland Surface Water Quality*; Goklany, "Strategies to Enhance Adaptability"; Goklany, "Saving Habitat and Conserving Biodiversity"; Goklany, "Richer Is Cleaner."

10. Grossman and Krueger; Selden and Song.

11. "Of sorts" because, as noted, E/cap and E/GNP are *leading,* rather than genuine, environmental indicators.

12. Bureau of the Census, *Historical Statistics*, 137.

13. Ibid.

14. Bureau of the Census, *Statistical Abstract of the United States 1998*, p. 421.

15. Trends in VOC emissions from residential combustion emissions per occupied housing unit may not be a good proxy for VOC concentrations indoors. See Chapter 2.

16. Greenwire, "Oil Drilling: FL Ruling Gives Enviros Victory," http://www.cloakroom.com, March 31, 1999; Greenwire, "Natural Resources—Oil Drilling: Florida Files Objections to Chevron Rig," ⟨http://www.cloakroom.com⟩, June 24, 1998; Greenwire, "Natural Resources—Oil Drilling: Florida Enviros Fight Chevron Rig," http://www.cloakroom.com, June 12, 1998; Greenwire, "Energy—Drilling: Offshore Gas Moratorium to Stay in Place," http://www.cloakroom.com, August 2, 1993.

17. Greenwire, "Worldview—Nuclear Power: Countries Looking for New Power Sources," http://wwww.cloakroom.com, February 16, 1999; Greenwire, "Worldview—Nuclear Power: EU: Enviros Call for Action on Climate, Eco-Taxes," http://wwww.cloakroom.com, July 14, 1998.

18. Such balancing need not be—and, in fact, is rarely—done formally. It can be done "informally" via the political process. See Chapter 8.

19. Goklany, "Richer Is Cleaner," p. 371, n. 4.

20. Goklany, "Strategies to Enhance Adaptability"; Goklany, "Saving Habitat and Conserving Biodiversity."

21. S. M. de Bruyn, J. C. J. M. van den Bergh, and J. B. Opschoor, "Economic Growth and Emissions: Reconsidering the Empirical Basis of Environmental Kuznets Curves," *Ecological Economics* 25 (1998): 161–75.

22. Note that the distance along the affluence axis between points T_B and T_A on the curve for country A depends upon its rate of economic growth, and it does not have to be equal to the corresponding distance for country B.

23. Several international agreements have differential obligations for nations—for example, the Montreal Protocol for chlorofluorocarbons, or the Kyoto Protocol for greenhouse gases.

24. Grossman and Krueger; Nemat Shafik and S. Bandopadhyay, *Economic Growth and Environmental Quality: Time Series and Cross-Country Evidence*, Policy Research Working Papers (Washington: World Bank, June 1992).

25. Goklany, "Air and Inland Surface Water Quality"; Goklany, "Richer Is Cleaner."

26. Mariano Torras and James K. Boyce, "Income, Inequality, and Pollution: A Reassessment of the Environmental Kuznets," *Ecological Economics* 25 (1998): 147–60. Dale S. Rothman and Sander M. De Bruyn, "Probing into the Environmental Kuznets Curve Hypothesis," *Ecological Economics* 25 (1998): 143–45.

27. Luxembourg is ranked first. World Resources Institute, *World Resources: 1998–99 Database* (Washington: WRI, 1998).

28. Organization for Economic Cooperation and Development, *Environmental Data Compendium 1997* (Paris: OECD, 1997). Ten of the eleven countries for which data are available are in the list of the top twenty wealthiest nations, which list includes the oil-rich nations and Hong Kong and Singapore. The eleventh country is the Czech Republic, which is ranked much lower.

29. Based on 1994 data from WRI, *World Resources: 1998–99 Database.*

30. I use 1993 because that has the most data points for the countries with PPP-adjusted GDPs greater than $18,000.

31. This analysis used data for Canada, the United States, Japan, Belgium, France, Germany, Luxembourg, Norway, and the United Kingdom (i.e., n = 9). The year 1993 was used because n shrinks to 6 in 1994 and to 4 in 1995. The GDP per capita data were obtained from OECD, *OECD in Figures 1998* (Paris: OECD, 1998).

32. Indur M. Goklany, *Do We Need the Federal Government to Protect Air Quality?* Policy Study no. 150 (St. Louis, Mo.: Center for the Study of American Business, Washington University, 1998), pp. 30–31; Torras and Boyce.

33. Indur M. Goklany, "Adaptation and Climate Change," paper presented at the Annual Meeting of the American Association for the Advancement of Science, Chicago, February 6–11, 1992; Goklany, "Strategies to Enhance Adaptability"; Goklany, "Saving Habitat and Conserving Biodiversity"; Goklany, "Richer Is Cleaner."

34. Torras and Boyce.

35. De Bruyn et al.

36. Intergovernmental Panel on Climate Change, *Climate Change: The IPCC Scientific Assessment* (Cambridge, U.K.: Cambridge University Press, 1990).

37. Indur M. Goklany, "The Importance of Climate Change Compared to Other Global Changes," in *Global Climate Change—Science, Policy, and Mitigation/Adaptation Strategies, Proceedings of the Second International Specialty Conference: Washington, D.C., October 13–16, 1998* (Pittsburgh: Air and Waste Management Association, 1999); Indur M. Goklany, "Richer Is More Resilient: Dealing with Climate Change and More Urgent Environmental Problems," in Ronald Bailey, ed., *Earth 2000: Revisiting the True State of the Planet* (New York: McGraw-Hill, 1999); Goklany, "Adaptation and Climate Change"; Goklany, "Strategies to Enhance Adaptability."

38. Goklany, "Factors Affecting Environmental Impacts."

Chapter 6

1. John P. Dwyer, "The Practice of Federalism under the Clean Air Act," *Maryland Law Review* 54 (1995): 1191,1193 (footnotes 32, 37). See also Richard B. Stewart, "Pyramids of Sacrifice? Problems of Federalism in Mandating State Implementation of National Environmental Policy," *Yale Law Journal* 86 (1977): p. 1197: "The failure of prior efforts (heavily dependant on state initiatives) to check air pollution prompted Congress to enact the 1970 Clean Air Amendments."

2. Robert V. Percival, "Environmental Federalism: Historical Roots and Contemporary Models," *Maryland Law Review* 54 (1995): 1160–61.

3. EPA, *The National Air Monitoring Program: Air Quality and Emissions Trends Annual Report, Volume 1,* Office of Air Quality Planning and Standards, EPA-450/1-73-001-a, 1973, p. 4-6.

4. Ibid., p. 4-10.

5. Ibid., p. 4-11.

6. Ibid., p. 4-16.

7. Environmental Protection Agency, *Monitoring and Air Quality Trends Report, 1972,* EPA-450/1-73-004, 1973, p. 1-6.

8. See notes 1 and 2 above (same references).

9. John H. Ludwig, George B. Morgan and Thomas B. McMullen, "Trends in Urban Air Quality," *EOS* 51 (1970): 468–75. This paper notes that it had been presented previously at a meeting of the American Geophysical Union in San Francisco on December 17, 1969. The authors include an assistant commissioner of NAPCA (Ludwig) and the director of the Division of Air Quality and Emissions Data, also within NAPCA (Morgan). Thus, it is somewhat surprising to see in the CEQ's first report issued in August 1970 (*Environmental Quality 1970,* p. 87) and introduced into the Congressional Record, and in a *Legislative History of the Clean Air Act Amendments of 1970* (Washington: Government Printing Office, 1974) p. 255, that instead of these (or updated) trends, there is a statement about how difficult it is to develop trends. Perhaps—like Sherlock Holmes' celebrated "dog that did not bark"—there is a story here, or maybe one is reading too much into this chain of events.

10. Percival, p. 1161.

11. It could be argued that more extensive monitoring would not have been undertaken without federalization; however, this cannot be used as justification for the wholesale federalization effected under the Clean Air Amendments of 1970, since as noted in the text, the forerunners of EPA had been monitoring air pollutants since the mid-1950s, and could have continued—and expanded—monitoring programs without the benefit of the 1970 act.

12. Environmental Protection Agency, *USA Air Quality Nonattainment Areas,* http://www.epa.gov/airs/nonattn.html, March 14, 1999.

13. Ibid.

14. See, for example, Richard L. Revesz, "Rehabilitating Interstate Competition: Rethinking the 'Race-to-the-Bottom' Rationale for Environmental Regulation," *New York University Law Review* 67 (December 1972): p. 1210; Peter P. Swire, "The Race to Laxity and the Race to Undesirability: Explaining Failures in Competition among Jurisdictions in Environmental Law," *Yale Law Policy Review, Yale Journal on Regulation, Symposium Issue: Constructing a New Federalism: Jurisdictional Competence and Competition* 14, no. 2 (Symposium) (1996): 67–110. The latter describes the "race to the bottom" as one that is simultaneously a "race to laxity" and "race to undesirability," and NIMBY as one that is both a "race to strictness" and a "race to undesirability."

15. This does not mean that in some jurisdictions regulations would not have been more stringent but for interjurisdictional competition. It does show, however, that the behavior is much more complex than that suggested by the Prisoner's Dilemma—that in fact jurisdictions were attempting to improve their quality of life, even if they risked adverse economic effects.

16. National Air Pollution Control Administration, *Report for Consultation on the Metropolitan St. Louis Interstate Air Quality Control Region (Missouri-Illinois)*, December 1968; *Report for Consultation on the Steubenville-Weirton-Wheeling Air Quality Control Region (Ohio, West Virginia)*, August 1969; *Report for Consultation on the Metropolitan Providence Interstate Air Quality Control Region (Rhode Island-Massachusetts)*, July 1969; *Report for Consultation on the Metropolitan Toledo Interstate Air Quality Control Region (Ohio-Michigan)*, November 1969; *Report for Consultation on the Washington, D.C., National Capital Interstate Air Quality Control Region*, July 1968; *Report for Consultation on the Metropolitan Chicago Interstate Air Quality Control Region (Indiana-Illinois)*, September 1968; *Report for Consultation on the Air Quality Control Region for the New Jersey-New York-Connecticut Interstate Area*, August 30, 1968.

17. Terry L. Stumph and Robert L. Duprey, "Trends in Air Pollution Control Regulations," in *A Legislative History of the Clean Air Act Amendments of 1970* (Washington: Government Printing Office, 1974), p. 1120.

18. Ibid., pp. 1110–1111.

19. Dwyer, p. 1223.

20. In response to the argument against "externalization" of control costs—namely, that politicians have to be careful not to burden their constituents with a higher cost of living lest the voters extract vengeance at the ballot box—it could be said that it is, at best, a weak argument, particularly for items less visible than automobiles since, by and large, regulations can and have raised their cost relatively unobtrusively. In fact, because several years may often elapse between the passage of legislation and consequent regulations becoming effective, it is possible for politicians to take credit for passing "symbolic" bills over one or more election cycles, before the bill to the consumer actually comes due. And even after that, it is unclear whether consumers would distinguish increased costs resulting from such legislation from those attributable to "routine" inflation. The strength of the argument and the counterargument can be checked by conducting an informal poll of one's acquaintances and asking them if they know what are the costs of the Clean Air Act. The chances are that most people, including the intelligent lay public, will be able to rattle off the numerous nonquantitive and nonquantified benefits of clean air more easily than they will be able to specify the resulting increase in the costs of various items.

21. Stumph and Duprey, pp. 1105–25. Process weight regulations generally specify, on a sliding scale, allowable emissions based upon the total material input to a process. The sliding scale gets more stringent as the amount of material input increases. This document, prepared by NAPCA, was included in a response to several questions addressed by Senator Muskie, as chairman of the Senate Subcommittee on Air and Water Pollution, to Secretary Finch, Department of Health, Education and Welfare, on April 8, 1970 (see *A Legislative History*, p. 1033).

22. Ibid.; Herbert F. Lund, "Air Pollution Criteria for Industrial Plant Equipment," in *Proceedings: The Third National Conference on Air Pollution*, Public Health Service Publication 1649 (Washington: Government Printing Office, 1966), pp. 212–13; and subsequent "Questions and Comments," pp. 221–22. See also Morton Sterling, "Current Status and Future Prospects—Foundry Air Pollution Control," in the same

Proceedings (pp. 254–59), who gives an indication of Los Angeles' aggressive approach to controlling air pollution—in this case, particulate matter from foundries.

23. James E. Krier and Edmund Ursin, *Pollution and Policy: A Case Essay on California and Federal Experience with Motor Vehicle Emission Control 1940–1977* (Berkeley, Calif.: University of California Press, 1977).

24. Krier and Ursin, pp. 138–69. According to Krier and Ursin, 11 counties with 80 percent of all vehicles registered did not opt out (p. 148).

25. Ibid.

26. Bureau of the Census, *Statistical Abstract of the United States 1996,* p. 417. In 1996, 74 percent of the nonfarm jobs were in sectors other than mining, construction, manufacturing, transportation, and public utilities. Note that the last two (transportation and public utilities) are classified by the *Statistical Abstract* as part of the "service-producing" sector.

27. Greenwire, "State Reports—Florida: State Seeks Complete Ban on Gulf Drilling," February 3, 1995; "Across the Nation—Gov. Signs Bill to Impeded Oil Drilling," May 30, 1997; both available at http://cloakroom.com/pubs/greenwire/extra/search.htm/Greenwire/Green.

28. This argument, with its focus on attracting new investments and enterprises, is somewhat different from the Florida example in the previous paragraph, where the concern was to retain existing enterprises.

29. "Best Places to Live, 1998, How We Decided," *Money,* http://pathfinder.com/money/bestplaces/how.html, November 8, 1998; Carla Fried, "The Best Places to Live in America," *Money* 26 (July 1997): 132–49; *Money* 25 (July 1996); *Money* 24 (September 1995): 139; *Money* 23 (September 1994): 136; *Money* 22 (September 1993): 134; *Money* 21 (September 1992): 115; *Money* 20 (September 1991): 140.

30. It is conceivable that if, in the future, air quality is "good enough" in most of the country, the ability to use air quality to discriminate between the quality of life in different locations could decline and the apparent importance of clean air could drop in *Money's* annual poll of readers, not because its real importance would be any less but because the fight over dirty air would largely have been won.

31. The latest survey uses a different methodology since it was conducted on the Internet. Because that as well as previous years' surveys were based upon volunteered responses, their results are probably not representative of the United States as a whole. However, see the following note.

32. Arguably, the average *Money* reader is perhaps more representative of the people who help make decisions about locating new businesses than is the average American.

33. Stewart, pp. 1196–1272, was perhaps most instrumental in advancing the race-to-the-bottom rationale for federalization. A very readable description of the game-theoretic model underpinning that rationale is provided in Kirsten H. Engel, "State Environmental Standard Setting: Is There a 'Race' and Is It 'to the Bottom'?" *Hastings Law Journal* 48 (1997): 271–377.

34. The Prisoners' Dilemma model, which is the basis for the race-to-the-bottom rationale, may be more appropriate for financial and business regulations; in those instances, because the general public has little or no interest in or understanding of the issues, it is possible for both states and firms to pursue one-dimensional strategies.

35. Engel.

36. For an action to be economically efficient, marginal benefits must be at least as great as marginal costs. It is therefore possible for aggregate benefits to exceed

aggregate costs and still run afoul of the economic efficiency criterion. As used in this paper, "overregulation" implies that marginal costs exceed marginal benefits.

37. Engel, pp. 279–300.

38. 42 U.S. Code, Section 7409 (b) (1994).

39. Some have argued that EPA, in fact, has, in my terminology, underregulated since it has shied away from imposing transportation control measures. See, for example, Martin Bern, "Government Regulation and the Development of Environmental Ethics under the Clean Air Act," *Ecology Law Quarterly* 17: 539–80 (see pp. 550–51). However, underregulation of transportation and traffic can coexist with overregulation of the industrial sectors. The inability of EPA to follow through on transportation controls, coincidentally, also shows that in the face of determined opposition, the federal government can fold almost as easily as any state government.

40. Arguably, the difference in air quality ought not to be more than trivial because state officials cannot afford a relaxation that would extend nonattainment or violate either NAAQS or PSD increments, since that would make them even less competitive with respect to attracting new industry.

Chapter 7

1. Environmental Protection Agency, *USA Air Quality Nonattainment Areas*, ⟨http://www.epa.gov/airs/nonattn.html⟩, March 14, 1999.

2. John A. Danielson, ed., *Air Pollution Engineering Manual*, 2d ed., AP-40 (Research Triangle Park, N.C.: Environmental Protection Agency, 1973). This reference is a testimony to the importance of the federal government's role in helping disseminate information related to environmental matters.

3. Danielson, pp. 919–21.

4. U.S. Environmental Protection Agency, Office of Policy, Planning and Evaluation, *The Benefits and Costs of the Clean Air Act: 1970 to 1990* (Washington: EPA, 1997) (cited hereafter as EPA Benefit-Cost Study).

5. EPA, "National Air Pollutant Emissions Trends, 1900–1996," EPA-454/R-97-011 (Research Triangle Park, N.C.: Environmental Protection Agency, 1997), pp. 3-8, 3-15; David Schoenbrod. "Administrative Rulemaking," Testimony before the Subcommittee on Commercial and Administrative Law, Judiciary Committee, U.S. House of Representatives, September 12, 1996, available at http://www.cato.org/testimony/ct-ds091296.html. Schoenbrod briefly describes the decade-and-a-half long struggle he led as a lawyer for the Natural Resources Defense Council to have EPA reduce lead in gasoline used by pre-1975 automobiles (unleaded gasoline was already required for 1975 and later models). He notes that EPA was, in effect, protecting emissions control devices—not children—from lead. EPA finally resolved this lead-in-gasoline issue for pre-1975 autos in 1986, by which time "most of [these older] cars . . . had gone to the scrap heap."

6. EPA Benefit-Cost Study, p. 14.

7. Randall W. Lutter, "An Analysis of the Use of EPA's Benefit Estimates in OMB's Draft Report on the Costs and Benefits of Regulation," AEI-Brookings Joint Center for Regulatory Studies, Comment 98-2, Washington, D.C., October 1998.

8. EPA Benefit-Cost Study, p. ES-7.

9. Bureau of the Census, *Statistical Abstract of the United States 1998* (Washington: Government Printing Office, 1998), pp. 118, 451.

10. EPA Benefit-Cost Study, pp. 57–58.

11. Tammy O. Tengs et al., "Five-Hundred Life-Saving Interventions and Their Cost-Effectiveness," *Risk Analysis* 15 (1995): 369–90; Tammy O. Tengs and John D. Graham, "The Opportunity Costs of Haphazard Social Investments in Life-Saving," in Robert W. Hahn, ed., *Risks, Costs, and Lives Saved: Getting Better Results from Regulation* (New York: Oxford University Press, 1996), pp. 167–82.

12. John D. Graham, "An Investor's Look at Life-Saving Opportunities," *Risk in Perspective* 7 (1999): 1–4. Graham's values are for dollars per "quality-adjusted life-year," which adjusts a life-year downward if the quality of life for the years by which life has been extended is impaired. Had Graham used dollars per life-year saved (as EPA used in its estimate), the value would have been smaller.

13. Ibid.

14. Bureau of the Census, p. 104.

15. Ibid., p. 451.

16. Ibid., pp. 118, 451. Note that these health expenditures do not include the share of the GDP devoted to controlling air or other pollution, although the rationale for those expenditures is largely posited upon improving public health. See Indur M. Goklany, "Rationing Health Care While Writing Blank Checks for Environmental Health Hazards," *Regulation* (Summer 1992): 14–15.

17. Bureau of the Census, p. 149.

18. Ibid., p. 451. The value of eliminating one case of chronic bronchitis was recalculated by using the GDP deflator.

19. R. A. Cohen and J. F. Van Norstrand, "Vital and Health Statistics: Trends in Health of Older Americans: United States 1994," *Analytic and Epidemiological Studies*, series 3, http://www.aoa.dhhs.gov/stats/agetrend/wk1.html#chap2, April 16, 1999.

20. Bureau of the Census, p. 149.

21. Cohen and Van Norstrand; John. G. Collins, "Prevalence of Selected Chronic Conditions: United States, 1990–1992," *Vital and Health Statistics*, series 10, no. 194 (Washington: Government Printing Office, 1997), p. 13.

22. S. Rappaport and B. Boodram, "Forecasted State-Specific Estimates of Self-Reported Asthma Prevalence—United States, 1998," *Mortality and Morbidity Weekly Report* 47 (1998): 1022–25.

23. Ibid.; David M. Mannino et al., "Surveillance for Asthma—United States, 1960–1995," *Mortality and Morbidity Weekly Report* 47 (1998): 1–28; Gretchen Vogel, "Why the Rise in Asthma Cases?" *Science* 276 (1998): 1645.

24. Mannino.

25. EPA Benefit-Cost Study, pp. 54–55.

26. This result is not substantially changed if I use data only from 1960 to 1970. The best linear fit for that segment is provided by the equation E/GNP = 0.588 – 0.0192 (YEAR – 1950) with R^2 = 0.97 and p < 0.001.

27. EPA Benefit-Cost Study, p. B-36.

28. Robert D. Brenner and Richard D. Morgenstern, "In Response to 'Clearing the Air,'" *Regulation* 19, No. 4 (1996) http://www.cato.org/regulation/reg19n4c.html, April 6, 1999.

29. This analysis uses E/GNP equal to unity in 1900. See Figure 4-3.

30. EPA Benefit-Cost Study, p. B-36.

31. Alan J. Krupnick, *The Proposed National Ambient Air Quality Standards (NAAQS) for Particulate Matter (PM) and Ozone (Panel 1)*, testimony before the U.S. Senate Subcommittee on Clean Air, Wetlands, Private Property and Nuclear Safety, Committee on Environment and Public Works, April 24, 1997, http://www.rff.org/testimony/remarks/naaqs1.htm, April 19, 1999.

32. EPA Benefit-Cost Study, p. B-37.

33. See also Robert W. Crandall, Frederick H. Reuter and Wilbur A. Steger, "Clearing the Air: EPA's Self-Assessment of Clean-Air Policy," *Regulation* 19, No. 4 (1996), http://www.cato.org/regulation/reg19n4c.html, April 6, 1999.

34. Lutter; Crandall et al.; George T. Wolff, "Guest Commentary: In Response to the PM Debate," *Regulation* 20 (No. 1) (1997), http://www.cato.org/regulation/reg20n1d.html, April 6, 1999.

35. Brenner and Morgenstern.

36. See, for example, Thomas Tietenberg, *Emissions Trading, An Exercise in Reforming Pollution Policy* (Washington: Resources for the Future, 1985).

37. Council on Environmental Quality, "New Source Performance Standards and the 'Bubble' Concept," *Environmental Quality* (Washington: Council on Environmental Quality, 1984), pp. 59–65.

38. Anne Smith, Jeremy Platt, and A. Denny Ellerman, "The Cost of Reducing SO_2 (It's Higher Than You Think)," *Public Utilities Fortnightly* 136 (May 15, 1998). Smith et al. note that although emissions trading under Title IV (for acidic deposition control) of the 1990 Clean Air Act Amendments has substantially reduced control costs compared to what they would have been under a command-and-control approach, it is premature to compare current costs with projections made at the time the amendments were passed since not all elements of Title IV regulations are yet in place.

39. "Overall, SO_2 emissions from all sources are more than 6 million tons below their 1980 levels. Not only are emissions reductions greater than expected, but compliance costs are now expected to be half that originally projected. The flexibility offered by the SO_2 allowance trading system deserves much of the credit." Brian McLean, *Fifth Annual SO_2 Allowance Auctions*, March 26, 1997, at http://www.epa.gov/acidrain/auctions/auc97tlk.html.

40. Indur M. Goklany, "Rationing Health Care While Writing Blank Checks for Environmental Health Hazards," *Regulation* (Summer 1992): 14–15.

41. Z. Meng, D. Dabdub, and J. H. Seinfeld, "Chemical Coupling between Atmospheric Ozone and Particulate Matter," *Science* 277 (1997): 116–19.

42. Alan J. Krupnick and Paul R. Portney, "Controlling Urban Air Pollution: A Benefit-Cost Assessment," *Science* 252 (1991): 522–28; J. W. Anderson, *Revising the Air Quality Standards: A Briefing Paper on the Proposed National Ambient Air Quality Standards for Particulate Matter and Ozone*, Issues Brief, February 1997, http://www.rff.org/issue_briefs/PDF_files/ozprimer.htm#ozprimer, April 19, 1999.

43. Z. Meng, D. Dabdub, and J. H. Seinfeld; National Research Council, *Rethinking the Ozone Problem in Urban and Regional Air Pollution* (Washington: National Academy Press, 1991).

44. CEQ, "New Source Performance Standards."

45. See, for example, Marvin Soroos, *The Endangered Atmosphere: Preserving a Global Commons* (Columbia, S.C.: University of South Carolina Press, 1997).

46. Richard L. Revesz, "Federalism and Environmental Regulation: A Normative Critique" in John Ferejohn and Barry Weingast, eds., *Federalism: Can the States Be Trusted?* (Hoover Institution, forthcoming); John P. Dwyer, "The Practice of Federalism under the Clean Air Act," *Maryland Law Review* 54 (1995): 1183–1225; Kirsten H. Engel, "State Environmental Standard Setting: Is There a 'Race' and Is It 'to the Bottom'?" pp. 285–87.

47. Office of Technology Assessment, "Acid Rain and Transported Air Pollutants: Implications for Public Policy" (Washington: Government Printing Office, 1984) p. 13.

48. Office of Technology Assessment, "Catching Our Breath: Next Steps to Reduce Urban Ozone" (Washington: Government Printing Office, 1989), pp. 3–26.

49. Brian McLean, *Fifth Annual SO$_2$ Allowance Auctions*, March 26, 1997, at http://www.epa.gov/acidrain/auctions/auc97tlk.html; Smith et al.

50. Ibid.

51. Council on Environmental Quality, *Environmental Quality 1997–1998* (Washington: CEQ, 1999); Environmental Protection Agency, *National Air Quality and Emissions Trends Report, 1997*, Office of Air Quality and Standards Planning, EPA 454/R-98-D16, 1999.

52. Gene E. Likens, Katherine C. Weathers, Thomas J. Butler, and Donald J. Buso, "Solving the Acid Rain Problem," *Science* 282 (1998): 1991–92; CEQ, *Environmental Quality 1999*, Environmental Protection Agency.

53. Carol Browner, speech before the Harvard University Kennedy School of Government Forum, Cambridge, Mass., February 24, 1997.

54. Smith et al.

55. Smith et al. also note that costs are lower because railroad rates dropped (which reduced the costs of hauling low sulfur coal across long distances) and because industry is engaging in a strategy of early emissions reductions in preparation for more stringent restrictions called for in Phase II of the program. Compliance costs will almost certainly begin to climb as Phase II restrictions come fully into force.

56. Dallas Burtraw, Alan Krupnick, Erin Mansur, David Austin, and Deirdre Farrell, "The Costs and Benefits of Reducing Acid Rain," Discussion Paper 97-31-REV (Washington: Resources for the Future, 1997), and accompanying "Summary of Findings," ⟨http://www.rff.org/disc_papers/9731.htm⟩, April 15, 1999.

57. Ibid; see also National Acid Precipitation Assessment Program (NAPAP), 1990 Integrated Assessment Report (Washington: NAPAP, 1991), pp. 9–164.

58. The rationale for the PSD program and Section 169C established by the 1970 amendments suggest a growing recognition of sulfates.

59. EPA, *Protecting Visibility: An EPA Report to Congress*, Office of Air Quality Planning and Standards, EPA-450-5-79-008, preprint, 1979.

60. *Acid Precipitation Act of 1980*, P. L. 96–294.

61. Greenwire, "Waste and Hazardous Substances—Asbestos: USA TODAY Concludes 4-Part Series," http://www.cloakroom.com, February 11, 1999.

62. W. Kip Viscusi and James T. Hamilton, *Are Risk Regulators Rational? Evidence from Hazardous Waste Cleanup Decisions*, Working Paper 99-2 (Washington: AEI-Brookings Joint Center for Regulatory Studies, 1999). This estimate uses EPA's conservative assumptions. Adjusting for those assumptions pushes the median cost to more than $1 billion per cancer case avoided.

63. Neil Franz, "Utilities Incensed, Enviros Pleased with EPA's NO$_x$ Rule," *Environment and Energy Weekly*, 28 September 1998, available at http://www.eenews.net, 27 July 1999.

64. Greenwire, "Spotlight Story—Smog: Court Panel Puts EPA No$_x$ Emissions Deadline on Hold." 26 May 1999, available at http://www.cloakroom.com, 27 July 1999.

65. Neil Franz, "EPA Proposes New No$_x$ Plan to Sidestep Court Ruling," *PULSE Monthly Update and Outlook*, 30 June 1999, available at http://www.eenews.net, 27 July 1999.

Chapter 8

1. Indur M. Goklany, *Air and Inland Surface Water Quality: Long Term Trends and Relationship to Affluence* (Washington: U.S. Department of the Interior, 1994); Goklany, "Factors Affecting Environmental Impacts: The Effects of Technology on Long-Term Trends in Cropland, Air Pollution and Water-Related Diseases," *Ambio* 25 (1996): 497–503.

2. Kenneth Arrow et al., "Economic Growth, Carrying Capacity, and the Environment," *Science* 268 (1995): 520–21; Dale S. Rothman and Sander M. de Bruyn, "Probing into the Environmental Kuznets Curve Hypothesis," *Ecological Economics* 25 (1998), 143–45.

3. Indur M. Goklany, "Adaptation and Climate Change," paper presented at the Annual Meeting of the American Association for the Advancement of Science, Chicago, February 6–11, 1992; Indur M. Goklany, "Strategies to Enhance Adaptability: Technological Change, Economic Growth and Free Trade," *Climate Change* 30 (1995): 427–49; Indur M. Goklany, "Saving Habitat and Conserving Biodiversity on a Crowded Planet," *BioScience* 48 (1998): 941–53; Indur M. Goklany, "Richer Is Cleaner: Long Term Trends in Global Air Quality," in Ronald Bailey, ed., *The True State of the Planet* (New York: Free Press, 1995).

4. Arrow et al.; Rothman and de Bruyn.

5. See, for example, Norman Myers, "Consumption: Challenge to Sustainable Development. . . ," *Science* 276 (4 April 1997): 53–55.

6. Greenwire, "Earth Summit + 5: UNDP Estimates Pollution-Control Costs," April 14, 1997, available at http://www.apn.com/greenwire.

7. Goklany, "Strategies to Enhance Adaptability"; Goklany, "Factors Affecting Environmental Impacts."

Index

Acid rain
   compliance costs, 143
   control program, 142–44
   OTA study (1984), 142
Affluence, societal
   relation of environmental
      degradation to, 88–89
   relation to environmental quality,
      102–5
Air exchange, indoors and outdoors,
   45–46
Air pollution
   under 1990 amendments to Clean Air
      Act, 39–41
   ground-level concentrations, 49
   historical perceptions of, 9–11
   indicators for, 2
   lessons in U.S. experience, 154
   with recommended emissions
      trading, 142
   reduction in urban levels
      (1920s–1960s), 31–32
   steam locomotive as source of, 18
   with technological change, 149
Air pollution control
   arguments for larger federal role, 33
   Chicago (1881), 13
   city, county, and state-level
      programs (1880–1980), 21–22
   early city ordinances, 13–16
   federalization (1970), 1, 4, 29, 31–32,
      36–37, 112
   Ohio ordinance permitting (1890), 13
   Oregon state-level program (1951), 26
   Pittsburgh (1868), 13
   prior to federalization at state level,
      111–14
   St. Louis (1860s), 13
   use of Ringelmann smoke density
      chart, 14
Air Pollution Control Act (1955),
   United States, 26
Air pollution episodes
   concerns related to, 34
   Donora, PA (1948), 24-25

London and New York (1950s, 1960s,
   1970), 26, 28–29
Meuse Valley, Belgium (1930s), 25
ozone alert in wisconsin, 29
Air quality
   growth of county and state programs
      (1960s), 151
   with improved dust collection, 116
   improvements (1957–97), 52–65
   improvements prior to Clean Air Act
      1970 amendments, 4, 33, 52–65,
      126
   influence of NAAQS on, 125
   outdoor measurements of, 2
   pre-1970 tightened opacity standards,
      116
   standards under Air Quality Act
      (1967), 30
   trends in PM, SO_2, and CO, 50
   trends in United States, 91–95
   See also Pollution; Pollution control
Air quality, indoor
   concentrations of pollutants
      (1940–90), 44–46, 91
   contributions of tobacco smoke to
      poor, 45–46
   improvements in non-smoking
      homes, 44–47
   as indicator of public health, 43–44
Air Quality Act (1967), United States,
   28–30, 32–33, 114
Air quality control
   under Air Quality Act (1967), 30
   growth of local- and state-level
      programs (1960s), 115–16
   state-level initiatives, 150
   See also Air pollution control
Air quality control regions
   under Air Quality Act (1967), 30
   interstate, 115
Air quality monitoring
   measures as indicators of air
      pollution, 2
   programs for, 49

as response to 1970 Clean Air Act
amendments, 126
Asthma
deaths and death rates associated
with (1960–95), 46, 134–35
relation to air pollution, 134
Ayres, Robert U., 23

Browner, Carol, 143

California
air quality with emissions standards,
27
CO air quality improvement (1960s),
113
motor vehicle emission and exhaust
standards (1966), 26–27, 117–18
Motor Vehicle Pollution Control
Board, 27
oxidant and ozone environmental
transition, 150–51
oxidant concentration levels, 60
smog alleviation, 26–27
trend in CO air quality, 58
Carbon monoxide (CO)
decline in levels of, 56–59
emission levels (1940–97), 83–86, 87
EPA trend analysis, 56, 58
sources and problems of, 28–29
transition prior to federalization, 150
Chicago
air pollution control (1881), 13
dustfall levels, 54
effect of Department of Smoke
Abatement regulation, 17
Clean Air Act (1963)
acid deposition control under 1990
amendments, 142, 146
1970 amendments, 1, 4, 29, 31–32,
36–37, 112
1990 amendments, 39–41, 60
failure of 1970 amendments, 125
HEW conference procedure, 26
NAAQS promulgated under, 112
NAAQS under 1990 amendments, 40
Clean Air Act (1956), United Kingdom,
26
Cohoe, B. A., 11
Continuous Air Monitoring Project
(CAMP), 49
Council on Environmental Quality
(1970), 36
Crandall, Robert, 33

Data
from air monitoring programs, 49
to determine trends, 51–52
EPA publication of ambient air, 50
Data sources
to construct real annual GNP series,
68–69
economic data, 68–69
emissions data, 67–68
EPA AIRS Executive Data Base, 62
Davidson, Cliff I., 19
Defoe, Daniel, 10–11
Degradation, environmental
after environmental transition, 96–97
causes of increased, 5
conditions related to levels of, 96–98
environmental Kuznets curve, 87–88,
98–102
peak in, 5
Dust
Cincinnati dustfall levels, 54
city ordinances controlling, 23–24
dustfall levels in Detroit, 54
Philadelphia dustfall levels, 19, 21, 54
pre-1970 improvement in collection
of, 23, 116, 151
Dwyer, John P., 116

Economic development, 89–90
Emissions
effect of climate on levels of, 51–52
effect of technological change on
levels of, 73–86
estimates as indicators of air
pollutants, 2
methodologies used to estimate
(1940–84, 1984 to present), 67
residential contribution to outdoor
exposure, 44
trends in PM-10 and CO (1940–97),
69, 71
trends in SO_2, NO_x and VOC
(1900–97), 69–70
U.S. trends in total (1900–97),
74–75
See also Fuel combustion emissions;
Motor vehicle emissions
Emissions per capita
as environmental indicator, 2
trends in United States (1900–97), 5,
69–72
Emissions per GNP
decline in, 149, 152–53
defined, 2

peak in, 4
trends in United States (1990–97), 5,
   72–86
Emissions reduction
motor vehicle, 126
under Toxics Release Inventory, 125
VOC and CO, 125
Emissions standards
federal preemption of motor vehicle
   emission standards, 16
for motor vehicles in California,
   26–27, 29
state-level motor vehicle controls,
   29–30
tightening at state level, 151
See also Motor vehicle emissions
Emissions standards, new-source
controlling, 38
new source performance standards
   (NSPS), 37–38
state-level actions related to, 142
tightening of federal, 142
Emissions trading
effect of recommended, 142
recommendation for expansion, 154
sulfate, 142, 144
Energy Supply and Environmental
   Coordination Act (ESECA) (1974)
amendments (1977), 39
requirements under, 39
Engel, Kirsten H., 120–21
Environmental indicators
decline in leading, 73–86
emissions as, 2–3
Environmental Kuznets curve (EKC)
relation to environmental
   degradation, 87–88, 98–102
relation to environmental transition,
   98–102
Environmental policy
Johnson administration, 35
Nixon administration, 35–38
recommendations, 6–7
in U.S. postindustrial era, 5, 89–91
See also Clean Air Act (1963);
   Federalization
Environmental Protection Agency
   (EPA)
AIRS Executive Data Base, 62
analysis of oxidant air quality trends,
   60
benefits and costs study, 127–39, 152
command and control regulations of,
   152

establishment of NAAQS (1971), 37
exceedance probability review
   (1972–73), 37
publication of air quality trends, 50
report on protecting visibility (1979),
   146
rules for nitrogen dioxide, 146
SO$_2$ and CO trend analyses, 56
Environmental transition hypothesis
   (ETH), 98, 105–9, 155
See also Transition, environmental
EPA. See Environmental Protection
   Agency (EPA).
Evelyn, John, 9–10, 35

Federal Energy Agency (FEA), 39
Federalization
of air pollution control (1970), 1,
   31–41, 111, 125, 150
arguments for, 1–2, 111–23
under Clean Air Act Amendments
   (1970), 36–37
dangers of, 146
effect in air pollution indicator
   trends, 3
effect of NAAQS, 125–26
of stationary source controls (1970s),
   113
time of federalization [t(F)], 3
See also Clean Air Act (1963);
   Environmental Protection Agency
   (EPA); Time of federalization [t(F)]
Fuel
cleaner sources, 15–19
increased use of fossil fuels, 38–39
increased use related to air pollution,
   11–12, 20
Fuel combustion
contributions to indoor air pollution,
   46
increased efficiency, 15–19
Fuel combustion emissions
as indicators of air pollution, 2–3
as indicators of indoor air quality,
   2–3, 46–47
Fuel consumption
cleaner sources, 20–21
coal consumption levels, 18
coal use in steam locomotives, 18
electricity as replacement for coal, 18
related to smoke, 13–23
in United States (1850–1995), 11–14

Graunt, John, 10
Griswold, S. Smith, 27–28

Haagen-Smit, A. J., 24, 27
Hadacheck v. Sebastian (1915), 14–15
Hays, Samuel B., 25, 89
Humphrey, Hubert, 34–35

Laitos, Jan Gordon, 29
Lead
  concentrations of (1975–97), 64–65
  effect of motor vehicle emission
    control on, 38, 126
  emission levels (1970–97), 85–86
London
  air pollution episode (1952), 25
  Coal Smoke Abatement Society, 16
  elimination of black fogs, 16
Los Angeles
  Air Pollution Control District, 24
  Los Angeles County Air Pollution
    Control District, 117
  O_3 as component of, 58
  ozone level trends, 27–28, 60–62
  smog problem, 24, 26, 117

McCabe, Louis, 24
Middleton, John T., 27
Motor Vehicle Air Pollution Control
  Act (1965), United States, 29–30,
  113
Motor vehicle emissions
  California standards, 151
  federal standards, 151
  reduction with federal intervention,
    126
  standards under Clean Air Act
    Amendments (1970), 37–38
Motor vehicles, catalyst-equipped, 38
Muskie, Edward, 36

NAAQS. *See* National Ambient Air
  Quality Standards (NAAQS).
Nader, Ralph, 35
National Air Monitoring System, 50–51
National Air Pollution Control
  Administration, 113, 116
  See also Environmental Protection
    Agency (EPA)
National Air Sampling Network, 49
National Air Surveillance Network, 51
National Ambient Air Quality
  Standards (NAAQS)
  extension of compliance deadlines,
    125
  as idealized goals, 7
  influence of, 125–26

  for lead (1978), 38
  for ozone, 60
  for SO_2 amd PM, 25
National Gas Sampling Network, 49
Nelson, Gaylord, 34
New source performance standards
  (NSPS), 37–38
New York City
  air pollution episode (1966), 26
  dustfall levels, 54
  levels of SO_2, 56
New York State Air Pollution Control
  Board, 30
NIMBY (not-in-my-backyard), 6, 95–97
Nitrogen dioxide (NO_2)
  EPA rules, 146
  mean annual average levels, 62–63,
    65
Nitrogen oxides (NO_x)
  as contributor to smog, 24
  emission levels (1900–97), 80–81,
    87
  Jacob-Hochheiser measurement,
    50–51
Nixon, Richard M., 36
  establishes CEQ, 36
Northwestern Laundry v. City of Des
  Moines (1915), 14

Office of Technology Assessment
  (OTA)
  1984 acid rain study, 142, 146
  1989 study, 142
Oil price shocks (1973, 1979), 38–39
Oxidants
  environmental transition, 150–51
  as pollutants, 113–14
Ozone (O_3)
  adjustment of data related to, 52
  as contributor to Los Angeles smog,
    24, 27
  environmental transition, 150–51
  formation and dispersion of, 58
  interstate transport of, 146–47
  trend in national mean levels, 60–62
  trends in Los Angeles (1956–72),
    27–28
Ozone Transport Assessment Group,
  146

Particulate matter (PM)
  effect of indoor emissions, 44
  emission levels (1940–97), 80, 82–83,
    87

federal-level monitoring and
  sampling, 49–52
methods to develop trends in
  airborne, 50
trends in air quality containing,
  49–50
Period of perception [p(P)]
  compared to period of transition and
    t(F), 91–96
  defined, 3
  determinants of, 3–4
  effect of, 107
  illustration of, 40–41
Pittsburgh
  Bureau of Smoke Regulation, 16–17
  dustfall levels, 54
Pollution, interstate
  acid rain, 142–46
  recommended methods to control, 154
  solutions, 142
Pollution, intrastate
  federal government role, 139
  recommended control methods, 154
  state-level role, 139
Pollution control
  devices for motor vehicles, 26–27
  San Francisco Bay Area air pollution
    control district, 117
Portney, Paul, 33
p(P). See Period of perception [p(P)].

Quality of life
  determinants of, 4–5
  race to top of, 5–6, 96–97
  rationale for race to the bottom, 151
  society's improvements of, 5, 88–89

Resources for the Future study, 143
Ringelmann, Maximilien, 14

Smog
  motor vehicle emission controls, 117
  problem in Los Angeles Basin, 24, 26
Smoke
  city abatement regulations, 14–21
  decline in controls (1920s, 1930s),
    20–21
  effect of control of outdoor, 149–50
  post-World War II controls, 21–24
  state and local control programs,
    30–31
  from steam locomotives, 18
  trends in city problems, 13–19
Smoke density chart (Ringelmann), 14,
  22, 24

Stern, Arthur C., 22
Sulfur dioxide (SO_2)
  decline in concentrations of, 56–57
  emission levels (1990–97), 76t, 77–78, 87
  environmental transition, 150

Tarr, Joel A., 21, 23
Technological change
  decline in emissions per GNP as an
    indicator, 149
  improvement in pollution control
    devices, 31
  influence on reduction of air
    pollution emissions, 72–73, 149
  related to combustion, 15–19
  role in environmental transition, 89
  T-factor measure, 72–86
  trends in emissions related to, 73–86
Time of federalization [t(F)]
  compared to transition and p(P),
    91–96
  defined, 3
  illustration of, 40–41
Total suspended particulates (TSP), 4
  environmental transitions, 150
  federal government program to
    monitor (1950s), 54
Toxics Release Inventory, 125
Transition, environmental
  country differences, 98–105
  determinants of, 104–5
  elements of, 5
  under environmental transition
    hypothesis (ETH), 98
  factors influencing, 89–90
  period of perception related to, 87–88
  periods of, 91–95
  for pollution indicators, 91–96
  relation to environmental Kuznets
    curve, 98–102
  in United States, 5
  variation in periods of, 91–96
TSP. See Total suspended particulates
  (TSP).
Tucker, Raymond, 24

U.S. Department of Health, Education,
  and Welfare (HEW)
  conference procedure under Clean
    Air Act, 26

Volatile organic compounds (VOCs)
  concentrations in nonsmoking
    houses, 46
  emission levels (1990–97), 78–80, 87

About the Author

Indur M. Goklany, who holds a Ph.D. in electrical engineering from Michigan State University, has over 25 years of experience working on air quality and environmental issues at various levels of state and federal government and in the private sector. He was formerly chief of the technical assessment division of the National Commission on Air Quality and a consultant in the Office of Policy, Planning, and Evaluation at the EPA.

The opinions expressed in this book are solely those of the author. They do not reflect the views of any organization with which he has ever been associated.

Cato Institute

Founded in 1977, the Cato Institute is a public policy research foundation dedicated to broadening the parameters of policy debate to allow consideration of more options that are consistent with the traditional American principles of limited government, individual liberty, and peace. To that end, the Institute strives to achieve greater involvement of the intelligent, concerned lay public in questions of policy and the proper role of government.

The Institute is named for *Cato's Letters*, libertarian pamphlets that were widely read in the American Colonies in the early 18th century and played a major role in laying the philosophical foundation for the American Revolution.

Despite the achievement of the nation's Founders, today virtually no aspect of life is free from government encroachment. A pervasive intolerance for individual rights is shown by government's arbitrary intrusions into private economic transactions and its disregard for civil liberties.

To counter that trend, the Cato Institute undertakes an extensive publications program that addresses the complete spectrum of policy issues. Books, monographs, and shorter studies are commissioned to examine the federal budget, Social Security, regulation, military spending, international trade, and myriad other issues. Major policy conferences are held throughout the year, from which papers are published thrice yearly in the *Cato Journal*. The Institute also publishes the quarterly magazine *Regulation*.

In order to maintain its independence, the Cato Institute accepts no government funding. Contributions are received from foundations, corporations, and individuals, and other revenue is generated from the sale of publications. The Institute is a nonprofit, tax-exempt, educational foundation under Section 501(c)3 of the Internal Revenue Code.

CATO INSTITUTE
1000 Massachusetts Ave., N.W.
Washington, D.C. 20001